FROM THE MOB TO THE MOVIES

HOW I ESCAPED THE MAFIA AND LANDED IN HOLLYWOOD

RICHIE SALERNO

D1073302

WILDBLUE
P R E S S

WildBluePress.com

FROM THE MOB
TO THE MOVIES

1

Let's Start With the Pleasant Stuff

It was great growing up in Brooklyn in the middle of the twentieth century, but only if you looked at things just right. From my experience, it was a marvelous time to be alive. The streets were always filled with the sounds of rock and roll, all kinds of happy music. You could walk the neighborhood with your loved ones and not worry about getting molested.

There was a reason. A special sense of protection, of being safe, ran through every part of our lives. It was fueled by the mob, the Family, the Mafia. Of course, now I know all about what I didn't know then—the violent criminality hiding behind that magical feeling of special protection. I was told the reach of it governed all the boroughs in and around New York. Back then, there didn't appear to be any reason to doubt it.

What it meant to us was simply that people could trust things to work the way they expected them to because a common structure of respect existed for everybody. That feeling was a comfort to a boy who didn't understand the mechanics. Plus for this kid there was the New York Yankees, the Giants, and my personal favorites, the Brooklyn Dodgers! I know it must be odd to read it, but in our mobbed-up neighborhood, the sense of community was powerful.

When mobsters are your idols, authority from the outside doesn't mean much. I remember how great it was to play hooky from school, hopping a trolley car to Ebbits Field to watch my beloved Brooklyn Bums, because, besides mobsters, baseball players were the heroes I looked up to.

I guess it seems strange, especially if you aren't from Brooklyn. Don't worry about it. It just means you aren't from Brooklyn. Because back then when I went to see a baseball game, a kid could wait for all the players at the side door and ask them for their autographs. Many a day my heart pounded when I watched the greatest baseball players of their time come striding out the door.

One day a scene unfolded there that became an abbreviation for the way my whole life was going to work for me. Jackie Robinson and Roy Campanella spotted me at the back door and challenged me.

"Kid, why aren't you in school?"

I just laughed and replied, "How come you missed that tag at home plate?"

Jackie chimed in. "Yeah Campy, what happened?"

Campy replied, not really angry but sort of pretending to be, "Man, that umpire blew the call! That guy was out!"

We all laughed at that. Imagine that—there were these famous guys, loved by much of the country, and they let me yank their chains like I was somebody. Even the athletes then knew about respect.

Jackie looked at me and said. "You've got to stay in school, you've got to learn, you got to get educated." He ruffled my hair. "I don't want to see you at this back door no more on school days."

I gave Jackie my best smile, but instead of agreeing with him I just asked, "Jackie! Can I get your autograph?" Quick as a whip I handed him a baseball card.

He could have ignored a kid like me. Nobody would have stopped him. But he signed it, and then Campy signed it, and then Gill Hodges walked up and *he* signed it, too! Last one out was the team captain, Pee Wee Reese. He signed and he did it with a smile. I almost died.

See, that's that I mean by the episode being an abbreviation for my life, right there. The Jews call it *chutzpa*. I didn't know I had it. It was just how I reacted to things. It was somehow part of my nature, early on, to always have this feeling that if I didn't step up and ask, I wasn't going to get.

Jackie turned to me and repeated, "Make sure you stay in school."

This time I nodded in agreement. "Okay, Jackie. I hear you."

Then I was running for the trolley car with their autographs tucked in my pants. Whether they could hear me or not, I yelled back, "Gee thanks, guys!"

Gee thanks, guys.

2

It's All Who You Know in The Neighborhood

I ran back to home turf and the first guy I saw standing in front of The Black Kitten was Joey the Blond, one of the top mobsters in the neighborhood.

"Joey, Joey! Today I got Jackie Robinson's autograph! Can you believe that?"

Joey grinned. "Sure. But did you go to school today?" Unlike the athletes, Joey didn't actually care about who was in school or not. So I just answered, "Did you break anybody's legs today?"

"No not yet, wise guy, but the next time I catch you playing hooky I'm going to put my foot up your ass." I figured any excuse would do.

But Joey smiled and rubbed my head. "Tell your ma and pop I said hello. Come to the Black Kitten tonight and bring your shoeshine box."

Now that was something! A chance to earn. "Gee thanks, Joey!"

So say what you want about my heroes, but the ball players and the mobsters told me the same things—play it smart, stay in school. These were guys who should know. Most of them lived close enough to the edge to understand how screwed they would be if they had to look for regular work at an actual job.

The neighborhood itself was a mixed bag of Jews, Irish, and Italians. Mostly it was Italian mobsters. My old man was married and I was single, but he was an unfaithful cocksman in addition to also being the neighborhood tailor, a pretty cushy job for a guy who liked the ladies. They called him Charley the Pick, and boy he could "pick" 'em; my father could spot a sucker a mile away.

Aside from his talent, he had a lot of weird ideas, like for some strange reason he thought because he sired me, I owed him payback. Let me tell you, he collected on the investment. By the time I reached eleven, he had me working my ass off.

He claimed he was getting me ready for the tough world out there, but I gotta tell you, working for the Pick was like entering a boxing ring, dodging the left hooks and overhand rights that came out of his mouth. And maybe a sweeping slap across the back of the head when I made a mistake.

So the Pick. Charley was his name and drinking was his game. My mom, God bless her soul, she would always defend him, saying "Oh, Son, Daddy only drinks on weekends."

Yeah, yeah, from one weekend to the next. She was in complete denial, but I still loved her. I loved her because I could see every day that she was doing the best she could with what she had. I have since met plenty of people with far more money and education than she ever had who don't do that.

Mom didn't have much schooling, but she was a gifted seamstress. It was her keen eye and skills that propelled their tailoring business. But her eyes and her skills had to do with fabric and thread. She couldn't see she was married to a hopeless drunk and that he would never get better.

So there I was at eleven years old, and my job—my actual daily job—was the same as Ma: survive the mood swings of Charley the Pick. His mixed messages became my daily lessons.

He could be friendly, he could be welcoming, and he knew "who you treat with respect." Problem being he also knew who he didn't have to bother to respect, and that included me. When his beloved steady customers came into his shop, he always offered them a drink. Mister Suave to the max. "Hey Philly! Come on in the back!"

But private drinks and quiet conversations were for the favored ones. He never told me, "Hey Richie, come in the back." The only time I went to the back was to clean up the messes left by him and the anointed ones.

I stuck pin holes in his rubbers to get even.

For awhile it was my favorite thing to do. One night I heard him screaming at Ma in one of his drunken rages, "Why the hell do you keep getting pregnant?"

Yeah, you read that last bit right. My father was asking the woman he plunked on a regular basis how it was that she kept getting pregnant. I realized early in life there might not be any geniuses in the family tree, and if there were, I'd have to be the first.

See, he could have tested out a rubber or two. Maybe blow it up like a balloon. Fill one with water to see if it had holes in it. He could have done anything at all, besides blame Ma. He didn't.

I could have stopped with the pins. I didn't.

They had three more kids.

It's fine if you want to hate me for that. I understand. And I'm sorry for your lack of a sense of humor.

I hit the streets early in life, and I was a happy soul out there because the people I met were so exciting. There's an unexplainable mystique about gangsters, specifically the gangsters of that time and place, and I got caught up in it all the way.

The mobsters in my neighborhood were all different individuals, like with any other way of life, but they had one thing in common: respect. Respect was what kept them from being a bunch of anarchists with guns. Respect made sure the people of the neighborhood accepted them and more or less cooperated. Respect was the spine of the community.

When you get respect, it means you belong. The code of respect was how they managed to deal with one another in spite of their criminal minds.

And so, to a kid who lived with constant disrespect and verbal cruelty, this was a beautiful thing. I wanted to belong. I wanted the respect. Treat a kid with respect—I mean actual respect, not pampering—then I believe that kid will not only follow you anywhere, that kid will try to figure out how to be like you. Other people can tell the kid you're a piece of shit, and to *that kid* those other people will sound like idiots.

A little respect can shape a whole neighborhood full of people to the point that, in Brooklyn at that time, there were no such things as car jackings, gangs of thugs stopping traffic, and junkies shitting in the streets.

Nothing like that ever happened there because everyone knew everyone. Kinda like a small town in that way. Except with us, the town sheriff wasn't our source of authority. If there was a problem, we went right to the candy store run by Frankie Five Fingers, who may or may not have actually made his living selling candy. Frankie was a made man, a man of high rank, and whatever the neighborhood problem, Ol' Five Fingers always took care of it. No matter what.

Example: guys that got caught raping a woman endured the somewhat depressing experience of having their "three piece set" cut off and fed to my grandpa's dogs. And that version was mercy. The version without mercy was for perverts who fooled around with children. They got themselves tossed off the roof from nice and high and therefore they tended not to come around. Because you did not do those things. Not to our people, not in our neighborhood. It really was that simple.

But that was then.

3

Joey the Blond and Nipples Galore

The rule of respect was invisible, but it covered everything. That night when I entered the Black Kitten with my shoeshine box, it was the middle of August and there was a hot wind blowing, the sort of weather that puts people on edge. The place was jammed with mobsters and their women, and as soon as I walked in, I was blinded by a sea of red. Whoever decorated the place must have used up all the red stuff in the city. I wondered if that was because when blood flew it would blend right in. That seemed to be the message. You know, just in case somebody forgot about respect.

I spotted Joey sitting next to Ernie the Hawk, a tall man with one eye. Ma said Ernie got the nickname when some guy shot him in the eye, and the bullet spun all the way around the *inside of his skull* to come out his fucking ear.

I guess for some people that's what passes for luck.

That night trouble started right away. When I walked around the smoke-filled bar, I somehow bumped right into Jimmy Bitts, the top numbers runner for Ernie the Hawk. Jimmy was tough, but he was also germ phobic and he hated to be touched.

I tried to turn the mistake into a profit by smiling up at him and asking, "Shine, mister?"

He sneered, "Get the fuck away from me! You need a fucking shower! Besides, you little punk, can't you see I'm wearing suedes?"

Oops. Okay, I should have looked first. But the next thing, Joey the Blond yelled over to me, "Salerno!"

I looked over to him. "Yeah, Joey?"

"Shine em' anyway."

I looked back at Jimmy Bitts.

The Kitten got real quiet. Joey the Blond had just ordered me to shine the man's shoes. It didn't make any difference what he was wearing.

So I just said, "What color, mister?"

Jimmy got embarrassed. He threw a twenty bill on the floor. I went to pick it up, but then Joey the Blond stepped on it.

"*You*," he quietly said, pointing to Jimmy. "I'm talking to you."

First reaction, Jimmy tried a tough guy response. Logical enough. Sometimes those work.

"*Me?*" He stood up, and he towered over the Blond. It would work on most guys and shut them right up.

The Blond didn't move. Didn't flinch. Didn't blink. He kept his voice really quiet. Clint Eastwood style: "Don't you *like* my shoeshine boy?"

Now this had to be odd for Jimmy. Even though he was much bigger than Joey the Blond, Joey the Blond wasn't backing off. And Jimmy's boss, Ernie the Hawk, wasn't saying a word to help Jimmy out on this one. Nobody had to ask why that was.

The Blond was a made man.

A dim light finally went on inside Jimmy's tiny brain and he got uneasy. "I just, I just, I like Carlo a lot better. And besides, Carlo is Gino's cousin from 10th Street."

Joey grinned at that. "Well I like Salerno here, so the next time you see Fat Gino, maybe you tell him that. You got it?"

Jimmy got red in the face real fast. "Aw well, that's different. Gee, I didn't know. I mean Joey, if I knew that? All this would've never happened."

But it was a little too late for Jimmy to walk out of this with a smile on his face. He forgot that little thing about respect, and he wasn't getting any help from me with that, either.

So I got ready to smear shoe polish on Jimmy's blue suede shoes while Joey the Blond watched me with a satisfied smile.

I asked him again, "What color, mister?"

* * *

Watching my old man in his shop was fascinating when he was fitting a blouse on a woman. It was the way he moved those fat fingers around each woman's breasts without ever touching a nipple. A teenaged boy notices these things. It was beautiful to watch. Because for me, the more he avoided those nipples, the more they stood up and sang opera to me.

I was always wishing he would make a mistake, just to see how the woman would react, but he was too damn good at what he did. Fat fingers and all, the nipples stayed untouched and he got the job done in style.

But it was in that shop where I discovered that it ain't just the men. Women can be a little pervy, too. The day I watched him pinning the blouse of customer Debra, I could tell she was deliberately moving her body towards him. I could see plain as day she was trying to get him to touch her there! But he moved too, just enough to avoid the dreaded nipple touch.

Let me tell you, her pervy nipples were rock hard. Did I mention teenage boys notice those things? Yet he either didn't have a clue or he wasn't buying.

Pop was often drunk at work, and even so, he could still navigate around the breasts. I knew he wasn't faithful to my Ma, and sometimes wondered if he was popping some of his customers. Or maybe not, maybe to get aroused he would have had to mistreat them the same way he mistreated Ma. I overheard my share of it.

Still, it was my old man who got me moved up from shining shoes. It happened on the day Tony Lap walked into the tailor shop and said, "Charley, I need a favor."

"What can I do for you, Tony?"

"I need someone to paint my basement. You know anybody can do that for me?"

You can relax. He actually wanted ordinary paint applied with brushes and rollers. This was not the "paint the basement" in the mob's usual sense of the word, meaning paint the walls with the blood of your victims. Those guys were paid real money. This was the sucker work. The back work. The monkey job.

So Pop stepped me right up. "Sure, Tony, no problem, I got just the guy for that job right here, my fifteen-year-old son."

Good ol' Charley the Pick loved doing this with the mobsters, performing little errands and feeling close to the action. I wasn't too happy about getting volunteered, or at least no more than any other teenage boy who is basically out for a good time in life. Even so, I thought maybe it was a way to get Pop's approval because of how much he loved those guys.

I loved them too, or admired them, at least. But I should have realized that fighting to get love from Charley the Pick was a losing battle.

4

The Venture

So I finally show up at Tony Lap's house, fresh and ready to go, figuring to knock off this painting thing fast and then get on my way to football practice.

To my surprise, the front door opens as soon as I knock. What I see almost makes me step back. Standing there with a paint brush in her hand was the beautiful tailor shop customer, Debra. S*he* was Tony's woman!

I had seen her kind in magazines, but now there she was standing right in front of me. The sight of her, the scent of her, completely engulfed my senses. I forgot where the fuck I was. I glanced, okay gaped, at her breasts, and her nipples were *oh boy,* just like on that day in front of the fitting mirror.

I thought, *my God, she's the real thing!* I can't overstate the appeal of seeing the wind ruffling her house dress, exposing part of her breast.

But right then she caught me gaping at her. Oops. Of course I expected a shit response.

Instead she just looked at me close. "How old are you?"

"Fifteen." And because I got *chutzpa* even though I don't know it yet, I keep going. "And you?"

She just grinned and handed me the paint brush. "Take this, wise-ass. It's what you're here for."

"Thanks. Is Tony home?"

She stood there smiling at me, so I waved the paint brush and tried to come on strong. "Come on, I ain't got all day!"

She just said, "I think you're very savvy."

"Savvy? What's that supposed to mean?"

She smiled again. "Savvy means you know when to back up and when to go forward. It means you know when to cry, how to cry, and who to cry to."

She saw the look of confusion on my face. "Being savvy might sound easy, sonny boy, but the trick is, you gotta know when to do it. That's how you stay alive. Now get your skinny little ass up on that ladder."

Before I got the chance to ask her to unravel any of that, Tony walked in. Saved by the bell, maybe. I was so relieved, I yelled out, "Tony! Long time no see! How you doing?"

He shook his head and replied, "Getting old, kid. Getting old."

Except I looked at the broad and thought, what a nice way to grow old.

Tony broke the trance. "Say hello to Debra."

I looked at Debra, wondering would she rat me out for staring at her back in my dad's shop, or for staring at her just now. I try to beat her to the punch and introduce myself.

"Hi, I'm Richie. My old man is the tailor."

She gave a little laugh. "Yes, I know. I heard all about you from your dad." But she didn't go any farther. We were okay for the moment.

Tony asked, "Do you also have time to rake my yard? It's full of leaves."

But with his deep, raspy voice, I could barely make out what he said. I turn to Debra for confirmation.

"What did he say?"

Debra just smirked at me. "He says you're very savvy."

What is this savvy crap? I couldn't meet her eyes after that, so I shot Tony a look. "Yeah. I'll do it, Tony. The raking, right? You want the leaves? I'll rake 'em up."

Good old Tony was missing all the undercurrents in the room and instead decided to show me the dirty basement. We got down there and it was a fucking mile long. The walls were grimy and crusty. I started thinking I could never clean this in one day. The entire basement was damp and full of junk, old newspapers and maybe for all I know a couple of dead bodies.

I told Tony I'd be back and hit the streets running. There had to be a way out of this mess. I turned the corner fuming, and ran smack into my friend, Fat Anthony.

"Salerno, where the fuck have you been? You give up football or what? The coach is really pissed at you."

Frustrated, I threw up my hands. "I been busy, just busy working. And now I gotta paint Tony Lap's basement."

Fat Anthony grinned, "Did you see the dame he's got?"

"Yeah, I seen her."

"Then smile! You got lucky, Salerno! You're gonna be around her! She is nice, I mean really nice. She has a body that never quits. I'd give up my best baseball card just to stick my head up her ass."

"How do you know what her fucking ass looks like?"

Fat Anthony laughed out loud. "Come here, Salerno, I got something to tell you! This is good, *real* fuckin' good. Now look, Tony Lap has a tree in his backyard and it sits right in front of her bedroom window."

"How do you know that?"

Fat Anthony giggled. "You know Benny the Bug? Lives over on Ryder Street? Benny is Tony Lap's gardener, so twice a week, every Saturday and Sunday night, me and Benny climb the tree and watch her."

"Watch her doing what?"

Fat Anthony laughed. "She takes her clothes off, she walks around naked, she looks at herself in the mirror, does a lot of poses. Then sometimes she lays on the bed and plays with herself. Salerno, you wanna go with me tonight? It will make your dick hard!"

"Oh hell no. I got no time for that shit."

"Then you wanna go get an egg cream?"

I waved him off.

"How can you say no to a fucking egg cream? Salerno, you are fucked up!"

I think to myself, *yeah that's right, Fat Anthony. I'm the fucked up one there.*

"Tell the coach I'll see him for sure on Sunday." After that I walked around the neighborhood a good long while, thinking about what I just heard about Debra, the tailor shop customer with the untouched nipples, who turns out to be the wife of Tony Lap.

My head started to spin, thinking maybe I could get lucky….

I pondered that while I walked into my ma's house, but inside all I heard was dishes and glass breaking. I stopped and stared. Shards were scattered all over the kitchen.

Then I heard voices, Ma screaming, "Stop, you're gonna kill him!"

I ran into the sewing room, and my old man had the cat trapped in a corner.

"What the fuck happened?"

Ma said, "The cat pissed all over Mrs. Lang's mink coat."

"So what?"

"That ain't all, Sonny sank his claws into the mink."

I laughed at her serious expression, but my old man shot me a look like I had on his smelly underwear. I started to say, "You know Ma, that's no big deal."

But the old man yelled out, "No big deal?! What the hell does *that* mean?"

"Pop, Sonny was only protecting his turf, that all. It's what cats do."

But he was outraged and frustrated and started screaming. "Protecting his turf my ass! He's only a fucking cat!"

He picked up a chair and threw it across the room. "I don't wanna hear about his territory anymore, I'm gonna snap his fucking neck!"

"Come on, Pop! So he pulled, made a few holes in the coat. Nothing to get all worked up about, is it?"

"You tell me, smart guy. That coat's worth ten grand!"

Oops. That stopped me. Ten grand. Shit. "Okay, but don't worry, Ma can fix it. You know she can fix anything." I shot my mother a look. "Right, Ma?"

But Ma just sat there, smoking and grinning.

"*Right*, Ma?"

To answer, she says, "Watch this, you two. Do as I do."

Then we all start walking around the room picking up pieces of shredded mink fur. Ma starts chewing bubble gum, one piece after another, until she can't get any more into her mouth.

She hands me some gum, so I chew all I can. My old man passed on helping. Maybe he didn't want to chew anything that might get in the way of his drinking.

After a while when our jaws were sore from chewing, Ma took the gum and spread it out, and then expertly molded the damaged pieces of fur into the soft texture of the bubble gum.

Then we waited anxiously for the bubble gum to harden. Ma kneaded the bubble gum and sewed it into the skin of the coat. Even with me helping, it took the two of us all night long. But at the end that coat was all in one piece again.

Ten hours later, bleary eyed and tired, I woke up Pop and showed him the repaired coat, "See that? I told you Ma can fix anything!"

"Good. Did you see Tony?"

"Yeah, I'm on my way, Pop." I ran down the stairs and passed into the sewing room. There was Ma, asleep with a cigarette still in her lips, and one in the ash tray. And there was Sonny also fast asleep, nestled in the mink coat.

* * *

I got to Tony's place and Debra was the only one there. She wore a skimpy outfit and when she flipped on the light, the words come out of me before I could stop myself. I smiled at her and said, "Now that's nice."

She shot me a look. "What did you say?"

"Well, the junk. Ready to paint in here. That's nice."

I stood there looking at her, forgetting what I was doing in the first place. She smiled and handed me a paint brush. "I think you're going to need this."

I watched her walk away, thinking *Fat Anthony is right, what a body!* I shook my head and went to work, with her brush in my hand and her bush on my mind.

After what seemed like an eternity, Debra finally reappeared. She was all showered, with a cold drink and a slice of pizza in her hand. I took a good look at her and thought *fuck the pizza.*

When I looked down from the ladder, I could swear she bent over on purpose just so I got a free shot down her blouse. Yeah, she was Tony's woman, but I wondered if maybe somebody should tell her that.

Now my mind was really racing—*Salerno, you better be careful! Make sure what you think is going on is real ....* Everybody knows a man's dick can give him hallucinations.

I didn't know what to do and my fucking dick wouldn't shut up. So I just looked at her and said, "Thanks, the pizza is good," scared she might know what I was thinking. It felt like she could read my mind. And maybe she could. Or maybe she was just watching the bulge in my jeans.

She asked me, "How old are you?"

"I told you, I'm fifteen."

I think she just wanted to hear it again. She gave me this dreamy-eyed look.

"Do you have a girlfriend?"

"Not right now, but I'm working on it."

"I'm sure you are"

I took a deep breath, and my whole world stopped. I had caught the scent of her skin. She was that close. We locked eyes a moment, but she never said a word. She didn't need to. Her spell was working on me and she knew it. She just stood there in her white house dress. I felt like I was in heaven.

Sure I was afraid, yet the desire was overwhelming. I couldn't take my eyes off her, even though my brain was blasting an urgent message. *Salerno, this is the Don's dame! Tommy Tomatoes always told you never fuck around with another man's woman!*

Just at that moment her perfume caused another short circuit in my brain. I started shaking so bad that I almost fell off the fucking ladder.

Somehow, I managed to steady myself. Then looked down again. There it was staring me right in the face. The blackest beaver I ever saw.

In one swift move, she unzipped my jeans and swallowed my dick. A moment later a happy little sound came from her throat and my dick exploded.

Without uttering another word, she left the room. Just like that. I just stood there and didn't know what to do.

She was already gone when I finally shouted, "See you tomorrow!"

There was no answer. I don't think she had any worries about whether or not I would be back.

* * *

I took off up the alley but I didn't get far before I ran into Gus Antico. Gus was a made man and naturally he killed people, and yes, in his case "paint the walls" was definitely *not* the same thing as what I was supposed to do for Tony Lap, but other than that, it deserves to be said, as long as nobody paid him to kill you Gus was actually a friendly guy.

"Gus! What are you doing here?"

"Your old man told me you'd be here, pretending to work while you scope out Tony's wife. Does he know you or what? Come with me. I got a job for you."

I cursed to myself. Just what I needed, another job.

But it was a lot more than that. So we drove the soggy streets of Brooklyn while my mind was still on the fucking ladder. Gus made some stops along the way, and each time he came out with a brown paper bag. He dropped them into my lap. "Keep an eye on these!"

In spite of my fantasy life, this experience was big for me. He was sort of trusting me with money. I was in another world.

He noticed. "Hey. You ok?"

I held the bags tight because I could feel the cash bundled inside. A lot of it. "Don't worry, Gus. It's in good hands."

He smiled. "I know that."

See that? He knew, all right. He saw into my soul. Because he knew I preferred to stay alive.

Even so, my mind went right back to Debra. All I wanted was to smell her, feel her, just to look at her. I was obsessed.

5

Reeled In

Gus then drove to a small house in the residential section of Bay Ridge. When we pulled up to a driveway, he pressed a button and a garage door opened, but when we pulled in, the door closed again. To my surprise the whole wall in front of us opened up.

What a move! That brought me back to reality. Gus just said, "The Money Room."

I was in awe. *This is where the action is?*

Gus seemed to read my mind. "This is the place."

Men inside were hard at work and the pace was swift. There must have been a million bucks in the room.

"What's my job? Can I count the money?"

Gus grinned. "No, I just want you to deliver it."

"Gus I can't, I got to do the school thing."

"You do the money thing *after* you do the school thing. Got it?"

I looked at Gus and because of my problem with this *chutzpa* thing, I asked him, "Was that an order, or what?" Well yeah it was an order, but it was a sweet one. He reached into a brown paper bag and peeled off six one hundred-dollar bills. He handed them to me.

"This is for today."

And just then, all the lights went on at the same time.

This is for today ....

* * *

Now I really had to do some fancy foot work to get this done without getting myself all jammed up. I had the school thing and of course I had to finish the paint job and Debra. I had to be everywhere all at the same time.

What I needed was a car. Then I remembered it would attract too much attention, in Gus's words. Luckily for me, when I showed up at Gus's to do the money pickup that afternoon, he was a guy whose thinking had been changed.

So I was to deliver money to different places all around the city, and Gus said no bicycle. Too dangerous. Instead his driver, the Snake, was going to take me.

"Gus, I have a better way," I told him.

Gus was semi-amused. "Okay kid, Let's hear it."

"A mobster and a kid in a car would draw too much attention. I think it's safer to use the bike."

The Snake chimed in, "He's right, Gus. Everything on the streets is changing. Not much respect these days. This kid travels with me, he'll have a target on his back."

Gus bought it. Right then I bonded with the Snake. We got to be a team. So every day, he pulled up at a street corner in his car and handed me a package along with directions. I took it from there by bike. Just a kid out riding.

It left me thinking how lucky I was. I mean, a kid like me moving a lotta money, and—spoiler alert—pumping a woman like Debra. I knew I was doing a stupid thing, banging the Don's dame, but when you got pussy up your nose, as my ma used to say, you forget what's right.

Later, after balling Debra into the wee hours of the morning, I got on my bike to go and all of a sudden, lights from a car flashed on and off. I thought *who the fuck is that?* When I looked up, it was the Snake. The son-of-a-bitch was following me.

My fault. I got sloppy. My heart sank. He must have known I was fucking the Don's dame. I watched him pull into the driveway. He motioned for me to get in.

"What about my bike?" I thought about taking off, but the Snake read me like a racing form.

"Kid, you can run, but you can't hide. Get in the fuckin' car."

"My bike."

"Fuck the bike, get in the car."

I did, and when the Snake headed for the old mill, I thought my life was over. We pulled into the marshy area, and all I could think was, *I am going to a watery grave here!*

I was scared for sure, but I wasn't gonna beg the Snake. After living with my old man, this was easy stuff. Funny, the shit goes through your brain when you think you're gonna die. Now here I was getting ready to meet my maker and all, wasting time thinking about my old man. I laughed at myself.

Snake asked, "You think this is funny? You fuck the Don's dame and you're sitting there laughing. Are you out of your fucking *mind*?"

"I wasn't laughing at you, just an inside joke. An inside joke."

"There you go with the fucking jokes. If the Don finds out you are fucking his dame, he'll cut your balls off and feed them to your grandfather's dog, you dumb fuck!"

Sounds grim, no? Not to me. I started thinking maybe there could be hope, here. Because obviously he hadn't told Gus yet! Otherwise, we wouldn't be here talking. He would've already clipped me.

Optimism was a tool for me as much as a hammer to a carpenter. I convinced myself there was a chance for me here.

The Snake pulled out a cigar, licked it, lit it, and started puffing away. He sat there looking at me a long time, then said, "Kid, I know that dame is a cunt. But still, what you're doing, that don't make it right. It's fucking plain stupid."

Snake leans over and speaks into my ear. "Never, never let this head (points to my dick) tell this head (points to my head) what to do. You got that, fuck-o?"

That was me receiving what passed for fatherly advice. Maybe a real dad would have said it nicer, but I guess the message would have been the same.

* * *

Friday was collection day. Every runner on the street had to have their accounts settled by 5:00 PM, and that included me and the Snake. If you came up short, you had to make up the difference. If you couldn't make up the difference, you were dead.

That was Gus's policy. Simple and effective.

Now here comes Mr. Smiley Ricks, the smoothest man on the planet when it comes to numbers. Smiley pulls me aside, "Salerno, where the fuck is the Snake?"

Usually Smiley was cool, but I could tell his tits were twisted. "I ain't seen him today, what's up?"

Tommy Tomatoes walked by right then and heard me. "Snake is two grand short. Find him now."

"Okay, Tommy."

"But first I want you to go to the track and lay off three thousand on a horse called Royal Anthem."

"Don't worry Tommy, I'll place the bet, then I'll find the Snake. I'll take care of it."

Tomatoes rubbed his bulbous nose. "Five tonight, just like always. Right?"

"Tomatoes, I got this, just like always."

Tomatoes grins. "Yeah kid, just like always."

I got out of there in a hurry, but I didn't really have any idea what to do. I roamed the whole neighborhood, looking, but it was a lost cause. Frustrated, I ran into Fat Sam's ice cream parlor. "Sam, the Snake—did you see him?"

Vinnie the Mook looked up from his booth and said, "I just left him, he's at the Good Shepherd Orphanage."

"Orphanage? What the hell's he doing there?"

"The Snake just bought all the poor kids at the Good Shepherd Orphanage a lotta baseballs."

What? Wait a minute .... "He did what?"

"Baseballs, Salerno. He spent two grand on baseballs. Vinnie nodded his head vigorously. "Yeah, baseballs."

"We better go get him before he does anymore stupid things."

"Don't worry, he blew all his dough on the baseballs."

6

Beautiful Belmont Racetrack –
the Wetting of the Beak

It was a damp day, enough to produce a muddy track. We were sitting in our usual lucky spot, which wasn't really that lucky, when I spotted Maxie Hirsh. He waved from his seat in a box next to us. He was one of our solid big betters.

I didn't believe what we were getting ready to do. Didn't fuckin' matter, there we were, sitting in the box seats and eating hot dogs like nothing ever happened. Like we all had clear heads.

The Snake looked at us and said, "Hey, don't gimmie those fuckin idiot *looks*, I was supposed to receive four big ones from my car accident. I thought I could put it back in time."

The Mook chimed in, "Snake, it's the little things that make the man. Being trustworthy is a fine thing."

"Ah, shut the fuck up, Vinnie. Whatta you know? Eat your fuckin' hot dog."

Vinnie replied, "I know a lot about money, *and* what to do with it when I have it. Not like some guys I know."

Then I jumped in, "Okay, let's knock off the bullshit. What's the big deal? Let's go to Gus and tell him we gave the money to a bunch a poor kids. He'll give us a fucking medal."

Snake shook his head. "No, no. One thing's got nothing to do with the other. I took the fuckin' money. That's all Gus is gonna hear."

Vinnie chimed in, "Gus don't put up with that kinda stuff! No exceptions period! Right, Snake?"

"Look," I said, "We know what you need. That's two G's in a hurry. Let's think about this."

Just then Maxie leaned in close to us and said, "You boys sound like you got trouble?"

"Yeah, Maxie. Money trouble. You got any?"

"Enough to match any bet you want to place. The question is how much do *you* have?"

Vinnie reaches into his black bag and pulls out a fat wad of bills and flashes them. "Maxie, are these enough?"

Maxie grinned and asked, "Who are you wonderful boys betting today?"

I jumped in, "Royal Anthem."

Maxie laughed. "Boys! Keep your money in your pockets. My horse is going to beat him today. Balls out."

Snakes eyes lit up at that, so I tried to slow him down. "Snake, aren't we in enough trouble?"

But Maxie really started adding fuel to the fire. He chimed in, "Royal Anthem is going to be the big favorite, and he can't win!"

I shot Maxie a quick look. *How do you know?*

"Why? Because he hates a muddy track."

"Maxie, a horse race is a horse race. Anything can happen, you know that."

"Boys, here's the deal: Royal Anthem *hates mud*." Maxie smiled. "Okay boys, how much you got in the black bag?"

"Three thousand," I told him.

Maxie took over. "Okay boys, here's what you do." Now all eyes were on Maxie, I mean we were hanging on his every word.

"Royal Anthem will go off the prohibitive favorite at odds of 1 to 9. Now if you take those odds and Royal Anthem loses, you win three thousand."

I asked, "And if he wins?

Maxie replied, "You have to come up with 600 bucks."

At that Vinnie the Mook shouted, "Salerno, that sounds like a good bet to me!"

I sat there thinking this is happening too fast. Three thousand, five thousand, six hundred, the numbers were clogging my brain.

But the Mook said, "I'm in, I'm in," and that did it. He yelled to me, "You better make up your mind fast cause it's almost post time!"

Suddenly the announcer's voice filled the air. Post time was already there! I took a quick look at the horses, then ran to the window and laid down the three thousand, but it was right then I heard the announcer shout, "And they're off!"

We never got the bet in.

I never got the bet in.

The thought hit me, *I'm a dead man.*

I stood there frozen. All I could hear was the Announcer screaming, "It's Vanquish on the inside! Royal Anthem on the outside! Aaand here comes Brightrock, splitting horses!"

All three of them hit the wire together. We waited out the photo check with the rest of the crowd, and it was the longest time of my life. At last the announcer bellowed with his professional excitement, "It's Brightrock by a nose!"

Anthem didn't win. Glory be. The clouds parted.

If I *had* made it to the window in time to place the bet, we would have lost it all, plus been on the hook for another six hundred bucks. Sometimes fortune smiles.

Not long after, zipping along on my new bicycle, I was thinking how I liked being around these mobsters. Seemed like if you had a half a brain, you could earn with them.

7

The Meet

It got serious for me when No Nose got himself killed. No Nose was a made man, and somebody started a rumor that I was behind it. Maybe it was because of my big mouth, maybe it was my overdose of *chutzpa* getting on people's nerves, but I received the kind of summons you don't ignore. There was going to be a meet regarding Salerno and No Nose....

The day of the meet was peculiar. Ma had me all decked out in my favorite suit. Just before I left, in walked my old man.

"This time, smart-ass, you really got yourself in some swindle. Joe Jelly is going to eat you alive."

Ma snapped, "Everyone in the neighborhood knows about this. Why don't *you* go talk to him? Isn't he your buddy? For Christ sakes, this is your son!"

"Oh, no. This is major stuff, it's out of my league."

"For Christ sakes, Charley, this is your son. I know you do business with that piece of shit all the damn time."

"Gracie, this is something that is beyond me."

And so I had to go to the meet without any backup.

When I got to Rosales Restaurant, the placed was jammed. I scanned the room looking for Tommy and Gus, and somehow found myself face-to-face with the old man Gambino himself. I nodded to show respect, and then made my way over to Joey the Blond.

Joey greeted me with a smile. He whispered. "You've come a long way from shining shoes."

I gave him a thumbs up, then moved along the bar.

Sitting there drinking a martini was Three Fingers Brown, the mob boss from Manhattan. We locked eyes for a moment. I figured he was going to preside at the meet.

Tensions were running high. This was heavy action.

As I approached, I saw Gus get up and move to the head of the table where Joe Jelly was seated. We locked eyes a moment, then the rotund mobster stuck a big Havana into his mug and asked, "How is your old man?"

I kept my face respectful. "I don't know, Joe. Last I heard he went to take a shit and the hogs ate him."

"Oh, you know, for a kid you got *such* a smart fuckin' mouth."

I walked away. Three Fingers looked at me, "Did you kill No Nose?"

"No!"

"Do you know who did?"

I was nervous, but I stayed cool and looked back at Joey and Gus a long moment, and then replied. "Yes, I do."

Joey the Blond slid over to me. "Kid, who was it?"

I pointed to Joe Jelly. With that, the whole room went silent. I could see the defiance in Jelly's eyes. He looked at me with murder.

All the mobsters went into a corner and started their own rap session. I would've given my right arm to be a fly on the wall. Surprisingly enough, I wasn't scared a bit. I was glad I fingered that fat prick; I knew he was gonna kill me anyway, thinking I took out No Nose. At least this way I had a chance.

Everyone returned to the table and it seemed to me the mood was tight. It looked like everything was decided, but it was hard to get a read on anyone. All the players had the same empty look on their faces. Now I started to get nervous. Jelly came over and sat next to me. I could tell from the look on his mug, he wanted blood.

Jelly whispered at me through his cigar-stained teeth, "If you didn't kill No Nose, then who did?" This time around I was ready for this meatball. I replied with confidence. "It was *you*! I could never forget that voice."

I turned to the others. "It was him. I'd know that voice anywhere."

With that, Jelly ripped into me, "Tell the truth, you little scumbag."

I jumped up, "I ain't no scumbag."

"Salerno, sit down!" Gus hollered. "Jelly, it's over!"

Jelly just glared at him.

Gus repeated, even louder, "It's *over*!"

Except it wasn't over. Not by a long shot.

I could see the defiance in Jelly's eyes. He looked over to the bar and yelled to the Blond, "Get the lemon squeezer and bring it over here."

Gus got to his feet. "Jelly, I said it's over."

But Jelly had rank on Gus. Jelly just snarled, "It isn't over while I'm alive."

I didn't know who all the players were, but I could sense there was definitely a power struggle going on. Jelly snatched the lemon squeezer. He gripped it so hard his knuckles turned white.

Jelly grinned, "Salerno! Now drop your pants. Let's see how much sugar you got in your draws."

I dropped them. I had to. Nobody moved. I looked at Joey the Blond, then Gus, but there was no help coming.

I quivered when Jelly inserted one of my balls into the squeezer.

Gambino looked at me and asked. "Kid, who killed my nephew?" Gambino nodded.

Jelly tightened the squeezer slowly. The pain hit like a spear to the crotch. The spear twisted. It was awful. I screamed and almost passed out, but not quite. I had to stand up to them.

Gambino asked again. "Tell me who?"

I pointed to Jelly. "I said it was *him!*"

Jelly just screamed, "You little scumbag!" He clamped down on the squeezer. I screamed from the bottom of my feet.

Tommy moved to stop him, but he was too late—Jelly crushed my testicle and left me with one ball in my nut sack. When poor Tommy tried to step in, Jelly snatched a fork from the table and slammed it deep into Tommy's voice box.

Such responses to heavy stress were not unknown among those people, but it never meant there wouldn't be consequences. His response to the accusation was strong, but it didn't do a thing to deny his guilt.

All he did was guarantee himself a heavy reckoning. Soon after, they found him in Plumb Beach. His head was stuck deep into the muck. A "Polluted" sign was jammed way up his ass for all to see, giving out a clear message: never cross the Gambinos.

Under the circumstances, I was fine with all of that. The Polluted sign was a nice touch.

* * *

My sacrifice became the talk of the neighborhood, and my old man was loving every minute of it. I guess in his warped mind I was some kind of a celebrity. This was the first time anyone could remember when a kid got the nod over a made guy. My old man was so stoked, he went so far as to crush a tennis ball and put it in a jar, and to this day he keeps that jar displayed on his cash register for all to see.

His little "nut display" turned out to be the bowling trophy he never won. But the strange thing was, when I would show up for work after school, he took the trophy down. Like he didn't want me to know he was proud of me. He knew I knew it was there. He knew I knew he was taking it down when I came over. But he kept it up anyway. I realized then, there was no sacrifice I could ever make to get him to love me.

And I needed to keep the other one.

8

The Woman for Me

It was now 1955 and the Brooklyn Dodgers had finally beat the New York Yankees. The bars were filled, people spilled out into the streets and danced until the break of dawn.

I was playing football on my seventeenth birthday, and as I was coming off the field, I saw a lovely blond just standing there all alone. The closer I got to her, the prettier she looked.

"Hi, I'm Richie."

She smiled. "I know, Crazy Richie, right?"

"That's right, I guess. And you are?"

"Lucille Esposito."

"Where you from?"

"Over on Avenue N." She smiled at me. "You looked pretty good out there today."

"You look good yourself. How about an egg cream? Fat Sam makes them the best."

"That would be nice, Richie, but I have to get home. I have to baby-sit."

At that moment, I just wanted to take her in my arms. "You wanna ride home?"

She grinned and pointed to my bicycle. "On that?"

"Why not?" I could see her reluctance, so I said, "Come on, Lou, get up on the handlebars, I'll show you."

She smiled at that. "No one's ever called me Lou."

We zipped along happily, at least I was, with the softness of her butt and the smell of her perfume. It was clogging my brain.

When we turned onto her street, she pointed to her house. Unfortunately, there was a Marine sitting there on the steps of the house across the street from hers. When we pulled up, he pointed at me and bellowed, "Who the fuck is *he*?"

Lucille snapped back, "None of your business, Jimmy! I told you, we're done!"

The irate Marine just gaped at her, so I added, "Tell me Jimmy, what part of 'done' don't you understand?"

Boy, that Marine was fast. I was on the deck before I knew what hit me. Then he stood over me to spit in my face, presenting his crotch for a quick right hand to his nutsack. I was, after all, the resident expert on nutsack pain.

Jimmy dropped hard to the ground.

It was only then that Lucille looked scared. "Salerno! You've gotta get the hell out of here! His brother is also a Marine, and they both have guns."

I waved her off. "So what? Everybody's got guns."

She grabbed me. "Richie, please go."

"Okay, are you gonna be all right? I mean, with that guy?"

"Trust me. Now get on your bicycle and get outta here!" I just stood there, feeling lost. I had never been this smitten over a dame before (Yeah, they were still dames then). Not even with Debra, who came on to a neighborhood rat like me while living in Tony's house. This was different. It felt real. I got on my bicycle, but as I was getting ready to take off, Lou came running back into my arms and whispered, "Come see me tonight."

I didn't understand. "What about your parents?"

She giggled and replied, "Oh, they'll be home. But my father parks his truck in the alley. It's right under my window …."

* * *

I came back later that night, of course. When I rode into her darkened street, it was well after midnight and my expectations were high. There was no streetlight, so now it was really dark. I crossed the street, pulled up in someone's yard to stash my bike, then scooted into Lucille's yard and climbed up onto the roof of her dad's truck.

I quietly tapped on her window.

Lucille appeared and helped pull me into her room. We immediately slid into her bed, where we hugged and kissed the night away. It was a beautiful thing. I wasn't even worried about my bike.

9

Birth of a Butcher

Me, Ma, and my uncle Sammy all crowded behind the kitchen door, trying to hear my old man and Mr. Esposito discuss my future. But all we could hear was a lot of mumbling, so I opened the door another sliver.

My Uncle Sammy saw me and whispered, "Richie, please don't marry her!" Then turned to Ma, "Gracie, Charley has plenty of dough. Let her get a fuckin' abortion!"

Ma snapped, "Sammy, shut the hell up!"

But Sammy kept going. "I know a great abortionist, he's real cheap, but good. He won't cut her up."

I chimed in, "Uncle Sammy, come on, gimmie a break. She's a nice kid. We can't kill the baby." Off my Uncle's questioning look, I added, "I'll marry her. It's the right thing to do."

"Richie, don't do it. You'll be sorry for the rest of your life.

We locked eyes a moment before he whispered, "Kid. Give yourself a break here."

Then Lucille's father shouted, "Marriage? Hey Charley! Now that your son has knocked up my daughter, tell me how the fuck he's going to make a living?"

I watched my old man compose himself while he took a few puffs on his stogie, then he calmly replied, "Well, you could always make him a butcher …."

And that's what put the butcher knife in my hand.

* * *

Mom and Pop had everything all set at the church. By then, Lucille was big. Tony Lap, our resident mobster of the parish, got the priest to do a special ceremony for us at the side altar next to the big altar.

By the time me and Lucille finally waddled up the aisle together, I could see the lines were drawn. Esposito and his bunch of hooligans were on one side and Joey the Blond and his mobsters on the other.

It looked to me more like a mob war. I could feel the tension ready to explode. But then Tony Lap's girlfriend Debra entered the church, wearing a black skin-tight wraparound. All the worshipers stopped and stared.

Esposito's half-witted son decided to reach out and pinch Debra on her voluptuous ass while she passed. He might as well have gone after her with a knife.

In seconds, everyone was slugging it out. My wedding ceremony poured out into the street. It took about ten short minutes before most of us were arrested for disorderly conduct or maybe it was inciting a riot.

Our wedding present from Tony Lap was me and Lucille spending our honeymoon together in a jail cell. That's right, couple's night inside a city jail cell for two. Tony's brother-in-law was the head detective on the night shift, so he had a nice cell set aside and all ready for us.

Joey the Blond made sure we had plenty to eat and drink until we saw the Judge. It was all so crazy that it was beautiful. None of it felt wrong. It felt like beating the odds.

10

Hanging with Harry

Hanging with Harry was the wrong kind of adventure. He was too unstable to be trusted. I went over to the Black Kitten to find Joey the Blond and tell him about what happened.

"Joey," I told him, "Harry the Ear has shit for brains."

Joey shot me a funny look, but I put up my hand. "Case in point, we went to stick up a plumbing supply joint. Harry walked in and made the announcement 'This is a stick up.' And guess what? Harry forgot the gun. So there we were with our dicks in our hands. Only this time I got wacked in the head with a snow shovel by a three-hundred-pound woman."

Joey laughed, "At least you didn't go home empty!" I got up to leave, but Joey stopped me. "Ah, come on Salerno, give him another shot."

"Joey, please. This is a guy that just knocked off his own wife."

Joey just frowned. I said, "Look, the way he tells it is he came home from the track late and he missed dinner. His wife goes nuts. They get into a beef, she picks up a baseball bat, and she nails him in his ear. In the scuffle, Harry picks up a fork, so she smashes him again in the ear. When the wife goes in for another swing, Harry raises the fork in defense and she falls right into the fork. The judge sentences Harry to twenty years. This is a guy you want me stepping out with?"

But Joey nodded. "Yeah. Now here's where owning a member of the police comes in. Good old Swivel Tooth manages to get department information and pass it along to Harry; Harry says he gives top-notch information."

"So now I'm stuck with him?"

Joey smiled. "Twenty-five percent for Swivel Tooth and twenty-five for me. Not such a bad deal. You got Swivel Tooth to help you on his end and you got me on this end. Kid, you got the best of both worlds."

"So now I have three partners, and I still haven't earned a fuckin' dime."

Joey laughed, "Twenty-five percent of something is better than one hundred percent of nothing."

And after all, Joey was right. Stealing is a full-time job. So I went to see Vinnie the Mook to show me how to use a gun. Vinnie was a war hero and an expert on guns, so I figured the Mook was the best guy to learn from.

Just then, Harry comes bursting in my front door and he was beaming with joy. "I got a good one! I got a good one."

"Harry, what the fuck are you talking about? Can't you see I'm busy?"

He pushed, "This is a great tip!"

"Harry, later, not now."

But Harry is too excited to use his ears. "She's only a dame, we are going to knock off a bookmaker that's not connected. It's a piece of cake."

My mistake that day turned out to have been bringing Lucille along on this visit. It was like a gun went off. She stepped back. Her face transformed. She looked at me like I was a demon. "My father was *right* about you!"

"Lucille, I'm just trying to get over!"

But it was not the first she had seen of this life. It was only the first time she had seen it from me. She laughed, "Yeah, right over the wall and into Sing-Sing!"

We went anyway, minus Lucille. All the way there, Harry kept mumbling, "This is it, I got this from my best connection. Twenty-five grand for openers. Salerno, I can feel it, this time we break our cherry. This time we get the fucking money!"

No guns, no masks, no nothing. Harry was right. When we got there, our target, Jimmy the Bookie, was nowhere around. There was only this sweet-looking dame with an ass that didn't quit.

She smiled in the doorway. "What can I do for you boys?"

I asked, "Is Jimmy home?"

"Jimmy doesn't live here. You're in the wrong place."

"Let's knock off the bullshit. I know what's going on here. Where is the cash?"

"You've been duped, sonny boy. Jimmy took the money and left. All of it"

I looked at Harry. "We been suckered! Jimmy took the money. He used us to cover his ass."

She replied, "You boys better be careful, Jimmy's cousin is a mobster."

Her powers of attraction were considerable enough to distract me a little from the fleecing we just took.

I looked at her. "Is there anything we can do for you?"

By the time I left, she was happy and I was happy.

So it wasn't a complete bust. The dame had such a good time she couldn't wait to tell us were Jimmy lived. Now I know why Tommy always told me, never tell your business to your wife, and *especially* not your girlfriend.

11

Trusting the Untrustworthy

We went to see Mr. Wise Ass, but as soon as we walked through the door, he squealed like a pig. "Don't hurt me! Please don't hurt me!" His wife snaps, "He did *what*? What did he do?"

Harry told her. "He sent us to rob his partner, Sweet Sally."

Her eyes widened. "Jimmy, who the fuck is Sweet Sally? Answer me, you pig."

He was shaking so bad I almost felt sorry for him. But we had to push him. "Where's the fuckin money?"

He finally replied, "On the floor of my closet you'll find a box of rubbers. The cash is in the bottom of the box."

Hearing that, his wife went ballistic. "Rubbers? Who are the fuckin' rubbers for? You never use them with me, you pig!" Then from nowhere, she gave Jimmy the best swift kick to the nuts you ever saw. He went down hollering.

We finally made a score and got the thirty thousand, but in the end we gave the rubbers to his wife. If they split up and she started dating, she might want them.

The joy was short lived.

When we got back to the neighborhood, my pal Joey the Blond told me Sally D, the boss in Brooklyn, wanted to see us about a bookmaker who got knocked off. I knew who this Sally D was, and I remembered the first time I met him in my old man's shop. Right off, he kind of reminded me of a spider. Like a guy who was always trying to pull you into his web.

I never trusted my old man, so why should I trust Sally D? Together these two worked all the card games that were held over at the Knights of Columbus. Sally D tried to get my old man into the Italian American League, but there was a beef, being my old man was only half Italian, so they threw him out.

Of course that didn't sit so well with Sally D and my old man, so Sally D got my old man a special dispensation from the pope. I don't know how he pulled that off, but there was the pope sponsoring a cold-blooded killer into a Catholic organization for the sole purpose of cheating.

Nice move, Pop, I thought. But make no mistake, my old man played the victim well—one of the reasons he was known as Charley the Pick. Sally D hated my old man's line of shit, but he sure loved the old man's slight-of-hand. Sally D once said to me, "Kid, you know what's so amazing about your old man? He has these fat beefy fingers, and he's as skillful as a surgeon. Go figure that one!"

I figured, all right. Especially about the old man's beefy-fingered skills around the ladies.

* * *

The Friday night card game at my old man's house was the game to play in. My job in those days was to answer the door from the upstairs window. If I knew who they were, I hit the buzzer. If not, I'd call Sally D.

Sally D loved that kind of attention. So now there I was going to see Sally D himself, a guy who I knew liked to cheat and kill people. And while I rode the rusty elevator up to his place, I was thinking *why the fuck am I here?*

It didn't take long to find out. When the ride was over, there was Sally D and my old man sitting in a high-stakes poker game.

In this game, there was a new mark, a face I hadn't seen before. I didn't begrudge them a little gambling. It was just a way to pass time while they waited.

Vinny the Cig whispered to me. "You're in big trouble."

I nodded, "Yeah, Vinny, it won't be the first time!"

"This one might be your last time, hot shot."

That didn't sound too good. Vinny the Cig spotted the worried look on my face and said, "This Johnny G is bad news. He's looking to make a name for himself. Looks like you're first on the list ...."

I nodded. I already knew Johnny G was a killer on the way up.

That why I had just gone to see Vinny the Mook and asked him for a derringer. The Mook had told me, "This move could get you killed. You never bring a gun to a sit down. You know they're gonna frisk you. You know that?"

"I know, Vinnie. Need it anyway."

I took the derringer, then went to see Ma. She sewed a holster to the inside of my jeans, right next to my fly, so I could slip the two-shooter into the holster. I thought, *at least now I have a chance, if something goes wrong.*

I knew I was alone in this thing, even though Sally D and my old man were friends. I still couldn't trust either of them. I didn't want to be just another dumb kid that got stupid.

At the meet, Vinny the Cig poked me in the ribs. "Salerno, see that big guy in the corner? That's Johnny G. You made a big mistake this time. Really big."

"Maybe. Who knows?"

"Wise ass, I told you sooner or later you would get your tail caught in the fuckin' door."

This time I ripped into him. "Vinny, you dumb fuck, now tell me what's that supposed to mean?"

Like if I scared Vinny, I could make this go away. ButI knew I was in some kind trouble. I looked over at the guy, and the son of a bitch was way to happy. Then he personally started frisking me, like he couldn't trust anyone else to do it.

"Gee, Vinny, why don't you start with my balls?"

He stopped short.

I asked in a very nice tone of voice, "What's the matter, tough guy? You afraid you might like it?"

Vinny smirked. "Wise ass. When Johnny G gets through with you, your balls are gonna be history."

Sure, I could have corrected him on that, but there didn't seem to be much point.

I caught my old man's eye, and I could tell he was in the middle of a scam. My old man and Sally D did it to everyone, even wise guys, and they were doing it there.

He always said wise guys were the easiest marks, because they believed they were invincible and let their guards down. What a joke that was, because here they were giving Johnny G the old one-two, and I could see it coming a mile away. Distraction was half the battle. One half of the team was sweating Sally D while the other end kept betting strong.

Now here it came, my old man dealt Johnny G three eights. The sucker saw his cards, then came out betting with both hands. Sally sat there with two red aces, raised the pot, and Johnny re-raised. Sally D just called. Johnny took two cards. The moron smiled.

Sally drew three cards. Johnny smiled again and came out betting. Now, I've watched my old man do this thing over and over. Here comes two black aces straight off the bottom of the deck and into Sally D's sweaty hands.

Johnny was dead in the water. Only he didn't know that while he pushed all his chips into the pot and said, "I'm all in."

I laughed to myself. Vinnie caught me and asked, "What's so funny?"

I just said, "Watch, you might learn something."

Sally pushed in his chips in with one hand. With the other, he produced the four aces. Nice.

Johnny G didn't appreciate that. I could see from the corner of my eye he was ready to explode. I decided to speak up. "Hi Pop, how you doing? Hi, Sally, you wanted to see me? What's up?"

Johnny G exploded. "Yeah, I'll tell you what's up, you piece of shit! Where do you get the fucking balls to rob my cousin Jimmy?"

I looked at him a moment, then I said, "Johnny! I didn't know he was your cousin, and if I did, I never would've made a move." Off Johnny's doubtful look, I added, "Your fuckin' cousin, Jimmy, robbed his partner, not me. He gave us the tip just to cover his sorry ass."

Johnny just stood there gaping at me.

"Johnny, you might want to sit down: your cousin is a fuckin' double-dealing scumbag."

Johnny turned the table over, flipped the thing, then came at me like a mad bull. I stepped back just as he got to me and I slammed a right hand into his pretty face.

All I felt was his nose collapsing. I walked out of there and fast, then roamed the streets all night long, thinking about what I just did to this "how you doing," tough guy. The kind of fool who thinks killing makes you tough, who doesn't realize how many killers are cowards and weaklings. Everywhere I went, all I could think about was, *Salerno, you dropped a guy who just made his bones! They kill for that.*

Right then, I remembered what the Hawk told me about this tough guy, Johnny G, when he was about to make his bones and whack some target. When it came time, he was shaking so much, Sally D had to hold his hand while Johnny pulled the trigger. That's the worst kind of a guy in the whole Sicilian universe to be trusted with a "button."

We called guys like Johnny G "disappointed dunskis." The term "dunski" referred to a made man, but this dunski had no balls at all. It would still be easy for him to whack me, because one: he had a reason, and two: I was a nobody.

Who could I trust? I called Joey the Blond, and he said to lay low for a while until things cooled off. Good old Joey, I knew I could trust him to keep quiet about me.

But I also called Tommy Tomatoes, and he just laughed hard when he said, "You busted him up pretty good, Salerno. I gotta tell ya, he doesn't look so good no more. So, lay low 'til Sally D cools off, got that? Remember, the man is Johnny G's rabbi, so you gotta be careful. Trust no one! There's a lot of people out there who want to get next to Sally D, to earn a favor. They would give you up in a *minute* to do that. Remember."

I knew not to call my old man with this. Who could tell what he would do in this situation? Good old Pop. I couldn't trust no one in the hood, not even my wife. So I made a left turn and headed for Far Rockaway. In those days, no one would think about looking for me in a black neighborhood.

12

Call It What You Want

When I walked into her office, I could see it was plush. I took one look at her and realized I had forgotten how lovely she really was. But she looked up at me with a frown.

She came to her feet anyway and walked over to hug me. "Salerno, look at you, what the hell happened? You look like you haven't slept for a month! What's going on?"

Her scent filled my nostrils. "Dante, will you marry me?"

She laughed. "If you weren't already married, I might think about it. What's going on with you? Are you in some kind of trouble, or what?"

"All I need you to do is let me hide out here until I can figure out what to do."

"Let's call my dad, he can fix anything."

"The Hawk? Oh, I don't know, Dante. He's pretty good friends with the guy that I hit."

"Salerno! You know you can trust him. Besides, he loves you. He's told me that many times."

That struck me. "Dante, in that case, first off, I gotta call the neighborhood and find out what's going on."

So I called Vinnie the Mook, and he said Johnny G was so pissed, he was looking for me all over the city.

"So wherever you are," Vinnie told me, "stay there!"

Dante's apartment was really small so we got used to one another fast. Almost too fast. I liked her company and she liked mine. But I decided after a few hours it was time to leave, just as soon as I finally had a plan.

That night, I was slowly slipping off to sleep when a soft hand touched my head. I opened my eyes and there was the Hawk, right there, smiling and looking relaxed.

"How you doing, kid? I heard you got trouble?"

"Yeah, but that piece of shit came at me. What the hell was I supposed to do?"

"You did what you had to do, now we have to do what we have to do."

"How do we do that?"

"Kid, this isn't going to be easy."

I snapped, "I'm not running from that wind bag!"

"Salerno, I know Johnny G since he was a kid. Win or lose, you made some enemies now that you're not even aware of."

"The same can be said about you, right?"

The Hawk didn't answer me right away. There was a long silence. So I added, "I did what I had to do."

The Hawk finally replied. "Better men than you have died for the same reason. I need you to be right."

I shook my fist. "I'm right, and that lowlife cousin of his set me up!"

The Hawk grinned again, "There's more to this than just being right. We have to get Sally D on your side."

Hearing that, I walked around the room shaking my head. The Hawk added, "Remember, he saw the whole thing, we gotta find a way to get to him."

I nodded. "Yeah, you're right. My old man and Sally are as thick as thieves. Sally D loves the action, loves the winning."

I looked at the Hawk. This sounded promising. I told him, "Go see my old man. You talk to him. I know he will listen you. In fact, I know he's scared of you. Every time I mention your name, his face twitches. Ernie, I tell you, my old can get into Sally's greedy head!"

The Hawk walked around the terrace. I could see his good eye pulsating while he thought it over. So I piled on.

"Ernie, Sally D loves running a good cheat more than he loves that fucking creep, Johnny G."

13

The Meet

Gus set the meet for a Friday night. On the Hawk's turf and in his joint. Hearing that was a relief. But the Hawk reminded me, "Johnny G will never be far away, so for the next few days you better watch your back."

Wherever I went, I packed my derringer and a fucking old-time hand grenade. I ran into the Hawk and told him, "Look! A fuckin grenade! I got it from Uncle Phil. He was a war hero, killed forty Japs all by himself."

"Some of us know about him," the Hawk said with a smile. "He was the smallest guy in the whole army, but he had the biggest heart."

When Uncle Phil found out what was going on, he came to see me and said, "Salerno, your mother would kill me if something happened to you." He also told me he would be at the Black Kitten just in case one of those mobsters gets stupid.

Knowing he would be in that room gave me the feeling that at least I wasn't alone. The Hawk smiled again. "Listen to this. Your mother told me your old man went to Florida until this is all over."

I shook my head and told him, "You know, Ernie, my old man is still true to form: a coward."

He shook his head. "Nah, he's not a coward; he just has a little sugar in his draws, that's all."

"Yeah, Ernie, did you ever wonder why my old man wasn't drafted? He got Jimmy Go, you know, the butcher's son, to piss in a bottle. Then when my old man got to the draft board, he poured Jimmy's piss into his bottle. Cost him a grand, but Jimmy had albumen in his urine. So two weeks later, my old man was classified 4-F. Now isn't that a fucking coward's move?"

The Hawk replied, "There are some people that might think that was actually a slick move. You follow my drift?"

Great. When I pulled up to the Black Kitten in my 1950 Mercury, I saw Lucille standing out front. She looked good, but standing there talking to her was Johnny Bath Beach. Not great. I got out and asked. "Lucille, what's up?"

"I wanted to see you, so I came here because this place seems to be your home these days."

I went to enter the Black Kitten, but Johnny stopped me. "Saturday nights is only for the wives. No dames."

This was an unexpected complication from the fact that I kept everything about my personal life as far from those mobsters as I could. As far as he knew, I was single. But now the jig was up. I eyed him. "Lucille is my wife."

He grinned and put up his hands. "Sorry pal, no offense. I just thought she was on the loose."

I nodded. Johnny eyed me, "You better put her on a leash, Salerno, you might lose her."

I guided Lucille to my car. "Who was that guy?" she asked me.

"Just some mobster"

"Now you're hanging out with mobsters? We're married four years and now I find this out?"

"Lucille. I got this covered. It's a piece of cake." We drove down to the old mill, our favorite spot, which I thought was a nice touch. That night our third child was conceived.

* * *

Friday night was the big sit down. Jittery anticipation was running wild in my body, but as I waltzed into the Black Kitten the joint was humming. That put me at ease.

Vinny the Mook was pouring drinks at a torrid pace. He moved toward me and said, "All the big bosses showed for this one."

I looked around. Mobsters lined the walls. Black Sam and Gandi were in deep conversation. Frankie Hollywood and the Andrezzi brothers were eyeballing me. Westo and Tony Ducks, the top mobster from Manhattan, were also there. A full house for sure. I wondered why the Manhattan made men were there. After all, this was a Brooklyn beef. That was strange.

Johnny Bath Beach walked by and said. "How's Lucille?"

I thought that was strange, too. So I just looked at him a moment. "Why the interest in my wife? I don't even know you."

He smiled. "Kid, right now you got more trouble than you can handle."

Then he walked off. The Mook slid next to me. I could see he was all excited. "Salerno, I think you got a problem with this Johnnie Bath Beach."

"Whaddya mean? What the fuck is going on? I got no beef with that guy."

The Mook whispers to me, "I think Johnny Bath Beach got the hots for your wife."

"What?"

"Yeah, from time to time she has been here looking for you. Then one stormy night she shows up, you were a no-show, so Johnny bought her a couple of drinks. Then after a while they went dancing at Max the Mayor's."

"What?" I just looked at the Mook. "What should I do?"

"He wants your wife. Get a fucking gun."

"You mean he would kill me, just to fuck my old lady?"

"Something like that."

"I never heard of that, that's fuckin nuts."

"Yeah, well Salerno, you're just a kid. You better get your head out of your ass and start to pay attention."

I moved across the bar to Sally D, but then Johnny G shot me a look. I knew he was at the top of his game. I just walked up to Sally D easy as you please, and whispered in his ear, "Sally, my old man is down in Miami. He told me to tell you he has a bunch of suckers all lined up."

Sally smiled at that.

"He's staying at the Hotel Johnna, and he said to call him." I knew I had Sally's ear now, so I went on. "Sally, I never knew Jimmy was Johnny's cousin. That fucking cop Swivel Tooth McGowan gave Harry the Ear the tip. Jimmy set this whole thing up just to cover his ass for the money he stole. That dame, Sweet Sally, was the one who gave me Jimmy's address."

Then from the corner of my eye I spotted my uncle sitting quietly all by himself, eating a slice of pizza. He nodded but he waved me off. I got his message. He also had his game face on. I stood there wondering how many grenades he was holding.

There were so many things going on in the bar my head started to spin. I walked out to clear my mind with some fresh air. It felt good, until I looked. Sitting right there in a beat-up Plymouth Fury was Swivel Tooth.

What the fuck is he doing here?

That's all I needed was for this guy to start breaking my balls. To make things worse, he had that penetrating look in his eyes. I got goose bumps and quickly retreated into the bar. When I got inside, the players were all arranged differently.

The Hawk, Tony Ducks, and Gus were all seated at a table talking. Sally D and Johnny G were at another table, sucking down clams. I could see from the way they were eating, their moods were very pensive. I'm sure the presence of the Hawk was also giving them something to think about.

I strolled through the Kitten and walked right over to Gus. In front of the whole bar, he hugged me like a teddy bear.

That was a big time move. Now everyone in that room for sure knew Gus was on my side. I whispered, "Gus, that cop Swivel Tooth is parked outside." I was pumped just like a kid at his first birthday party.

At that moment, Swivel Tooth finally made his entrance. I thought, *here's another player in the puzzle.*

All of a sudden, I wasn't scared anymore. I could see things clearly. I walked right over to the Hawk and sat down just like I belonged there. The move was bold, but I was making my own statement to that scum-sucking cop and everyone else in the room. Including myself.

The Hawk spotted Swivel Tooth at the bar, and then while he watched the cop approach, he reached under the table and pulled a snub-nosed thirty-eight from his pocket. He jammed it between Holly's legs. She was one of the local girls and she had seen a lot, but now the pistol sent her wide-eyed.

The cop moved toward the Hawk and grinned. "Nice little gathering." He looked at me. "I see you're still alive. Not bad, kid. You might be three-to-five to stay alive."

The Hawk just smiled. "Mack, how about a drink?"

"Not when I'm on duty." Then he looked at Holly and said, "Ernie, tell me, how do you rate something as fine as this woman?"

Holly shot back, "It's called class, mister, Something I'm sure you don't know anything about that."

Swivel Tooth snickered. "Lady, it all depends on how you define the word class." He spotted Johnny G and shouted across the crowded room, "Johnny, I heard you were busy the other night. Seems like your buddy Willie Wide Eyes, took one in the back of the head. I also heard there was a good-looking wop sitting in the back seat. I guess that was you."

He swaggered toward the mobster. "Looks like something you would do, since he got it from behind."

Johnny sat stone-faced. I thought, *isn't there anything this cop don't know?"*

The Hawk just sat there smiling at the killer cop. There was definitely an acknowledgment of respect between both men. Swivel Tooth turned and looked Johnny G straight in the eye, and I mean close. "Good morning, sunshine. Remember this: when I give it to you, it'll be from the front 'cause I want you to see it coming."

Johnny G snapped at the cop, "Yeah, well, *you* remember: bullets fly both ways."

Swivel Tooth chuckled and turned to the Hawk, "That wop there is going to give your joint a bad name." Without further ado, he turned and left the room, taking along whatever infection was poisoning his brain.

Holly leaned over to the Hawk, "Get this fucking thing away from me before it goes off. I think you're just as crazy as that cop."

The Hawk chuckled and whispered to her. "What's that supposed to mean?"

She smiled like you do when you don't feel like smiling.

* * *

Getting ready for the sit down was like watching some strange stage play. I thought that underneath it all, this must be a struggle for power. What else could it be?

Tony Ducks, a powerful boss from Manhattan, was selected by Gus because Tony was tough and never took sides. For him, it was the facts and only the facts.

Now I saw it: the guy I robbed was located in Manhattan. That was in Tony Ducks' backyard. That was why Tony was there. These wise guys were all very territorial. Gus knew Johnny G was way out of line on this, but it was a very sensitive subject. Johnny G was a made guy.

Me, I was just a young street punk who just happened to have some nice wise guys in my corner. Not much of a contest.

Gus motioned to Johnny G to join the table, and Sally D, Johnny G's rabbi, also got up. Gus quickly eyeballed Sally D, letting the Brooklyn mobster know it was time to sit down, which meant *you're not wanted.*

All this was a very subtle move, yet effective. Sally D was not invited, and from the expression on Sally D's face, I could see that for him, that was a definite sign of disrespect.

Just then the tipster, Johnny G's cousin, Jimmy the Mole, came strutting into the crowded bar. I could smell his stinky perfume clear across the room, like in a cheap hotel. I watched him sweating. By the time he reached the table, he was washed out, like an old Charles Town claimer, which is one of your broken-down racehorses that has seen better days.

Jimmy the Mole looked like he wanted to go lie down somewhere and die. But before he could run off, Tony gave the Mole the seat of honor, right at the head of the table. Believe me, from the look on the Mole's face, I could see he wasn't comfortable with that at all.

Now, his cousin Johnny G was seated next to him. The sight of that pair side by side confirmed my suspicion—*wise guys gotta find a better way to recruit new blood.*

Tony Ducks eyed the daily double while he casually asked Johnny, "Why did you go after Salerno?"

Johnny D replied, "Because that piece of shit pistol whipped my cousin, took all his cash, and then raped his girl. You don't do shit like that and expect to live."

Right then, I wanted to belly fuck this lying son of a bitch.

Tony Ducks snapped. "Salerno, what about that?"

"Tony," I told him, "Johnny doesn't know what really happened. His cousin Jimmy robbed his partner, not me. On the other hand, the girlfriend was a good-looking chick."

Tony asked, "What does that mean?"

"We talked."

"What did you talk about?"

"Mostly bullshit, you know dis and dat, then after a while, we had a couple of drinks, and the next thing you know we were all in the bed having a good ol' time. But Tony, a funny thing happened while we were getting ready to leave. Sally handed me Jimmy's address."

"What, she did you both?"

"In a New York minute. Now as far as making Jimmy look bad in front of his wife, yes that I did do, but we never ever disrespected his wife in any way. Tony, the whole time we were there, all Jimmy did was whimper like a baby."

"Why was he crying?"

"I don't know. That you'll have to ask him."

Tony looked at the Mole. "Well, Jimmy, what about it?"

The Mole just sat there awaiting the arrival of general shit. Never a word passed his lips.

Tony looked away. Then shot me a look. "Your hands, why did you use them?"

"Tony, I hit Johnny because he gave me no choice. He knows that. He came at me like a crazy man, so I dropped him and took off."

The Duck asked me, "Where is the stuff you took from Jimmy?"

I told him, "Harry the Ear took his end, all except for the rubbers. He said he never uses them, then he split. Tony, the Ear don't care about respect. He's just a redneck! The cop, Swivel Tooth, gave Harry the tip."

The look on Tony's face made me keep going, "You know these rednecks; they live by a different set of rules. Gus is holding my end."

Ducks looked at the daily double a long time, while the room anxiously waited. Tony finally got up and walked over to Johnny.

"You bring me here to defend a rat bastard?" He leaned close to Johnny G's face, "How could you not know your cousin set up his own partner?"

At that moment, Johnny got a lot of sugar in his draws. I know the look, the face turns a pale gray.

His voice was shaky. "Tony, I swear my cousin never told me a fucking thing."

Tony just glared at him.

Johnny shouted, "Tony! I swear on my mother's eyes! If I knew he was selling out his own partner, I would've wacked him myself!"

Reacting to Tony's doubtful look, Johnny went on, "Tony, he never told me a fucking thing!"

"You mean you never asked him a fucking thing? You just did this all on your own?"

Nobody was going to sallow that. Jimmy was left holding the bag. Knowing he was in deep shit, he bolted from the table and went for the door.

I was on him right away, and as soon as I snatched him, he started crying again. Worse, the smell hit me and I realized Jimmy had shit himself. So I just dropped him on the floor. He lay there, whimpering and mumbling, "Please don't hurt me! I can't take the pain!"

I actually felt sorry for the guy. The Hawk looked down at the Mole. "What about the pain you caused?"

Jimmy started squirming on the floor, mumbling, "Please, no more! I was only a kid when they shot my old man and threw him in a hole! Please, no more pain."

I stood there dumbfounded, wondering what the hell was going to happen. I didn't have to wait long.

Tony Ducks and the Hawk picked up the Mole and took him outside. I never saw the Mole again.

14

Why Don't You Work For The Government?

Johnny G got demoted. The last I heard, his goombah Sally D sent him to Jersey, where he was slinging hamburgers in some greasy spoon. The Hawk got the Sinatra records. Tony Ducks got the cash for his church and I got the finger without a single rubber. Once again, I went home broke. But at least this time, after that night my stock went up in the neighborhood.

Just like a movie star after you win an Oscar, like the night Marlon Brando won the Oscar for *On the Waterfront*, the whole fucking joint went nuts, standing ovation after standing ovation.

When I got my neighborhood Oscar, the only ovation I got was when I gave Tony Ducks my end of the score. Wherever I went, night and day, there was plenty of respect. I was really a little uncomfortable with the whole thing because I knew sooner or later, one of these made guys was going to try to recruit me. And if I refused the offer, he might get pissed off and kill me. I was very nervous about that. Same notoriety, different set of rules. Those were the rules and I knew it.

I just wanted to be my own man. It was hard to do without belonging to someone, which would cancel out independence anyway.

This newly acquired respect finally paid off when I was offered the part of a lifetime. Bobby Dees was humming, the atmosphere was smooth as silk, and then in walked Joey the Blond, the Hawk, Vinny the Mook, and an old friend from the neighborhood, Philly Fish. He strolled in with a good-looking dame I had never met.

Joey hugged me and said, "Good job." Then he kissed me. I smiled and moved on. I thought for sure he was going to ask me to come join him and his brood. Then a familiar voice bellowed above the sounds of the Bobby Dees band.

"Salerno! Salerno!"

I looked up standing there looking me straight in the eye was my old football buddy, Louie Sagulbinnie. "Louie, my main man, what is up?"

"I'm running numbers. Easy stuff. The Hawk here is my bank."

We all moved to the saloon's big bar, next to Philly Fish and this sweet-looking dame. Louie went off with the Hawk. I went right after the dame. Philly stopped me and said, "My sister wants to talk to you"

But a waiter interrupted me with a telephone message. After that, I said, "Keep her on ice, I just got a call from my ma's neighbor, I'll be right back."

I made the turn onto Avenue P, and all I saw was smoke coming from my mother's bedroom window. I ran into the alley and through the back door, up the stairs, and straight into Ma's bedroom.

There was Ma sleeping like a baby, I ripped the smoking drapes from the wall and beat out the rest of the flames, then threw them out the window. Thank God Ma slept through it all.

In the morning, I took her to Fat Sam's for some bacon, eggs, and egg creams. It made me smile to watch Ma guzzle those egg creams like they were going out of style.

"Ma, what's new in the neighborhood?"

She looked up smiling. "You'll never guess who I met the other day. Mrs. Saglumbinnie! You remember her?"

I nodded.

"She told me all about her son, Louie"

"What did she say?"

"You will never believe this. Louie works for the government! He's a G-man, and he gets a pension and also a 401k."

I looked away, but Ma grabbed my hand. "Salerno, listen to this: he also gets all the health benefits too, all for nothing. Ma saw the look on my face she asked. "Son, are you ok?"

Hearing that about Louie was making it hard to breathe. This news was a killer. I was between a shit and a sweat. *If I tell the Hawk about this, he kills Louie. Then we got the feds all over us. If I try to warn Louie to get out of dodge, he will just tell me to go fuck myself.*

Ma was good at this kind of thing. She knew the ins and outs of motherhood to the max. She planned a get-together over family dinner. So I made a killer marinara sauce which I learned from my grandma. Funny, I was the only one who could duplicate how she made it. The secret was high heat and you must use only frying pan, not a pot. I could never understand why people never got the heat thing.

Anyway, Ma made her wonderful lasagna and then she invited Mrs. Saglumbinnie and Louie for Sunday dinner. Once the table was set, Ma made sure everyone was eating and drinking, then she dropped the bomb. She looked at Louie and asked, "Louie, you love your mamma?"

At the moment, Louie had a mouthful of Ma's pasta. He frowned at the question, but then with a face full of sauce he grinned and said, "Yes, Mrs. Salerno. Very much."

Ma snapped, "Good! Then tell your mama that you and my son are both in trouble. If you boys keep this up you'll both wind up dead."

Mrs. Saglumbinnie jumped up, "Oh my god! Mary, what is going on?"

"Maria, your son is in big trouble and he doesn't seem to realize it. He's investigating a bunch of mobsters, and my son found out."

Louie jumped up and started to storm out the door, but Ma stopped him with her thirty-inch arms. "Louie, your mother knows there is only one way out of this, and so do you. Remember, my son's life is also at stake here."

Louie started to leave again.

"Look Louie, just tell your boss you blew your cover. It's that simple."

I could see the wrinkles on Louie's forehead were all scrunched up.

"Louie, hear me, you have no chance against the Hawk and this bunch. You nail him, there's always another one to take his place."

Louie ripped into me, "Salerno, you're just walking on quicksand and you know it!"

"I do, but it's my fucking choice, Louie. I know you love your mom, so just go investigate someone else. You can't win this one. It's as simple as that."

We never made it to dessert.

15

Needing a Bigger Gun

People said Philly Fish's sister was a fox, which sounded wrong until you saw her. At first, I thought she was after my body, but I soon found out she was after my brain. I was impressed by her perception, because Geri was a slim chick with big tits. No fakes here, those puppies were the real thing. She was always impeccably dressed and kept her hair in a French roll.

Thing is, she was a bank clerk by day and a devil by night. Her dynamic personality changed with each hair style, and for sure this dame knocked me off balance. I was never sure what she had on her mind and never knew what to expect. Then, after one hot night of lovemaking, she whispered into my ear.

"I want you to rob my bank."

This might sound like a strange remark to you, but women love to confide in me. I don't know why that is. Right then I knew I needed a bigger gun. So I got up and started for the door. She asked where I was going.

"I got to see a guy."

She just stared. "At three in the morning?"

"… he works nights."

* * *

Vinny the Mook opened his door looking half asleep. He gradually focused his gaze on me. "Salerno? It's the middle of the night! What the fuck is going on?"

"I'm going to rob a bank and I need a bigger gun."

"You fucking nuts? Whatta you know about robbing a bank? What you need is a bigger brain, not a gun. Now get outta here so I can get some sleep."

No help there, so I took off. When I scooted into the Black Kitten, there was Joey the Blond and Swivel Tooth drinking at the bar. Joey looked at me like he wanted to see me. Swivel Tooth was drinking pretty heavy, so I just waited for the Blond to give me the high sign. Then Swivel Tooth eased over to me.

"Kid, I heard you broke your cherry."

I just smiled. Joey got there just in time. He looked straight at Swivel Tooth. "Ok, what's the deal?"

Swivel Tooth looked me dead in the eye. "Twenty grand, five grand for you and me. Ten for the kid."

I frowned. This was offensive.

"What the fuck are you making faces for? It's more money than you have ever seen in your miserable life. You greaseball, I should put my foot up your fucking ass!"

Joey jumped in. "Okay, slow down, I heard you. Now what's the deal?"

Swivel Tooth slugged down another double scotch, then cleared his throat. "There's ten moving trucks parked on Avenue U. The Fellini Brothers. You knock them out of commission permanently, we get twenty big ones. He looked at me and then said with a sneer, "Can you make that happen, hot shot?"

"Does that famous old bear still shit in the woods?" Swivel Tooth looked at me and went into a fit of drunken laughter. "The bear in the woods! I like this kid."

Four a.m. and here I am, pounding on the Mook's door. Vinny answers looking annoyed, as usual. "What *now*, Salerno?"

"I'll tell you what now, I'm gonna rob a fuckin bank! That's what now!"

That really set him off. "You already told me that! We went thru this *yesterday*, at four in the morning! So tell me, Salerno, what the fuck are you talking about? Last week you were in your old man's store sucking farts out of people's pants. And now you gonna rob a bank?"

The Mook went to close the door I stuck my foot in and stopped him. I spoke in a quiet voice. "So I'm nuts, Vinnie? Listen to this: I just got twenty grand tonight to do a job!"

That got his interest. "Twenty? What kind of a job?"

"I gotta put ten trucks out of commission for good."

"For that, you get twenty G's?"

"Well, five for the tipster and five for Joey the Blond. I get ten! You in?"

"You fuckin' a, I'm in. This is sweet."

"Good, now how do we make sure these fucking trucks never drive again?"

The Mook grinned at that. "Apple pie! All we have to do is go to the supermarket and buy 20 bottles of pancake syrup."

"Get real, Vinnie, this is twenty grand."

"Then we pop the caps on the gas tanks and pour this sweet stuff into them. In the morning, when they start up those big engines and everything gets nice and hot, the syrup hugs those pistons and sticks to them like piss on a wino.

"But that's not the good part. Because when they turn them off for the night, the engines cool off and everything goes to sleep, the engines go to sleep, we all go to sleep. And then the next morning when they try to start those engines, all you hear is a humming sound. Nothing works, all the engines are seized up tight as a crab's ass."

"How much for helping me with this?"

Vinnie smiled. "Twenty dollars for the syrup. A G-note for the info, and two large for the pistol you're gonna need for the bank job.

"Vinnie, you're a genius."

16

Ma the Moll

The Blond was happy about the trucks going out of business. Swivel Tooth even bought me a drink. I had finally made a score. I was feeling good and when I walked into Fat Sam's to get a soda, sitting there was Ma, smoking over her favorite chocolate egg cream.

She looked me up and down. "Why the long face?"

I blurted it out. "Ma, I think I'm gonna rob a bank …."

"Why?"

"Because I ain't got nothing better to do."

"Uh-huh. Did you ever rob a bank before?"

"No."

"Well, if you do this, you'll have to do this job right. You can't go around the neighborhood looking for help. One wrong word, one slip of the tongue, and you'll have so many partners leeching onto this thing, it'll make your head spin."

I just nodded.

"Oh, yeah!" she added. "One other thing. Kids in the neighborhood help mobsters keep their fingers on the pulse of things, so keep your big trap shut around them."

"I know, Ma. I'm gonna need a guy with balls, speed, and brains."

Ma chuckled at that. "Son, I'm looking right at him. You do this thing, you do it alone. Now give me the layout."

"The layout? Did you ever rob a bank?"

"No, but I saw enough bank robberies on TV to know what to do and what not to do. Now stop with the questions and give me the layout."

"Ok! According to this dame, Geri-"

Ma interrupted, "Geri who?"

"Geri Swartz, Ma. Philly the Fish's sister."

"The Jews from 25th Street?"

"Yeah. Any problem with that?"

She took a second to sip on her egg cream and didn't say anything.

"Look, Ma, Geri's been planning this for a long time."

"Salerno, I hear ya. Just give me the layout."

"Okay, according to Geri, the layout is pretty simple. One retired cop, his gun is rusted tight in his holster, and he's the only security. No silent alarms, no cameras, and get this: the bank is in the middle of nowhere! You're not gotta believe this one, Ma, but the police station is located *two towns away*. That's twenty miles!"

Ma looked at me a moment then says. "This all seems too good to be true. I'm a little uneasy. How could all this money just be laying around? Call this bitch."

"Ma, she's not a bitch."

Ma chuckled. "Oh, my son is in love." Then she snapped, "Now call that bitch and get the rest of the information."

I went to get up, but Ma stopped me. "Remember, that's too much money to just lay around doing nothing. Find out where the money comes from. One more thing. Before you do this, you'll have to get the bitch's pussy out of your nose."

Before I could react to that, Ma changed the subject and called out, "Sam! A couple more egg creams for me and my son."

* * *

I called Geri, and we agreed to meet in Penn station at some hot dog joint. I sat and watched her approach. She was dolled up, but as soon as she spotted me, she became all business while she walked over and sat down.

"Why the call?"

"Business," I replied. "Madam, I would like to know more about the employees."

She sneered, "Knock off the 'madam' crap"

"Well then, loosen up. Now what about your employees? Are there any heroes sitting on one of those stools? Any starry-eyed secretaries in love with the boss, or maybe an employee ready to lay down their life for somebody else's fucking money?"

Geri sat there munching on a double hot dog loaded with onions and relish. She said nothing for a while, but I could see she was thinking.

Then the iceberg cracked and she smiled. "You know you're a bright kid, my brother was right about you, I like that. So here it is: there are four women, all married with families. I'm the only single person in the bank. What these woman do all day long is count money and try to set me up with a date. They could care less what happens to the money. Seems to me they're all worried that I'm gonna end up an old maid."

"What about your boss?"

"What makes Stanley's day is if he can cop a feel. Paddy, the security guard, is a nice old guy and a good friend. Don't hurt him, you got that?"

"Got it. Where does the money come from?"

"I don't know. When we show up for work, the money is always there in the back room. Just for the record, Salerno, this is a one-time thing for me. I don't ever want to be poor like my parents and have to struggle for the rest of my life. So do *not* fuck this up." She leaned close to me. "You do, and I swear on my mother's eyes, I'll kill you myself."

I watched Geri walk away and decided she wasn't exaggerating. I had no doubt that if I blew this caper, she was capable of coming after me for real. If the cops didn't get us both first.

* * *

Mouse's Marinara Joint, featuring old-world Italian pizza, no oil used. The joint was packed. I walked in and yelled, "Half a dozen pizzas to go!"

The Mouse looked me in the eyes and didn't laugh, smile, or in any way encourage me to continue being a dick. "Brother, you didn't come all this way for a slice of pie."

I smiled and hustled him to the back room, where I whispered to him, "Mouse, I'm going to rob a bank and I need you. You're a guy I can trust."

"Brother man, I think you are out of your fucking mind. Have a slice of your grandma's pie; you'll live longer."

I laughed. "Brother man, are you in for two thousand bucks?" I can tell you that got his attention quick. The Mouse studied me a moment then relented.

"For that kind of cash, you can have my black ass wrapped up in salt pork and collard greens. But what bank has that kind of loot?"

"Mouse, this is on the square, God sent me an angel."

"Or maybe the devil."

"Mouse, this is square business. I got the inside word, as inside as you can get."

"Not so fast. Where the fuck is this bank?"

"Long Island!"

"Long Island? There ain't nothing out there but a bunch a fucking rednecks."

"You gotta trust me on this."

He thought for a second. Just a second, though. "When do we go to make this score, brother?"

I smiled. "I'll be in touch. Brother."

* * *

The best gun slinger in the neighborhood was a fat little sausage of a man called Baldy, for the usual reasons. Baldy was born about a hundred years too late, in my opinion, but that was part of what made him just the man I wanted to see. He really knew about guns, and I needed a special kind of a gun.

I had to be careful not to arouse his suspicions, because he loved mobsters, and if he smelled a bank job, he'd run right to Fat Anthony and spill the beans, for a taste of whatever they extracted from me. I would get stuck with expensive do-nothing "partners" in a heartbeat.

Baldy was a sweetheart of a guy who would give you his right arm; but at the same time, fuck with him or his dog and he would blow your head off. I knew I had to be very careful with this walking time bomb.

"Baldy, I'm moving to the country, part time, anyway, so I'm thinking I need a dart gun to knock off the mountain lions. You know I got kids, so I gotta be careful! I even heard they got a couple of fucking bears roaming around out there."

"Fuck that dart pistol and fuck the bears. I'll get you a real gun. I got a 45-70 with a long barrel. You'll knock them sons of bitches off, one-two-three."

"Oh no, Baldy, I can't do that. My wife, she's an animal lover. If I knock them off, she'll get pissed and then I won't get no pussy. I'm in a bad spot. You got to help me."

Baldy thought a quick moment. Most men understand the need for a direct line to the pussy in your life. "All right. I see what you mean." He pointed to the cellar. "You're just in time for target practice. Follow me."

The smell of gunpowder greeted us as he led me down into his inner sanctum. I looked around his arsenal, a real collection, and spotted some old World War II hand grenades. "Baldy, the grenades? You expecting a fucking war?"

He grinned. "Never know. You gotta be ready all the time."

He drew two pistols and started to rapid fire at a target on the wall. BAM, BAM, BAM, BAM, BAM, BAM. Six shots, all hit dead center. I thought for sure I was gonna go deaf. Then he pulled out the other pistol and ripped off another six shots.

This dude was fast. I'm talking Billy the Kid fast. He gave me a sly grin then went to a table and picked up two dart pistols. "Nice, ain't they?"

"They look great, but how do they work?"

"Easy. Just take six pellets and slip em in the cylinder. Lock it down, and you're ready to go."

"How much juice is in one of those pellets?"

Baldy chuckled. "Enough to stop a horse."

"What happens if I hit one of my kids by mistake? Would they be okay?"

"I dunno." He pointed the dart gun at me and fired.

I came around a half hour later. My mouth tasted like I had been smoking my socks. When I looked up, there was Baldy eating a salami sandwich dripping with olive oil and roasted peppers. He grinned at me. "You wanna bite?"

* * *

Ma slid into the booth and whispered, "What's the story?"

"Ma, the story is two hundred thousand dollars."

She took a deep drag on her cigarette. "Where does that amount of money come from?"

"Ma, it's a drop bank!" I knew I had to talk fast. "This is on the square! On the first Monday of every month, this bank is popping at the seams with money. Wait till you hear this: all the other banks, loan companies, and businesses in the area drop off their cash at *this bank*, to be picked up every Monday morning by an armored truck!"

"Where are the money bags stashed?"

I laughed, "This is the best part! The bank bags are dumped into a storeroom adjacent to the bank. I watched them. They handled the bags like garbage. The door I can pop open with a screwdriver. No alarms. No lights. I never saw a cop or a cop's car any time I was there!"

"When are you gonna do this?"

"Sunday night. Me and Mousey."

Ma dropped her head. "Mousey! My *mother's* Mousey? He's as dumb as a box of rocks."

"I trust him."

"Trust *me*. And besides I'm a better driver."

"What? Ma! You want me to take you? The old man would kill me."

She leveled her all-business gaze at me. "Forget about him. I'll kill you if you don't."

* * *

When we pulled up into the sleepy little village with the bank, I drove up and down the street a couple of times so Ma could see the town. When she finally spotted the bank, she was shocked to see it was no bigger than a strip mall store. A small sign in the window read, "Bank of Massapequa." Across the street was a grassy, well-kept park. The best part was that a motel and a coffee shop fronted the bank.

"So that's it, Ma."

She smiled. "This bank doesn't have a chance in hell."

There was no moon that night, so me and Ma, like two little pixies, popped the back door of the bank and slid into the back room and pulled the shades. We went to work nice and easy without breaking a sweat. It took hours and it seemed like a lifetime, but we finally emptied the room of twenty-four bags of cash. It was still dark out when we drove back to Brooklyn just as pretty as you please.

* * *

Counting the money was another story. I took the bags and slit them open, then emptied them all into the bathtub. It was a sight to see. I wanted to take a bath in the stuff. Ma counted the hundreds and I counted everything else. I told her we should pile the money into three bundles.

"Why three bundles?"

"Well, the tipster on this gig gets a full end."

She snapped when she heard that. "A full end? My ass! What the hell happened to the good old ten percent?"

"Ma, she put a lot into this score."

She waved me off. "Come on Salerno, all she did was sit on her ass all day long!" I could always tell when Ma was getting too hot under the collar because she started calling me "Salerno" like everybody else in the neighborhood. It was just another one of the things that set her apart from regular mothers.

"She brought me into this!"

Ma stopped me cold. "That's what tipsters do. *We* did all the work. *We* took all the risk. If *we* get caught, *we* go to jail, not her."

"Come on Ma, she's a nice kid."

Ma choked on that. "Nice kid, my fat ass! She's a diabolical bitch! All she did was pussy-whip you so you'd do this job! You sucker! I always told you not to let any woman get her pussy up your nose. Wake the fuck up! She used you. She could've sat on that bank stool for the rest of her life and never found another sucker like you. That bitch flat out used you!"

I just smiled. "Ma, look at me, I'm covered from head to toe with 100-dollar bills."

There was a long silence, then Ma asked, "How much?"

"Close to a hundred eighty grand, give or take a couple of bucks." No response, no nothing just more silence. I yelled, "Ma, are you dead or what?"

Ma answered, "On the other hand, that's sixty grand apiece."

"Give or take a couple of bucks here and there."

At this, she finally smiled. And we stashed our haul in the usual place: under Ma's girdles.

17

A House Somewhere In Brooklyn Away From The Mobsters

So with a pocket full of cash, I went to see Dante. I was sure she could help me find a house without raising any suspicion about where I got the money. One slip, one mistake, and I would have a couple of whiners up my ass looking for a handout and backed up by the mob.

The new offices of the Rockaway Beach Vigilantes were very impressive. Watching Dante approach made me remember how beautiful this woman was. She threw her arms around me, then asked, "What can I do for you?"

"I need you to help me find a house somewhere in Brooklyn away from the mobsters."

She laughed. "There's no such place."

When I went back to the neighborhood, I was finally gonna get my wife a house. The good feeling lasted a couple of hours.

That same night, loud ringing noises stung my head. I reached for the phone. "What?"

"Richie, this is Althea!" That was Dante's mother. "You have to wake up!"

I mumbled, "It's the middle of the night!"

She just shouted, "Dante's been hurt!"

That was enough to make me jump up, fully awake. "What happened?"

"I don't know! They found her beat up, maybe she was raped."

"Jesus. Is she alive?"

"Thank the Lord she's alive, but they found my baby in the back of a stairwell, in the Panchen Ave projects."

"Who the hell-"

"Wait, I ain't done. Salerno, the Mouse is in Coney Island hospital."

"Him too? What the fuck is going on?"

"Don't know, but someone dumped him on the hospital steps minus his three-piece set."

My mind went blank for a moment. I couldn't understand what she just said. It was like I went deaf. She continued on, "He damn near bled to death."

Things were happening fast, even for my scheming mind. I finally asked her, "What's the Mouse been getting into?"

"All I know is, he's been running with some white woman from Jersey City. I warned him she was nothing but trouble."

"What woman are you talking about? Do I know her?"

"I don't know her name, but the Hawk told me her daddy is some big Mafia dude, Funzie from Jersey City."

Things weren't making sense. "The Mouse never told me a word about her. Where did he bump into her?"

"Right here on the boulevard. Her daddy and the Hawk were doing business. You know, with the pizza parlors."

"*That* chick? I told Mousy she was a wacko."

"And right from the start, I told him that kind of woman loves men, period. I know the kind, I could see it in her eyes. Mousy just walked away from me. I told him, that kind of woman will make a man crazy. He shrugged me off, went to Rocky, borrowed five grand, and took the bitch to Europe."

It was four in the morning. The streets were just starting to come alive. And so was I. I jumped into my hot rod and sped up Avenue P, then as I passed the old man's store, I saw the sign in the window. "GONE FISHING." But when

I zoomed past Henry Street, a couple of blocks from Ma's, all of a sudden, out of nowhere, I got broadsided.

I jumped out of my car already pissed off, but when I looked up the words never left my mouth. My old man's 1937 Lasalle was embedded into the side of my car. I slammed his car with my fist. "Two million people living in this fucking city, and my old man with his drunken compass has to find a way to smash into me?"

He was full of drunk indignation when he rolled out of his hearse. Finally, his whiskey-scarred brain got the message. "Oh! Yeah! My son, my son. Yeah! My son. This is my son?"

With that revelation under his belt, Pop lets go one of the most horrendous farts God ever created. Well, let me tell you the mixture of his all-night boozing and a little excitement must have been too much for this midnight crusader, because following that, Charley the Pick shit his pants.

In the middle of the night there I was, lugging this fucking bad-smelling drunk up the street to Ma's. We were still in sight of the wrecked cars when I looked up at Ma's place—only to see smoke bellowing from her bedroom window *again.*

I immediately dropped the drunk and screamed, "Ma, wake up!" Then it hit me: *Ma's girdles! My cash!* I ran up to the front of the house as fast as my legs would go, then leaped right through the open bay windows, scooted into the smoke-filled house, and up into Ma's bedroom.

I fought my way through the flames and dense smoke, and when I pulled Ma from her bed, she was out cold. Her valiums and cigarettes once again did the job. I got her out, but in the end Ma's bedroom was gutted by the flames from a dropped cigarette. Fire took it all. Ma's girdles, the cash, and all.

18

Forever a Beggar?

Tony Martin's tunes were blasting from the jukebox when I walked into the Hawk's joint, dead broke. The Black Kitten was glum. Vinnie the Mook's usual high energy was nonexistent. The Hawk sat alone, facing the street. You could see it on his face, the news of his daughter Dante had his insides twisted.

I had never felt this kind of heaviness before. The air was so heavy I was almost afraid to breathe. Something big was going to happen. I watched the Hawk move to the jukebox and play his favorite song. *Norman, Norman my love.* The tune didn't match the mood at all, and that gave the room a dark surreal feeling.

The Hawk still stood at the jukebox playing that tune over and over, until this parcel post driver shows up. The driver took one look around the room, dropped the package, and scooted out the door. He never said a word.

The Hawk stared at the package a long time before he opened it. When he did, his lone eye flared hot. I took a look, and it was Mouse's three-piece set, all wrapped neatly in a plastic bag.

Things were happening too fast. Why were the Mouse's family jewels delivered to the Hawk? Why was the Hawk's daughter Dante raped and Gus wasted? What was the fucking connection?

I finally decided to tell the Hawk what I thought. He was still looking at the remains of Mouse's future when I approached. A look of rage was stamped solid on his grill.

"I'm thinking we better get Dante off the street before whoever did this tries again. I also think my place is the safest because no one will make the connection."

The Hawk just nodded. We went to get Dante. On the way, I asked. "What do you think is going on?"

He took a deep breath. "It's the neighborhood they're after. Rockaway Beach is virgin territory."

"Who's after it?"

"So far, I only know the why. Not the who."

"Gus got hit. It has to be another crew wants in."

We drove along Rockway Beach Boulevard mostly in silence, each with our own thoughts. I could tell the Hawk was filled with rage. When we finally arrived at Althea's, we saw Dante curled up in a chair. After they talked for awhile, the Hawk gently asked, "Sweetheart, do you have any idea why someone would want to do this to you?"

Dante's face was swollen, her nose smashed. "Dad, all the pizza joints and business places are in order. There was no reason to do this over money."

"Think a moment, sweetheart. If anything or anyone has been out of order, no matter how small."

She thought a while, then responded, "Well Dad, our marketing managers, Mr. Beech and Mr. Dow, were having a heated discussion about Mister Dow's investment strategies."

"What about the strategies?"

"When I asked Mister Dow what was going on, he snapped at me kind of funny. Like I should mind my own business. But I didn't think anything was wrong. I just thought it was business as usual."

I said to the Hawk, "Ernie, we better go see Mr. Dow now. We can drop Dante off at my house."

When we all pulled up to my house, I saw Johnny Bath Beach leaving out my front door. I knew they had dated a long time ago, but it rocked me to see him there just then. We all watched my wife, Lucille, and Johnny making small talk, and then he reached over and kissed her. My heart sunk.

Seeing my face, the Hawk asked. "You know that guy?"

"My wife and Johnny used to date."

It was too much to deal with under the circumstances. We watched the mobster pull away before we all entered.

"And who is this?" Lucille asked.

"My friend Dante, she's the Hawk's daughter."

"Didn't know you had any black friends."

"I didn't know you had mobsters for friends."

"Oh, Johnny? I was broke and you were nowhere to be found, so I called him."

Dante reached into her purse and pulled out a roll of bills.

"Hi! I'm Dante, take this please."

The Hawk smiled. "Lucille, take it."

Money always talks. There was an awkward silence until Lucille softened. "Thanks. Would anyone like a cup of coffee?"

* * *

This high-priced suit was living in a fucking huge mansion that fronted the beach. I whistled. "Wow! What a joint this is!"

The Hawk shot me a look. I shut up quick. When we walked in, we didn't even knock. We just strolled in, as easy as you please. There was Mr. Slickster busy sunning himself on his private beach. The layout was to die for. On his journey along the way, the Hawk had picked up a pitcher of ice water. He doused Dow, who snapped to attention. "What the--?"

The Hawk spoke slowly like you do to an idiot. "Mister Dow, I understand you have been investing our money,"

"*Your* money?"

"Yes, our money, *my* money."

I chimed in, "Yeah, his money, you scumbag! Who gave you permission to invest that money?"

"Gus did."

"You lying scumbag!" I hollered. "Gus would never do that. Ernie, I'm gonna get the lemon squeezer. This piece of shit is lying."

I ran to the bar, got the item in question, and showed it to Mr. Dow. He just sat there confused. Smiling I reached over and ripped his shorts off and out popped his weenie.

"My oh my. What do we have here?" I reached down and put his tiny nuts in the vice. Before I even squeezed on them, he fainted.

The Hawk immediately doused him with another cold shower. Mr. Dow opened his mouth babbling, "It was one of your own boys came to me in the middle of the night and said I was to skim all the interest earnings. From the schools, the pizza parlors, and businesses in the city, then put it into the county's general fund. Then I gave the young man vouchers so he could draw monies from the fund. I was told not to say a word. He threatened my whole family!"

The Hawk asked quietly. "Do you have a name?"

"Nobody gave me any names, but he was an extremely good-looking young man, very Italian, with a mole on his cheek."

"Ernie, that's Johnny G. He's talking about the mole, it has to be him."

"You're right, but that fucking idiot could never pull something off like this."

I agreed, "You can bet he's getting plenty of help from someone."

Ernie asked Dow, "Were does the money go from the general fund?"

"All over the city! Wherever it's needed."

The Hawk smiled. "I'm sure you own a business or two that has been funded?"

Dow nodded.

I said, "Tell me, Mr. Dow, how many other businesses did you fund?"

"I don't know. The tall man with the dark eyes always came to my home and gave me a list where to direct the funding."

I grinned. "I'll tell you what I know: Johnny G is going to be minus his third leg. You can bet on that handicapper."

In a swift move, the Hawk sent Mr. Dow upstate to Needles Malloy, an old buddy of Swivel Tooth, to keep him on ice. The way I heard it, Needles was an ex-cop acquitted by the city for killing a mentally ill woman who came after him with a crowbar. The fortunate family got a million and Needles got the shaft.

Later I walked into my house to see Dante curled up asleep on the couch. Light glared from the muted television, but there was an eerie silence in the room. I stopped to listen.

I ran upstairs. no Lucille! No kids!

I woke Dante to ask what was going on. She told me, "Lucille's whole family showed up. The mother and a car full of brothers. They packed up the kid's clothes and they all left, without saying a word to me. Not even Lucille. They just left, just like that. Not a single word the whole time they were here. I couldn't stop them. I sat on the sofa the whole time."

It occurred to me that I was way behind on mastering my family life, or even understanding much of it. If I had made more progress with all that, I would have stayed home. I should have stayed home. I did not stay home.

19

The Gulf of Mexico

There I was, thinking *what am I doing out here in the middle of the fucking ocean in the middle of the fucking night?* I'll tell you what the fuck I was doing: running guns for the CIA. Sitting there, seasick and wondering how the hell I ever got myself into this mess, running guns to Cuba for government spooks. Me, a sharp kid from Brooklyn, freezing my ass off out in the middle of nowhere, for a G-note per trip.

I realized I must have been outta my fucking mind to get on that boat. The worst part was the constant cold spray of sea water that chilled us deep down to the bone. I looked over at the Hawk, who appeared comfortable enough. He manned a fifty-caliber machine gun like he was watching a football game.

I shouted, "When we hit the island, how do we tell the good guys from the bad guys?"

He just grinned. "All depends which way the guns are pointing!"

"How do we even know that?"

"When we get to the other side, then we'll know."

I nodded like I understood or approved or something, and thought *that's real fucking nice.*

It's a piece of cake to zip along at 60 miles an hour in the freezing darkness in a cigarette speed boat filled with guns. Who the fuck ever said that?

The Hawk, on the other hand, was a former Navy SEAL. To him this was a walk in the park. "Come on kid, take a ride with me. We'll make a couple of bucks. This is easy money."

Easy money, my ass. When we approached the middle of the fucking ocean there was a sound like I never heard before. It was like being in the bowels of an engine room in a huge old tanker. The closer we got to the Gulf Stream, the louder it became. When we finally entered the jaws of the Gulf Stream, it felt like we were being sucked into a massive tornado.

The wind and the currents were so strong that I screamed, "How the fuck do we get across that?"

The Hawk beamed at me. This guy was really in his element. "You just watch!"

He powered the boat along the top of the waves in a wide arc. "It's called 'tacking,' Salerno. You have to skim in a wide arc to get across the Gulf Stream."

I realized why those poor immigrants on home-made rafts hardly ever made it to the other side. Out there they had no real chance.

But the Hawk played Mr. Cool, guiding the cigarette along the coast of Cuba, and it made me realize how strong in the mind he really was.

His lone eye scanned the shoreline, looking for a signal. Once he angled closer to the shoreline, we finally heard a hushed voice call out from the bushes on the shore, speaking in Spanish.

"Where is the bathroom?"

The Hawk answered, "Around the corner," in perfect Spanish.

The Hawk steered the slick speed boat around the bend and into a beautiful secluded cove. Standing there on a flat rock was Pedro Guerrio, AKA "the Roach." And believe me, this poor guy had nothing on a roach. He gave me the willies. I got right behind the fifty-caliber machine gun and racked a round into the chamber.

The Hawk tapped me on the shoulder. "Stay loose."

The Roach grinned at us and jumped aboard.

What happened next, I wasn't ready for. The Roach and the Hawk started hugging one another like long-lost friends. Now I understood why the Hawk was here. These two had a history. Next the shoreline came alive with about a hundred rag-tag Cubans.

I thought, *I don't think I have enough bullets in this gun.* In a matter of seconds, they swarmed all over that 5000-pound cargo of guns like flies on a loaf of bread. The determination I saw in their eyes made me realize these dudes were on a fucking mission. Wouldn't every general want soldiers like that?

I said, "Ernie! These guys can win."

"What makes you say that?"

"Take a good look at these fuckin' guys. They are stoked! Look at the determination on their faces."

The Roach chimed in, "Funny you should say that, because just the other day, I saw one of these rebels blow his fucking brains out, rather than get taken alive."

"What does that mean?" I asked.

"Means you're right. They can win."

"What side are you on?"

"Whatever side pays me the most *dinero*."

But there was to be no more *dinero* coming for Pedro. Gunfire ripped the air that nasty way it does, and he hit the deck already dead. Five rebels emerged from the shoreline, picked up his body, spit on him, and then dumped the dead Roach into the swirling sea. He had led them to the guns, but apparently that wasn't enough to earn him any sort of reprieve from whatever beef they had with him.

* * *

Dawn on the Gulf of Mexico was a breath-taking event. The sight was all the more relaxing after the terrible, near-lethal trip the night before.

The Hawk was sitting supreme at the helm. He hadn't said a word since we left the Roach floating in the cove. We just watched the rebels take their booty and go.

He suddenly bellowed, "We got company!" A Cuban gun boat approached. To me, the gunboat looked like a big-time prize fighter maneuvering for the early knockout.

"Salerno, concentrate on their cannon."

I watched and waited, trying to figure out where the knockout punch was going to coming from. Then a loudspeaker from the gunboat pierced the morning air and we were ordered to stop. Chills ran up my spine when I saw the smirk on the Hawk's face, I thought, *this guy is gonna play cat and mouse with these fucking Cubans?*

Just then I could feel the speedboat's powerful engines start to rumble. He bellowed out, "Put a couple rounds across her bow." I had to laugh despite my nerves because it reminded me of a scene from Captain Horatio Hornblower, when Gregory Peck, out-gunned and out-manned, said, "Put one across her bow Mr. Twig," and Twig replied, "Aye, Captain!"

So I bellowed, "Aye, Captain," and proceeded to squeeze. The trigger. "POP-POP-POP-POP!" What a fucking rush.

At that moment, I was thinking this game was like baseball. We just gave up five turnovers and we were behind twenty points, but we were still going to prove ourselves. I ripped off a few more shots, watching the surprised Cubans hit the deck.

But this was no fairy tale, this was the real thing. The Cubans quickly responded with cannon fire, the Hawk hit the gas and yelled. "Adios, amigos!" The canon fire felt short when he put that puppy into overdrive. It flew across the Gulf like a hurricane wind.

After that 45-mile adventure, it sure felt good to be on the American side again. I was feeling great because I knew the Hawk had such faith in me. He had known I could do this even before I knew it. With the game on the line, the Hawk sent his rookie sensation to the plate in the bottom of the ninth with two out, facing the best pitcher in baseball.

Everyone thought he was crazy, but the Hawk recognized the kind of talent I had, so he handed me the bat. Now I understood what makes a great coach. It's the ability to see the potential in any given player, and the guts to use that player in a pressure-packed situation.

The Hawk was putting his life on the line because he had the uncanny ability to judge a player. When the Politician arrived at the boat, he had the look of a team manager who just won the World Series. "How was the trip?"

"It was a piece of cake," I joked.

With that, the Politician did something I had never seen him do before. He cracked a smile. He actually grinned, then said. "Ernie, this kid has a sense of humor. I like that." For me, that was a bonus because he acknowledged me.

The Blond asked, "Which way were the guns pointing?" I jumped in. "The right way."

The Politician burst into laughter. "I love this kid." We all laughed at that. It was a fine feeling of being accepted.

Now, the Politician, alias Ralphie the Pimp, was a very serious fisherman. From New York he shipped in Eddie the Rope from the Mott Street Boys to be his first mate, and Tommy the Bull from the Five Points Gang in the Bronx to be his second mate.

The Rope and the Bull had furnished this forty-foot yacht with the all the modern appliances one could want. Fish finders, sonar, and fishing poles that automatically traversed in the water so all we had to do was drink and bullshit all day long.

We were three days out to sea and not a nibble so far. Not a fuckin' nibble.

I was no great fisherman, but I figured I could do better than these guys. They had no talent for it. My grandpa, who had a wooden leg, was still the best fucking fisherman in the neighborhood.

But I just couldn't make myself speak up. Who would listen to a kid from Brooklyn? They were the fucking pros, not me.

The Pimp was getting a little frustrated, because he had brought his prized gun collection on board, intending to spend his downtime shooting fish. Only thing was, there weren't any fish.

We had no dames for our recreational activities. When I beefed about no broads, the Hawk replied, "We got porno. Having porno is better than a stick in the eye."

Still, I needed something better to do with my downtime than choking the chicken. It was definitely not good for the brain. Finally, bored out of my tits, I whispered to the Politician that I had my own ideas about how to catch a fish. He replied, "What makes you think it's fish we're after?"

That knocked me on my ass. Then the Hawk, Tommy the Bull, and Eddie the Rope all appeared in scuba gear.

The Hawk said, "The Rope spotted what we're after."

The Pimp grinned. "It's about time. I thought we lost it." In a matter of minutes, all three slid into the waters of the Gulf.

I looked at the Pimp. "What's up?"

The Pimp just smiled and changed the subject. "What kind of bait do you use to catch fish?"

I replied, "Eels. You chop 'em up, then let 'em sit in the sun a couple hours until they are good and ripe. Then you throw 'em into the water. The smell is so powerful, it will attract every fucking fish in the ocean."

Just then, the Hawk rose up from the ocean carrying a cage filled with packages of cocaine. He grinned at the Politician and hollered, "This was a great drop and pick up!"

I looked at the Pimp, wide eyed. "Nice catch!"

He laughed. "Yeah, and no eels."

Just then the other divers surfaced, also towing cages of cocaine. Now the Politician got really pumped because he spotted another yacht closing in, too close for comfort. We finished the work and got out of there in a hurry.

As soon as got back to shore and docked, we heard from the government guys that Batista had been sucking Cuba dry. Meanwhile, Castro got pissed at the mobsters because they were in the casino business with Batista. So when he took over Cuba, he told all the mobsters, get the fuck out of my country.

20

Married to the Streets

When I got back to the U.S., I ran into Gail Lissome, an old street hooker from the neighborhood. Gail had stepped up her game. Pick Six Benny told me Gail went by a new handle. She was now called "Madam Lissome." That got my interest real quick.

The way Pick Six laid it out was Madam Lissome and some new dame called Miss Sarah had set up a string of classy female ornaments from Florida. High end hookers only. I wondered which mobster was protecting her.

I finally went home. When I walked through the door, much to my surprise, Lucille met me with open arms. I handed her a bag of cash, and she went right to her stash. I thought, what a dame. She made me feel like a million bucks. I was doing a half-assed job in the marriage department. I thought maybe it was time to settle down. After all, I did have four kids.

Funny, I never thought I was married. I mean, like Lucille was just my girl. I loved my kids, even though I was a kid myself and I didn't do the things normal people do with their children.

I guess I never knew who they were. The truth is, I was married to the streets. It was like if I wasn't on the streets, I would miss something, because I never knew where the next opportunity to earn would come from, and I had no idea how to play the game in a conventional way of living.

For me and Lucille, things were cool cause she was from the streets herself. So we did things differently than most people did. We were young and didn't have much information to go by, especially as far as sex was concerned. Who was I gonna ask? My old man was a total blank in that department. All he knew was you made babies when you went to bed. That was it. Nothing about fancy fucking.

Here's the kind of help I could get from Pop: I was driving down Avenue P to go show Ma my new car, a 1950 Mercury hot rod with black skirts covering the tires. I zoomed around the streets until I spotted my brothers playing baseball on the stoop. At that moment, a ball hit a neighbor's car, owned by a Marine who got pissed off and kicked my brother Billy in the ass.

When I saw that I immediately jumped out of my car. "Never do that again."

"Fuck you!"

So I stepped in and knocked the Marine on his ass. "Never touch any of my brothers again!" Then we all went back to playing baseball on the stoop. I hit the ball hard and it rocketed across the street and right through a neighbor's window. The neighbor, Mr. James, got mad and called my father, who immediately jumped into his Buick and flew down the street like a crazy man. When my brothers saw my father's car roaring down the street toward them, they got scared and ran into the alley. They ducked into our garage with my old man in hot pursuit.

I started chasing him, yelling, "You drunken fuck, leave my brothers alone!" Meanwhile my brothers hid under the ping pong table. But my old man was in such a rage that he ran into the garage and pulled the table over, exposing my helpless brothers. He started kicking the shit out of them.

I ran into the garage yelling, "You crazy fuck, leave them alone! You're gonna kill them!"

He turned and took a swing at me. I ducked and caught him with a solid left hook to his jaw. He went down hard with a broken jaw. My brothers just huddled in fear.

When I went to help them, my old man picked up a snow shovel and wacked me across the side of the head, splitting open my scalp. Blood flew all over the garage. It took fifty-two stitches to close the wound.

Sure, I got over it. But that's about how much I learned from the old man. That, and how to keep your fingers off the nipples until it's time for it.

So thank God for Mrs. Dermer, because if it wasn't for that dame, I would've been a total blank in the bedroom myself. Most of the time the information on positions and sexual situations that we got came from porn books. That was the extent of our sex education. Relationship education was done by example and picked up on the fly, if at all.

Little did I remember, but it was my twenty-first birthday that day in May when I came home and my wife got me what she said would be the ultimate birthday present. She introduced me to her cousin's wife, Dr. Vera Lugano, not a bad looking dame. I thought, what a wonderful threesome this is gonna be.

I hugged Lucille and whispered into her ear, "Thank you, baby."

Lucille pushed me away. "Thank you for what? This is about birth control."

"Okay baby, that's a positive thought, 'cause all you do is have kids."

"I'm not talking about me. I'm talking about you"

"… Me?"

"Yes, you!"

"Lou, you know we can't use rubbers."

"I know that, so my present to you is a vasectomy."

"What the fuck is that?"

"It's a new procedure for men."

And it was new, then. I had no idea what she was talking about.

Lucille spotted the wrinkles on my brow. "Salerno, no sweat. This method of birth control is completely reliable."

"Who says?"

"Dr. Lugano told me it's working wonders with monkeys and gorillas. Unless you want to tie that thing in a knot? After all, I can't keep getting pregnant all the time. This procedure is a no brainer. All they do is snip you!"

I jumped up. "Snip *what*? All I got is one nut as it is."

"What's the matter, tough guy? You chicken?"

"Look, Lou, you know I ain't no fucking chicken, but this Dr. Waco of yours is making me very nervous. She wants to make me her guinea pig and fuck with my *one nut*?"

But my bride had me in a corner and I didn't know how to get out. I ran it through my head and realized this was one of those moments in life that you gotta do what you gotta do, otherwise the dame shuts you down.

So me and Lucille went to see the good doctor. As soon as we walked into her office the first words out of her mouth were, "We always start with a testicle exam. Later, I'll show you how to do it yourself. It can save your life."

"My sex life at home, maybe."

21

Kill the Pigs

It was only a few days later when Lucille and I hit the New Jersey Turnpike. Every time you entered New Jersey there was always a great smell to greet you: pig farms. No matter how far a person traveled on the Jersey Turnpike, that smell was always in the air. A little gift from Jersey. The pig was king.

We were driving along when Lucille excitedly shouted, "Salerno, look there. The Motel on the Mountain!"

When I didn't answer right away, she shouted, "Hey, Salerno! Where the hell are you?"

"Right here, baby." I swung that hot rod into the driveway and took her right up to the Honeymoon Suite. What the hell, it was about time we went on a honeymoon, so I carried her in.

Inside, we took one look around and both laughed. Mirrors lined the ceiling and walls. Dim lights engulfed the room with an atmosphere that gave me a tingle. To top it all off, a huge heart-shaped bed sat in the middle of the room. I dropped my bride onto the bed and shouted, "Happy honeymoon, honey!"

All of a sudden, POP-POP-POP! Three shots rang out, shattering the wall mirror. I pushed Lucille to the floor, then picked up a huge Tiffany lamp, threw it through the window, and followed the lamp through the hole in the glass. I landed in a rock garden, and more shots rang out. POP-POP-POP! My heart went into overdrive. Finally upright, I ran around the building toward the suite.

The gunman turned the corner just when I did. I saw his pistol start to come up, so I leaped in his direction and snatched his hand. Once I got control of his hand, I jammed the gun down and between my legs. He squeezed off a shot, but it went straight into the ground.

We both struggled for control. Finally, I felt him lose his balance, so I kept pushing against his body weight. His legs gave out, then we both went crashing into another rock garden.

I saw a foot smash into his face, then felt him release his grip. I looked up. There was Lucille.

"Who the fuck is this guy?" she yelled. I finally got a good look at him and then it hit me, this was Cockeyed Louie, from 16th Street. He was a wanna-be from Black Sam's crew.

Our uninvited guest started to stir. Lucille stomped on his face again.

"Babe, take it easy! We need him alive."

She shouted down at him, "Hey, tough guy, who sent you? Scumbag, if you don't tell me, I'm gonna beat you up and take your eyes. Who the fuck sent you?"

But there was still no answer from the mug. Incensed, my bride now pushed the heel of her foot deep into his eye socket.

His eyeball popped out and bounced around like a yoyo on a string.

Lucille was not fazed. "Goombah, how about that?"

So you can see why I loved her.

The gunman made no reply. She went on, "Okay, then how about we go for the *other* eye?"

"Please, no more! Vinny the Cig sent me. That dame, Gail. Her and some chick they call Sarah said you ripped them off in Florida."

Son of a bitch. Now I knew why Gail never contacted me after setting herself up as a madam. She'd been setting me up to get wacked!

Lucille looked at me hard. "Salerno, what the hell did you do to her?"

"Lou, it's business. Just business." This was a time when "just business" would actually put an end to the conversation. Business was acknowledged as a personal and private occupation.

So we quickly dumped the intruder into our trunk, less one eye, then tied him up like a pig, fitting for New Jersey. But me and my bride had to postpone our honeymoon.

After I dropped Lucille at home, I headed straight to the Black Kitten. The joint was hopping. I scanned the room, and there nestled in the corner were Gail, Vinny, and Sarah. Snug as bugs in rugs.

The Hawk came out of the back room holding a plate of spaghetti. Just when he was getting ready to serve it to Gail, I ran up and grabbed the plate of spaghetti, then jammed it into her face.

When the hot spaghetti hit, Gail screamed and fell to the floor. Vinny the Cig went to move, so I jammed my gun into his ribs, whispering, "Try something and you're dead!"

Sarah reached for a bottle of beer and started to get up, looking all aggressive, so I happily clipped her on the chin. The Hawk yelled, "What the hell is going on?"

"Ask this punk, Vinny!" The Hawk's lone eye zeroed in on Vinny. I could feel Vinny squirm. So I poked him.

"Tell him, Vinny, because I got your man, Cockeyed Louie, outside in my trunk. And you, Gail, stop staring at me like you don't know what's going on. You sold me out to this bunch. You bitch!"

So yeah, I made a scene, a big scene, and such a thing was not considered respectful. Not to anybody. I broke the rules, even if I felt justified that I was in the right. That move made me unpopular with certain people and set me up to get a bad beating, or worse, unless something got fixed.

It forced a sit-down to deal with it. Gail, Sarah, and Vinny the Cig were allied with Black Sam, so there wasn't much I could do against them without help.

I headed straight to Bobby Dees to see if Tony G, the undertaker's son, was there. He owed me big time. I waltzed in and to my surprise, there was Joey the Blond, Swivel Tooth, and Tony G all at the bar surrounded with a squad of good-looking dames.

I quickly put a lock on my cock and headed straight for trouble. Swivel Tooth blasted out, "Look who's here, the Floridian Flash in the flesh."

I waved him off and focused on the Blond and Tony G. "Tony, I got a problem with some of Black Sam's people."

The Blond chimed in, "Kid, you got a big problem with Black Sam himself."

"I know, Joey. That's why I need to see his old man."

Tony jumped right in. "Let's go see him right now."

"Do you think he'll help me?"

"Only one way to find out."

Two weeks later, me, Tony G, and the Hawk all waltzed into Black Sam's joint, a smelly pool hall. I spotted him at his favorite pool table, smiling and flashing a set of tobacco-stained teeth.

He looked up and gestured toward me. "I been hearing good things about this kid."

When I heard that, I finally knew I'd live for another day, thanks to Tony G.

Black Sam even went on to say, "I could use a sharp kid like him." He looked straight at Vinny and said, "I got a lotta fucking stupid people in my crew that do a lotta stupid things. Maybe those people overstepped with Salerno here."

Tony G replied, "You want the kid to join you, you gotta ask him."

Black Sam looked at me. "Well, kid?"

I was never in a spot like this before, but I always knew if I lived long enough it could happen, and there it was.

I took a deep breath and said, "Sam, I appreciate the offer. I really do. But I have to say no."

His rotund face dropped. Now I could see why they called him Black Sam. It wasn't about skin color, it was about personality. His face was scary enough to stop a runaway train.

So I went on, "Sam, the reason I have to say no is because of my wife. Since the incident on our honeymoon, she got into a very bad head. I don't want to lose her, Sam. We got four nice kids. I'm sorry, but I told her I would get a job and get off the street. I gave her my word."

I was lying like a motherfucker, but it was the only way out of this spot.

Black Sam was so taken with my speech, he told Vinny that if anything was to happen to me, he alone would be held responsible. Holy shit, what a turn of events. Because to a guy like Vinny, when the captain of a crew gets his ass opened up for doing something stupid, that's one thing. But for him to have it done in front of me was another thing altogether.

In our backwards world, by threatening Vinny on my behalf, Black Sam had unknowingly just given me an enemy for life. Now I needed for Black Sam to live a long and prosperous life of his own. After that sit down, the Hawk and I decided to walk all the way back to the Black Kitten.

He said, "You know, Salerno, that was a hell of a speech you gave back there. Did you ever think about becoming an actor?"

"No. Never thought about it."

"Well you should."

"You think so?"

"I think you're quick and very good at improvisation."

"What the hell does that mean?"

"Means you can bullshit pretty good. That's what that means. Now, my Sicilian wop friend, you gotta go out there and actually get a fucking job. Make no mistakes about what just happened back there. Black Sam will be checking on you all the fucking time and Vinny the Cig will make sure of that. He finds out you lied about going straight, he kills you for the insult. You got that?"

"Yeah, yeah I got it."

The Hawk looked at me and said. "I don't know of anyone who ever told Black Sam no and lived to talk about it."

22

The 14th Street Meat Market

Five a.m. comes around very fast when you gotta go to work. All I heard walking down 14th Street were horns blasting from huge tractor trailers. As I approached the 14th Street Meat Market, the ringing was still in my ears. I saw nothing had changed in that place. The fucking traffic made me want to turn around and go home.

Then I thought about Black Sam breathing down my neck and my story about going straight, so I decided to keep on walking. But the sour stench from the cobblestone streets started to make me sick. Overwhelmed, I stopped to get ahold of myself and while I did, I happened to notice a big guy loading meat as he slung a meat hook around his neck then disappeared into the jaws of the trailer. In a matter seconds, the mouth of the trailer became alive with hindquarters of beef sliding out on the truck's overhead rails at two hundred pounds apiece.

I stood mesmerized watching these mammoth meat loaders handling those big hindquarters of beef. Then all at once a huge side of beef came speeding down the rail and, in the process, jumped off. I stood there frozen while it flew right at me. A huge hand snatched me away just in time. The giant's sweaty face cracked a smile, then gently said, "Son, you gotta watch yourself on this street."

I stood there knowing I was a complete fish out of water, so I asked him, "Where's Wexler Meats?"

"It's that building over there."

"Thanks." I shook his hand for saving me.

As I approached Wexler Meats, I saw Solly Wexler, the six-foot-two, self-made owner, directing all the traffic. I remembered once when Esposito tried to park there, Solly ripped him a new asshole. This guy was no creampuff. I walked up to him and spoke in humble tones. "Solly, do you remember me?"

At first, he just frowned.

"I'm Esposito's son-in-law. The greasy guinea gorilla that told you if you fuck with his truck he was going to kick your Jew ass all over the 14th street meat market. Remember him?"

Solly thought a moment then smiled. "Yeah, I remember him and a lotta guys just like him. So what can I do for you?"

"I got four kids and I need a job."

"Are you a union man?"

"Yes, sir!" I lied. He turned to his head scaler, he told him, "Sammy, watch the store. I'm going to show this kid around."

I was stoked. This guy was for real. Here I just met him and he's taking me on a fucking world tour. Or did he have something up his sleeve?

Just like when a four-star general commands an army, Solly strolled onto the cooler as easy as he pleased. I followed, and happened to overhear the fat scaler say, "Banjo! Hurry up with that box of steaks."

This move got my attention real fast. A big-boned worker appeared carrying a huge box. I watched Fat Sammy quickly look around the cooler, then say, "Come on, hurry. We got to do this fast." The guy dropped the box into an open trunk.

Seeing that move, I knew right then they were up to no good. Then the worker says, "Okay, Mick? Tell Paulie we're even for this week."

When I heard that, I thought, *I know that rap.* Tonight, someone was getting a good dinner. Then, as I went to leave, some guy stuck his head out. I recognized him.

Bingo! I would know that mug anywhere. Mickey Scaparrotti! He was Paulie Scaparrotti's nephew, and Paulie was a big-time mobster from Brooklyn.

I started thinking the fucking street follows me no matter where I go. Next Solly escorted me into another massive cooler that was hustling with activity. Butchers were everywhere, expertly cutting into hindquarters of beef. Truck drivers and customers were waiting impatiently.

Solly had everyone moving at a quick pace. I thought this guy is a fucking general, for sure. He waved a huge knife at the guy and shouted, "I need these forequarters cut and boxed by noon."

The guy just nodded. I smiled. *They're slipping meat out the back door and raking in the profits.* Now I knew exactly what Solly was about.

I changed the subject. "Solly, these guys are awfully quick with a knife. I don't know if I can do that."

"This is the Major Leagues, son."

When he said that, I got sick inside. He must have seen the look on my face, because he replied, "Don't jump to conclusions, kid. It's not as tough as it looks. Be here tomorrow morning. Five a.m., sharp."

Pay back is a bitch. I was now a working stiff in a cooler dialed to thirty-five degrees.

Walking into that cooler at 5:00 a.m., I actually looked comical, dressed in a white butcher coat and sporting a black sailor hat and gloves. I felt like an overstuffed animal watching the knife-wielding men buzzing down the floor. They were smooth, and they cut flanks from the hindquarters of beef with the ease of a breeze.

I went to work on the other end of the cutting floor, where I fucking struggled big time. Pretty soon, every time I put my knife into a piece of meat, it felt like my hands were going to fall off. I was a strong guy, but cutting into those sides of beef was tough work.

Finally, after a couple of hours, my hands went dead. Tired and embarrassed, I went to Solly and said, "Solly, my hands have had it. I'm fucking done."

He actually laughed. "Come on, kid. Let's go for a cup of coffee and a shot of schnapps."

* * *

Getting up at 3:00 o'clock every morning was a killer, but waiting in the cold for a bus was even worse. Then, to top it all off, there was the Eighth Avenue subway. That, in itself, was an adventure in misery while all the burned-out workers shuffled on and off the train.

Every night, I had to jump into a bath of hot Epsom salt just to get my body ready for the next day. I was struggling and my ass was dragging. Finally, it was time to speak up.

"Solly, I'm sorry. I just can't do this anymore."

Solly snapped, "Salerno, I never pegged you as a quitter."

"I'm not, Solly, I'm not."

"Well, Salerno, it's the fourth quarter and you're down three points with a minute to go."

So there I was right in the middle of unfamiliar territory. My hands were barely able to grasp a tit, so how was I going to hold a knife?

I turned, Solly was gone. So I struggled through the cooler thinking *why can't I get tough like the rest of these guys?* As I approached the scale, I saw Fat Sammy push four 200-pound hindquarters onto the scale. He weighed them, then pushed them out onto the loading dock.

At first, I just kept walking. But then I saw Fatso do it again, and this time he didn't weigh them. I thought *Whoa, what a fucking move that was. I know how to add, and that's 800 pounds of meat that nobody else but Fatso knows where it goes.*

I stopped a moment, contemplating the move. I started thinking that after my talk with Solly, he was never going to let me quit, so now he had me bagging hindquarters. That job was like putting a huge condom on a stiff dick. I never stretched and farted so much in my entire life.

Solly walked over. "How you doing, kid?"

"I've been better"

He just smiled. "Stay with it."

Solly was giving me the chance of a lifetime and I didn't want to disappoint him. I was also sure Black Sam had an eye in the sky watching me.

At lunch time I dragged my ass out to the loading platform and sprawled out. Then I saw Danny Dimes, the dispatcher, pushing a flatbed of boxed meat.

At the moment, he couldn't see me because I was laying down on the other end of the platform. But then he looked around in what I thought was a very suspicious manner, dropped the boxes into a truck, and walked over toward me.

"What the hell are you doing out here?"

I played the dumb guinea. "Can't a guy get some shut eye around here?"

"Go find someplace else to sleep!"

I got up, but I wanted to crush his cruller so bad I could taste it. While I walked off, I could feel the eyes of Danny Dimes, the sneak thief, burning a hole in my back.

23

Crooks With Long Knives

So I kept on working and my hands gradually toughened up. After about a month on the sidelines, the coach came to me and said, "Salerno, I think you're ready for the big time." I looked at the field general and thought, *why couldn't he be my old man?*

"What's up?"

"You're ready for the cutting room floor. Your hands to me look like they've toughened up. Have they?"

"Yeah Solly! '14th Street ready,' as they say."

Later on, I was moving along the cutting floor at warp speed when I heard, "I see it, but I don't believe it!" Standing there with that stupid grin on his face was Mickey the Slug.

Hearing Mickey's voice, good ol' Banjo the meat thief went white in the face. He spit out, "I'm sorry, Mickey! I'll get some money tomorrow! I swear, I got a couple of irons in the fire. Tomorrow for sure!"

I laughed and called out, "Mickey, I see you're still a fucking slug!"

But Mickey ignored me and stepped in to slam the unsuspecting thief across the face, knocking him to the cold concrete. The guy leaped up and raised his huge blade. I jumped over and kicked it out of his hand, then spun around and slammed a right-hand dead into Mickey's soft underbelly.

"Go on, beat it, you piece of shit, before I hamburger your face!" Solly caught the move and came running over.

I figured he would jump me, but to my surprise, he grabbed Mickey by the neck.

"Didn't I tell you I never wanted to see you in here again?"

"Mind your own business Solly, remember you got too much to lose."

But in the blink of an eye, Solly tossed Mickey's ass into the greasy street.

I grinned. "Solly, that was a hell of a move!"

"You know that guy?"

"Yeah. We come from the same street. He lives a block away from my mother's place." I looked at Solly. "None of my business, but Mickey the Slug? How did Banjo ever get mixed up with *that* guy?"

"That is a long story, my friend."

"Solly, I'm pretty good at paying attention to long stories, and if this is the kind of long story I think it is, I would like to know."

That obviously put Solly on the spot, so he eyed Banjo, his wounded warrior, and snapped, "Banjo, finish up this load. You still got a lot of wood to chop." Then pointed at me. "I'll see you in my office."

As soon as I walked in Solly's office I felt nothing but tension. "Goddamn it, Salerno, this has to end." He angrily threw a financial report on the desk. "Look at that report. I'm getting robbed blind. My monthly pilferage has gone up almost a hundred and fifty percent!"

Solly sat down, looking spent. This was not the Solly I knew. I tried to change the subject. "Solly, tell me how the fuck you ever got hooked up with Mickey and his uncle Paulie?"

Solly just sat there. I could see he was struggling.

"Solly, I know Paulie a long time, ever since I was a kid. He's partly a businessman, but he's mostly a fucking cutthroat."

I could see Solly was embarrassed. "In a way, he's into my business."

"What way?"

"That Mickey character was working for me as a truck driver. I got into a little difficulty when some of my customers were late paying me. As a result, I was a short in my bank draft. Those cattleman in Iowa want cash for their cows. Simple: no money, no meat. The next thing I know, Mickey introduces me to this Paulie character. This guy was a gentleman in every way possible. He fooled me. I was totally impressed."

"How did Mickey know you were in trouble?"

"I got a big mouth and walls have ears. Before I knew it, there was Paulie Scaparrotti with the cash in hand. So, like a *schmuck,* I took it."

"Didn't you ever hear of a bank?"

"Bank don't lend money to meat wholesalers."

"Why not?"

"Because meat is a perishable item. It can't be insured. Too risky for the banks, period. And those cowboys down in Iowa and Colorado want the cash up front or a certified bank draft."

"That's it?"

"No, wait! This gets better! Write a check, and one of the cowboys will get on his fucking horse and high-tail it to the bank to make sure the check is good. No money, no meat, end of story. But I kept taking money, to stay afloat. After a while, Paulie came to see me and asked if I wanted him out of the loan. He made me understand the note would have to be paid in full. All done very smooth, over a cup of coffee. That bastard knew he had me over a barrel, so I just kept paying the juice. And the juice is killing me."

"Solly, you've been good to me. So if you'll trust me on this, I know a guy that can help us.

"You can do that?"

"Yeah, I know a guy who can help you."

He looked doubtful. "You sure about that?"

"I got this!"

"Salerno! Please, I don't need another mobster up my ass."

"Solly, you're in a no-win situation right now. All you're doing is shoveling horse shit against the tide. You'll never get even with Paulie."

"What does that mean?"

"It means you got set up. I know Paulie is behind everything. This is how he operates. He's very smooth. He makes you feel like he's doing you a favor. But in reality, he's just putting the slow squeeze on you. Paulie sent in his nephew, Mickey the moron, to keep you off balance. He must have known you were in some kind of financial trouble. But the pilferage here, that's different. That's an inside job. You got to keep an eye on this guy Danny Dimes."

"Now it makes sense, all the money he's given me."

"Paulie wants to take over your business. This take-over was planned right from the beginning. Mickey isn't that smart, but he was the key, because Paulie planted him here to find out what was going on. Looking for your weakness. You never saw this coming."

Solly's rage got to him. He cleared everything off his desk with one sweep of his arm.

* * *

On my way to the Hawk's place, I kept trying to think of some cool way to get him involved. I needed an outside interest to make a deal that would keep everyone from killing one another. I knew Solly was ready to explode on all of them, but I told him he had no chance against Paulie. I assured Solly that me and "my buddy" could outsmart Paulie.

But I needed the right leverage. These guys didn't play by the rules. I explained this to Solly and he mostly agreed, but he was also taking the wait-and-see attitude. I warned him, one wrong move and you're dead.

He took the hard line and replied, "I'm not going to give up my life without a fight!"

"That's very gallant, but I got the perfect rabbi for this."

When I arrived at the Hawk's home, right away I got the feeling that all was not well. Tina led me into his study.

It was my first time in there and, to my surprise, in spite of the Hawk's single eyeball, he was unusually well-read. The walls were lined with books of the masters: the works of Charles Dickens, a copy of *Vanity Fair* by William Thackeray, and the complete works of Shakespeare.

But the most striking thing was a huge portrait of General George S. Patton hanging on the wall. I was looking at the portrait of this imposing warrior when the Hawk appeared. He spoke reverently, "That man was the best strategist the world has ever known. He always did the unexpected. Patton knew what his enemy was going to do even before they did."

I looked at this one-eyed fan of great strategy and knew he was the man I needed for this job. But I could also see there was something stuck up his ass.

Just then Tina came into the study with Swivel Tooth in tow. I knew it was time to leave, but when I started for the door, the Hawk stopped me.

"Wait on the balcony."

Okay then. I stepped out, pinned my ear to the window, and listened. This was obviously a very, very personal thing between these two killers. It seemed the Hawk's seventeen-year-old daughter was being bullied by some wacked-out pothead she had rejected.

When I heard that, I thought for sure Ernie the Hawk was going to head over to that school yard and handle the bully himself. Wrong.

No, he told the cop, Swivel Tooth, that he wanted the kid picked up, taken into custody, and given the full treatment.

Swivel Tooth actually smiled.

"Be my pleasure, pal. I have the perfect maneuver for this bully. Vaseline could do wonders to help him get through a night in a jail cell full of sodomites. Only there will be no Vaseline on the menu." Swivel Tooth left there with a satisfied look on his face. Some stupid pothead had earned himself a truck load of bad karma.

He left me with no doubt the kid would never look sideways at her again.

* * *

I went back to the study and hatched my plan. I went right for the Hawk's passion: the Scam. I told him about Solly's situation with Scaparrotti, and that I wanted to get someone else to pick up the note.

But that someone had to have that kind of cash, and they would also have to be happy with just two points a week.

The Hawk grinned. "What kind of money are we talking about?"

For me, this was already cool. I was enjoying every minute of it. "Three hundred thousand."

"That's way out of my league."

"I don't want your money. All I need from you is to be the mediator, at ten percent of the original note, which is two hundred thousand. So you would get twenty grand for your end."

Oh yeah. The Hawk kept on grinning. "Where are you going to get that kind of money?"

"Black Sam."

And the Hawk still had that grin on his face. "No chance. Black Sam is tight as a crab's ass."

"Except I found out from Benny the Bug that Black Sam hates Paulie with a passion. Now correct me if I'm wrong?"

The Hawk still sported that smile. "I see you've done your homework."

"Good. We agree on that. Now Black Sam's crew has a lotta cash. I been nosing around pretty good. Pick Six Benny told me Black Sam has all those hotels up in the Catskills locked up. He also told me Billy the Brew's wife is a Jew. So is Black Sam's wife! So those dames got all the synagogues in the neighborhood locked up. And what do they all do on Tuesday nights? Bingo. Tuesday night Bingo. Lotta cash, a lotta prizes. If I go to Black Sam with this deal at two points a week, he'll jump all over it, but I cannot pull this off without you. With you involved, it would be a slam dunk."

The Hawk nodded. "And he'd make me and only me responsible." But even though he said that, he continued smiling.

So I kept going. "Another thing with you handling this deal: Paulie would never know where the cash came from! And besides, he'd be too fucking scared to ask. Right?"

I was still getting no response, so I kept going, "Remember, he wouldn't dare insult the Hawk. Plus, I would get two percent of the outstanding note, which is three hundred thousand, that I would collect from Solly."

The Hawk just sat there grinning. He slowly started nodding his head.

24

Black Sam Loves the Kid

The Nineteenth Hole was the name of Brooklyn's hottest night club at that time. Mirrored walls, illuminated dance floor. Mobsters and their dames filled the club. When I walked in with Lucille, I whispered, "Babe, this is where the elite meet to greet. We're on Black Sam's turf."

"Which one is Black Sam?"

"The big guy sitting in the corner. The one with the pocked face."

Over at Black Sam's table were Vinny the Cig, Weinberg, Gandy, and all his henchman. Before long they were all watching me and Lucille dancing. Maybe not me. I could see their eyes were glued to her sculpted body.

Lucille had sensuous moves. She was basically leading me through a rock-and-roll number when Vinny decided to move onto the dance floor and come up to her. He dared to talk to her like I wasn't even there.

"Baby, get rid of this kid," Vinny said.

Lucille moved expertly around me and replied. "After you get a new face." She said it loud enough for others to hear. Vinny lost it. He raised his hand to strike her. I snagged his wrist and told him if he tried anything, I would snap his neck.

Lucille pulled me away and together we ripped up the dance floor. Gandy, Black Sam's captain, caught the action and quickly moved in. "What happened out there?"

"No big deal, Vinny just got a little stupid."

Gandy then ushered us to Black Sam's booth and, to my surprise, Black Sam actually got up off his fat fucking ass and greeted us. Now that was a big move, especially for all the wanna-bes hanging around him. You bet that caught their attention.

"Sam, this is my bride, Lucille."

Sam looked her over. "Is he treating you right?"

Lucille laughed and said, "He has his moments, but I can handle him."

Sam chuckled and planted a surprise kiss on her. "The first time he doesn't do the right thing, you come and see me."

I already knew Black Sam had an insatiable appetite, especially when it came to a young, sweet cherry like Lucille. So without further ado, I excused myself and escorted her to our booth. We sat down and I kissed her.

She whispered, "Love of my life and pain in the ass of my life, take me the fuck out of here. Then take me home and make love to me." I wanted to comply, but instead I reminded her I had vital business with Black Sam.

That went over like a fart in church. I quickly scooted over to Black Sam, sitting with the Hawk. He looked up and growled, "The Hawk here tells me you want to make me a lotta money. But I gotta ask why. Why would you want to do that?"

"Why the fuck not? It's good business."

Black Sam erupted into laughter. He turned to the Hawk. "I swear, I love this kid."

I took the opening. "Sam, it's not only good business. See, my boss is a good guy and he needs a fucking break. Besides that, I'll make a little cash for me and my bride."

Once again Black Sam bellows laughing. "For his *bride*. This kid would make a great fucking politician."

I kinda thought Black Sam was playing with me so I decided to play his game without insulting him. "Sam, you'll be putting up the money, the Hawk will protect your investment, and I will keep a close eye on everything else."

I looked right into his pocked-marked face. "Sam, Paulie Scaparrotti is a pimp. He doesn't deserve to have the meat market all for himself."

Vinny the Cig erupted, "He just insulted Paulie! Sam, what makes you think this kid can pull this off?

"Vinny, I got this, I know how to do this thing. I got this, but if you're smart enough to solve this riddle I'll tell you how the fuck I'm gonna pull this off."

"You little mother-fucker, fuck you and your riddles. Stick 'em up your herniated ass." He turned and stormed out the door.

Black Sam turned to me. "Kid, you know you just made an enemy. By the way, what was the riddle?"

"No riddle. I was making that part up."

That one put Black Sam over the edge. He looked at the Hawk and laughed again. "Ernie, I'm in. I love this kid."

* * *

Four a.m. on a cold and desolate morning is not the time to be in a place like the 14th Street Meat Market.

There I was, in the middle of a ragged crowd of working stiffs all running from the subway in a race to catch the on-coming bus. Every one of us knew if you missed it, you were fucked.

They were all running to work, and so was I, but on this day it was a different kind of work. I was playing detective.

I approached the meat market while it was still half asleep, and took a position across the street, where I snuggled up in a doorway. From there I could keep a watch on the entrance to Wexlor Meats.

But when the wind from the East River started ripping thru me, I thought, *Salerno what the fuck have you gotten yourself into?* In a way, it made me laugh. The street was where I was most happy, anyway. Then I saw someone approaching Wexlor Meats: Solly's son, Jerry. Right on time and full of energy.

I watched while he methodically opened the plant and moved inside. Despite the cold, I decided to wait a while and see if there was anything else going on.

After freezing my balls off for an hour, I was tired of playing detective, so I entered the building. Inside, I spotted Jerry sitting in his office. His head was buried in the racing form. I hung back in the darkness.

I didn't have to wait long before I heard the front door squeak. I stepped farther back into the shadows, but the overhead lights went on, so I slid between two hindquarters of beef. Several long minutes passed before I saw Fat Sammy and Fat Eddie Burns, the packing room manager, pushing a flatbed cart loaded with boxes of beef.

Fat Sammy leaned into Jerry's office doorway and pointed at the racing form. "Yo, Jerry! You got a good one for me?"

Jerry called out, "Horse called New Shares in the fifth at Santa Anita. He loves the turf. Should be a slam dunk."

Once Sammy was in position blocking the doorway, there went the other fat guy, pushing a load of meat right past the unsuspecting horse-junkie. *Nice little score,* I thought while I ran up a flight of stairs and looked out the window.

There was good old Mickey the Slug waiting with open arms. I watched the boys load up, then Mickey handed them a wad of bills that could choke a horse.

I was smiling when I came out of hiding, thinking *Boy, these guys got a racket going. Solly doesn't have a chance in hell.* I went straight to see Jerry.

As soon as Jerry saw me walk through the door, he called out, "Salerno what the hell are you doing here this early?"

"Early bird gets the worm."

"What the hell are you talking about? I'm here every morning."

"Yeah. But while you had your head buried in that fucking racing form, I already caught me a couple of worms."

Jerry jumped up at that, "What racing form?"

"The one you're sitting on. Take it easy tiger, your dad asked me to help him find out who's been robbing him. Now I know it ain't you because I know your bookie, Charlie A., and he told me you're only a two-dollar bettor. So it ain't you and it ain't me. I already have a good idea what's going on. So I'm asking you to help me."

Jerry looked relieved. "I'm in. What do we do? When do we start?"

"Hold your horses. I've already started. Now, here's what I need you to do. I want you to check all the windows in the building, then brick them all up. We don't need them. Then check all the vents and skylights. They're old and need help; a lotta help. Make sure they're all encased with steel wire mesh. No holes in 'em. This way, no one can slip any meat through em. Got that, Sherlock? You gotta make sure they are all sealed. If not, get them welded shut.

"Now get your pen out and write all this shit down. The next thing is the daily pilferage. From now on, all the butchers are not allowed to wear their white coats, going out the door. Got that, handicapper?"

"Why not?"

"That way they can't hide any meat under those coats, like fillets of beef. You should know, they strap them to their legs then put on the white coat. You never see the meat walk out the door."

"How do you know that?"

"Because I do it all the time. Now just do it, then move the timecard machine away from the cooler and over to the front office so you can see who is checking in and checking out. Very important to know where everyone is at all times.

Remember now, when butchers walk through these doors they will only be in their work cloths. No coats. *Right?*"

Jerry was trying to look offended. I had to stop that one cold.

"Jerry. They all do it. Including you. No more meat, period. Then have a new timeclock put up, with a buzzer that will sound every time someone enters the building."

I gave him a friendly smile. "This way no one can sneak past you while you got your nose buried in that fucking racing form. By the way, make sure from now on, you and *only you* have the keys for this joint. I'm holding you responsible for that. No one gets a key, not even your old man. If he beefs about it, tell him to see me. Only me and you will have keys."

Jerry went white. "I could never talk to my old man like that. He'll dump me in the meat grinder."

"Then at least until we find out what's going on, trust no one."

"Look, Salerno, what do you know that I don't?"

"First off, from now on you weigh in *all* the beef that comes into this joint, Jerry. Every fucking pound. Got that? Fat Sammy the scaler is the key. I already caught him in the act."

"What did he do, Salerno? I know Fat Sammy twenty years."

"Nice. Now listen. Let's say he puts two 200-pound hindquarters on the scale. But let's say he only weighs one hindquarter and never reports the other. That gives him 200 pounds of beef he can steal. Right? Then he goes to Fatso Burns and tells Fatso, my man, you have 200 pounds of beef to work with. Right? Then Fatso boxes 200 pounds of beef which goes to Danny Dimes, the dispatcher. Then Danny Dimes has his truck come and pick up the boxes. Simple, nice and easy. That is a sweet operation they got going, right? Now Jerry, tell me, how long have these guys been working here?"

"A long, long time. My Dad is going to be sick."

"Maybe we don't have to tell him. Let's see how these changes shrink the pilferage around here."

Jerry said, "Salerno, you work the scale, I'll work the packaging room. I know it better than anyone else. I discovered this system when I was at Michigan State. I'll make Fat Eddie and Fat Sammy box all the meat after I weigh it myself."

I smiled. "That's a nice touch, but these scumbags have beat your dad for a lotta rubles. So be careful."

"I know the party's over, but my dad is not the kind of a man to put anyone in jail. That's just not his style. But that don't mean he'll take it lying down. If he finds out what his friends have been doing to him, he will be so disappointed. I can tell you that. There will be *hell to pay*."

A solid month flew by while Solly made the changes, with me weighing in the meat and Jerry in the packaging room. It was working like a Swiss watch. The threesome of thieves never said a word and we never did either. Call it a truce.

At first, Solly was taking in the changes better than we thought he would. But then he came bursting into the office with news. "Just when the pilferages slowed down, I get a call from this Scaparrotti character. He wants another point! Well, fuck him and the mother that made him. I'll kill that blood-sucker with my own two fucking hands!"

Jerry caught my eye and whispered, "Wow. My dad has really picked up on your lingo."

I waited for Solly to cool off, then said, "Solly, it's time I called the Hawk."

"Salerno, that would only take me from the frying pan into the fire. In the end, he'll be putting the squeeze on me, too."

"Solly, you're in a no-win situation, but the best of two evils would be to deal with the Hawk. Solly trust me. The

Hawk would never fuck me around. Like it or not, that's the way the mop flops for this."

Solly turned to Jerry. "I worked all my life to have to have somebody tell me, 'that's the way the mop flops.'" Solly walked out. He called back, "Set the meeting. If you need me, I'll be at the Luxor baths."

Great fucking idea. Turkish baths. A nice clean environment for such a dirty bunch.

I called the Hawk and set the meeting.

25

Unfinished Business

Now it was time for some unfinished business. I met Jerry upstairs. Together we stormed into the locker room. There was Danny Dimes, Sammy, and Fat Eddie adding up their daily take.

I laughed and called out, "Pickins ain't what they used to be, right boys? The fucking party is over!"

Danny Dimes got up. His huge frame seemed to engulf the room.

"What's that supposed to mean?"

Jerry jumped in, "Solly Hirsch ain't gonna be supporting your habits anymore, that's what it means."

The quiet giant eyeballed Jerry. "What are you talking about?"

Jerry sat on his nerves, so I jumped in. "Big guy, he's talking about you blowing three, four hundred a day up your *schnazolla,* that's what he's talking about."

"And you, Sammy, you gotta quit gambling," Jerry added.

I turned my attention to Eddie. "Eddie, you I don't trust. Because if they suddenly stopped while they're walking, I'd have to take you to the hospital to get your fucking nose yanked out of their ass."

Danny Dimes stood there smiling. "That's a nice speech kid, real nice, but if you think I'm gonna let some punk like you tell me what to do you gotta be fucking crazy." He flipped the table across the room and started to come at me. I backed up enough to give me a second to slide my hand into my open fly and pull out my derringer thinking, *thanks Ma, you're always there when I need you the most.*

Danny Dimes eyed the derringer and laughed. "Kid, what are you going to do with that pea shooter?"

Everything in the room stopped. It got quiet real fast. Jerry said, "I'm going to take a shit and while I'm gone, I want you guys to hit the highway. If you're still here when I get back, I'm going to rip off your fucking skulls and take a second shit in the eye sockets."

I couldn't believe what I had just heard him say, but I thought he made himself pretty clear. A lot of these mob guys had a gift that way.

The three wise men did a wise thing. They packed up their booty and hit the highway. Jerry looked at me with a smile and asked, "How did I do?"

"Not bad. Where did you learn to rap like that, Michigan State?"

"Michigan State my ass, I learned it listening to you."

* * *

I was sitting in the steam room naked as a jay bird and drinking a delicious Dr. Brown's Cream Soda when the Hawk sauntered in. He had a wet towel draped over his head.

"Salerno, when Paulie finds out what's going on, I don't think he's going to take this lying down. You have to keep an eye on his nephew Mickey because I know he's a loose cannon."

"Ernie, I don't know why Scaparrotti is associating with his nephew because I know for a fact he's a stool pigeon."

"What!"

"Square business. I read his trial transcript. Mickey got nailed for bank robbery, turned state's evidence, then testified against Benny the Jet and Leroy Johnson from Staten Island."

"How did you find that out?"

"Benny the Jet is the numbers guy for Frankie Five Fingers. HeeHE asked me to look them over, so I sent them to my buddy Jerry the Jew, a legal beagle from the Kings County bug house. Now get this: Mickey is now the bartender over at Nicky's joint, you know the Tango Lounge down in the mill basin? Well, I told Nicky he was no fucking good, but Nicky just shook it off like he didn't give a fuck."

"Maybe so, but Nicky is a three-time loser. The joint beat him for his brain. Did you know he did twenty-two years for stealing a pizza?"

"He knew Mickey was no good, but he also knew Mickey was a bowling whiz. The story I got was, Nicky is backing Mickey in big-money tournaments."

Just then Mickey and Paulie waddled into the sauna, so we had to shut up about it. I took one look at Paulie's body and thought *Boy, this man should never take his clothes off in public.*

The Hawk pointed at Mickey, a la "get that rat the hell outta here." Mickey looked indignant and stared at Paulie a moment before he dropped his head and walked out.

That was a hell of move on Paulie's part. You never bring a rat to a sit-down. Paulie knew Mickey was a rat, but Paulie always did what Paulie wanted to do. Now he turned to the Hawk to try to explain. "I only use him for certain things."

"Look Paulie, a rat is a rat, period. You know that." Paulie got real uneasy with that remark. He was miffed and he didn't like being questioned. But this was a whole different deal. Especially dealing with the Hawk, who was a complete renegade.

Now the Hawk smelled Scaparrotti's uneasiness, and he moved in for the kill.

"Paulie, I'm taking over Solly's note."

That hit Paulie hard. He was completely unprepared and he didn't move. He just sat there with a look of disbelief. Here's a made guy that just came to a sit down with a rat, then got his asshole reamed for doing so. On top of that he got ordered what to do and told what was going to happen. That was too much for Scaparrotti. The gas he emitted soured the whole fucking steam room.

Solly enjoyed every minute of watching the overtaxed mobster squirm, belch, and fart. Solly said, "Mr. Scaparrotti, you should do something about your indigestion."

I added, "Small meals, several times a day."

Solly said, "Also, try nibbling on healthy snacks. Fruits and veggies."

It was sweet, listening to Solly killing Scaparrotti with kindness. The overweight mobster sat there without a clue. I gotta tell you, the feeling I had in that room was as good as it gets.

In fact, there are those inexpressibly sweet two or three seconds just before ejaculation and this was one of those moments. I felt like I died and went to heaven, watching this heavy-hitter getting worked over with nothing but kindness and generosity.

I thought, *This is a moment I'm going to tell my great-grandchildren about, if I live that long.*

Then the Hawk gave Scaparrotti an offer he could not refuse: either his nephew Mickey's tongue or his signature would appear on the note.

Scaparrotti signed the note.

The Hawk handed the note to Solly. "I think this is what you came for?"

Then the Hawk left. Not another word. No goodbyes, nothing.

26

What a Difference a Day Makes

Nefarious mobster Paulie Scaparrotti met a fiery death when the car he was driving exploded in flames. When Solly heard the news, he came running into the packaging room. "Mr. Scaparrotti! He got French fried!"

Among the spectators at Scaparrotti funeral, which was packed with every dignitary in the criminal world, not a word was discussed about the business meeting we had at the Luxor Baths. The Hawk and I paid our respects to Paulie's widow, then respectfully left.

Not one of Scaparrotti's captains said a word to the Hawk about the note. Matter of fact, nothing was discussed about anything with the Hawk.

Black Sam was among the mourners. He asked, "Why did he never come by for the money"?

The Hawk just replied, "Guess things just never got worked out." It was like that meeting never happened.

Mickey the Slug couldn't rat because he wasn't present. All he knew was his Uncle Paulie wanted to spend a day at the baths.

The Hawk told me Scaparrotti always kept his business to himself. So at that point I realized no one knew about this business meeting, period.

The only ones who knew what really took place in that steam room meeting were Solly, me, and the Hawk. Near as I could figure out, he didn't kill himself. When Scaparrotti left the bath house he was depressed and embarrassed, but was *that* enough to drive him to choose the most aggravated and ferocious way to end it all? I don't think so. A lotta questions were spinning around in my head.

It was like someone hated him. I don't know who. On the other hand, Solly despised the son of a bitch so much that I wouldn't put it past him either. I told the Hawk, maybe Solly held the lighter himself. Scaparrotti himself was a coward, so I'm sure he didn't do it.

That left the Hawk as the main suspect. This was his kind of M.O. The whole episode reminded me of the Aesop's fable about the Tortoise and the Hare. In the end, Solly finished first. He got what he wanted. I got my two percent. And the Hawk, I never asked what he got. That was between him and Solly.

* * *

Working in a cooler in the early morning hours always gave me the willies. It was like looking down a silent street populated only by rows of dead meat hanging on cold steel hooks. The silences worked on your mind like a slow drip water torture. So on this morning, I was startled to hear sounds of shoes on the salted concrete. I looked around the sweating pipes and yelled out, "Jerry, is that you?"

Out stepped a short man sporting a massive skull. I challenged him, "Who the fuck are you?"

"Where's the money, butcher boy?"

I lifted my ten-inch blade. "I don't know what the fuck you're talking about."

A voice echoed from deep in the cooler. "He's lying."

I heard Jerry's voice say, "I swear mister, I ain't got no money." Just then Mickey steps out of the darkness holding a gun to Jerry's head.

"I swear, mister, we don't have a dime. Wait for his dad. He's got plenty of money! You'll see, I fucking swear!"

"Did you lie to me?" Mickey demanded of the short guy with the large skull. And then without waiting for an answer, he put one between his eyes.

But one instant later, an eerie sound echoed across the cooler like a giant bee on coke. Mickey hit the deck hard. And from behind a hindquarter, out steps the Hawk, with a smoking gun in his hand. It was mounted with a silencer bigger than the pistol.

"I never trusted this punk, so I been keeping an eye on him. I had a hunch he was up to no good. It wasn't me who torched old man Scaparrotti. That piece of shit on the floor probably recruited that fag from Benny the Blade's joint. Probably gave sweet balls over there a line of shit, and he fell for it."

What happened next, I was not ready for. Jerry stepped over to the bodies and said, "Let's put them in the meat grinder.

The Hawk smiled at me. "I like the way he thinks."

I couldn't believe my ears. "Jerry, are you nuts?"

"How are we going to explain all this to my dad? Fuck them, Salerno."

The Hawk nodded. "Butcher boy, get to work. Let's see how good you are with that blade of yours."

We dragged Mickey and the short dead guy into the boning room and employed the skills we had, then slid them onto the conveyer belt. I hit the button and watched their armless bodies slide into the number seventeen meat grinder. This puppy had an insatiable appetite. There was only one problem. The skull on the midget was too big, even for this grinder. So I had to get a massive hog splitter and cut his skull in two, then all you could hear in the cooler was the echo of bones snapping and cracking. After we ground them up, we took the remains to my grandfather's dogs.

27

Don't Piss in the Corned Beef Barrel

My instincts told me life at the 14th Street Meat Market was starting to suck me under, so I decided to move on down the road. I thought a nice job in some local butcher shop someplace would be cool and offer a much better chance at staying alive. No stealing, no scheming, a time to rest.

Two days into working the new gig, I got my orders from Tony Tituli, the boss. My job was for big cash and a lotta prizes, but the catch was they had to be earned and there was massive risk involved.

Cutting meat for this guy was secondary. Stealing was his first love. I thought, *Here we go again, Salerno.* "If you're not stealing, you ain't trying." That was Tony's motto.

Beating people in the butcher shop was easy, but nickel and diming people was hard for me to do, giving the customer a big smile at the same time. When you put the meat on the scale and wanted to do a rip-off, that's where the fun begins. If a customer wanted you to weigh out a pound of chopped meat, there was a two-ounce weight included.

Now, if it was three or four chickens you put on the scale, you can bet there was at least a five-ounce weight stuck up one of those chickens' butt. Now, for the really irritating customers, Tony had a special surprise. On Saint Patrick's Day when the whole world was eating corned beef. Tony had a special barrel filled with a mixture of corned beef brine and piss.

I had a problem about pissing in the corned beef barrel so I quit. Before I left, I told Tony my reasons for leaving. He laughed out loud. He looked like he lived in the same world, but the one he saw was nothing like mine. His working life was nothing but one, long, chicken-shit maneuver.

So it was good to feel the neighborhood beneath my feet again, but I decided to hang out in a different part of town for awhile. I walked into The Night Owl Lounge. Only the best con guys in the city did their business there. The place had a mob influence to it, but there was more of an atmosphere of the scheme. Head work. I liked that.

I was alive with anticipation and listening to the sounds of Ray Charles, when a sweaty wise guy named Tony Dags approached and asked me, "Did you bring me the meat?"

Tony Dags always liked it when I brought him free meat. For some reason it made him feel very important. I smiled. "Tony, how could I forget that?"

As I moved through the crowded bar, I could hear familiar noises of a card game going on in the back room. I hated cards but I was stoked just to be there so I moved into the smoke-filled room.

Lo and behold, there was my old man sitting in a high stakes poker game. Now that wasn't bad enough, but what really threw me for a loop was that my mother was also a player.

I yelled, "Ma, whatta you doing here?"

"Playing cards, son. What's it look like? Come here and give your mother a kiss."

My mind was moving fast. *What the hell is Ma doing here?* Then it hit me. Aw shit, she's the shill for my old man! So I guess after Sally D disappeared, Pop started using Ma. Very dangerous work. Get you killed if you do it wrong.

I got a little sick to my stomach. What if they got caught? At least when Sally D was playing, Pop didn't have to worry. Sally D himself was Pop's security blanket.

Then a tall guy I never saw before entered, and Tony Dags greeted him with open arms. Jimmy Quinn was his name, and conning was his game. Jimmy was a slender, good-looking Irish fellow. "Irish Jimmy!" Dag's yelled. "You're just in time! I got the steaks on the grill."

I laughed at that remark. Irish Jimmy scanned the room, then the game and its players. He remarked, "This game looks like easy money."

Ma pointed to an empty seat. "There's room for another hand, especially if you think it's easy ...."

Irish Jimmy eyed Ma, then said, "Some chips, please." He pulled out a wad and ripped off two thousand. Ma caught the move. "You think that's enough?"

Jimmy snickered. "Well, ma'am, we are going to find out real fast."

Sitting next to Ma was a resident con man. Jimmy looked at him. "Gooch, you broke?" Gooch nodded.

Jimmy chuckled. "You mean you let this bunch take you? Shame on you. I thought I taught you better than that."

Jimmy handed the sleek Italian a thousand. Gooch replied, "They are a pretty sharp bunch," but Irish Jimmy waved him off.

Now my eyes were glued to old beefy fingers, knowing he was gonna split this Irish guy in half. Irish Jimmy reached for one of Ma's cigarettes. She casually moved the pack like she never saw his hand coming, leaving Irish Jimmy with his hand in the air.

Tony Dags asked Jimmy, "I hear you're going out with a new girl, what's-her-face's sister.

Ma jumped in, "You're going out with a new girl? Oh! That is so nice." Boy, did she sound interested.

Jimmy nodded and looked at his cards. Ma went on, "When am I gonna meet her, this new girl? Is she a nice Irish girl?"

Irish Jimmy looked at his hand again. Three aces looked back at him. "Soon, Ma. Real soon."

I knew right there, sure as God made little green apples, Pop slipped him those Aces.

Gooch looked annoyed and threw a hundred into the pot. He looked at Ma. "Ma, this is a card game, not a lonely-hearts club. Pot's open!"

Irish Jimmy raised. Ma re-raised. Irish Jimmy grinned, then gave his cards another look. "To tell you the truth, Mom, may I call you Mom?"

Ma smiled. Nobody called her "Mom," for the same reason you don't name your killer dog Sniffles.

"Sure. Call me Mom," She did not add, *sucker,* because in that company she didn't need to.

"Mom, I'll have to find out her schedule."

Ma just smiled, God she was sweet, then she gave her hand another little peek. "That's very respectful. She must be a nice girl." She glanced at her cards again like she was still trying to remember how they worked. "Yes, very nice."

Irish Jimmy re-raised. Ma re-raised. Gooch was caught in the middle, so he just saw the bet.

Irish Jimmy turned to Ma again. "Then the second time we went out, she took me to Kings County hospital to visit her sick aunt."

"What a nice girl! She takes time to go see someone who's sick." Ma checked her hand, barely a glance this time. "Oh! That's wonderful."

Jimmy turned to Ma, "You think that's wonderful, wait 'til you hear this: I went over for dinner on Sunday. She wound up taking me to the best Irish wedding I've ever been to."

Jimmy checked his hand, and the fool actually allowed himself to smile. I think he hoped it would look like he was smiling at the thought of his girl, but I knew better. He was staining his shorts over those three aces.

"I do love her, Mom. I just love her."

Gooch snapped, "Love her later! Let's stop all the bullshit and play cards."

"Easy Gooch," Irish Jimmy told him, acting like he was the one who stood clued-in on things. "It's only a card game."

Except it wasn't.

I watched Pop give the Irishman two cards, both fours, taking his hand to a full house, aces high. Ma drew one card. Gooch stayed pat and then checked.

Irish Jimmy had a head of steam on, now. He came out betting strong and dropped five hundred into the pot. Ma raised. Gooch saw the raise. Jimmy re-raised. Ma saw that raise as well.

Gooch went all-in and confidently laid out his hand, a full house with kings high. "Kings Full, lover boy."

Irish Jimmy beamed and laid out his three aces and two fours. "Sorry partner. Aces Full." Jimmy made the orgasm face and started to rake in the pot, but Ma stopped him by waving her finger in his face and shaking her head.

"No, no, no, sweetie!" In a single motion, Ma fanned out her hand to show four of a kind. "Four deuces never loses."

Jimmy got up and caught Ma winking at the old man, which cancelled out their genius scam. It was not only a fucking amateur move, but I could tell Jimmy caught the play.

Funny enough, Jimmy didn't look especially pissed off about it. "Well I guess this game wasn't as easy as I thought, eh?"

Ma winked at him. "I hope your girl is easier than this poker game was for you." But again, instead of spouting off, this slick Irish guy chuckled, bent down, and kissed Ma on the cheek.

"Mom, you're the best." He shot a look at the old man. "You two are a great team."

I just nodded and said, "I told you this was a tough game."

Jimmy smiled at me. What the fuck? It was a sincere smile. Then he whispered in my ear. "Can your mom and pop do this all the time?"

So, then.

I didn't know this guy that well, but I knew his reputation. He was a solid con man. So I took the bait. "My old man has the best hands in the city."

"What a great team! With them, I could clean out half the country."

That stopped me. He was looking at things on a much grander scale than my folks were. I got nervous. "Look Jimmy, that level of play sounds rough. I mean it's my ma, for Christ's sake."

"I got one in mind that's an easy play. You, me, and the Gooch riding shot gun. We protect the working team of your mom and pop. We move in on a place, hit fast, and move out faster."

"Who holds the guns?"

He gave me a sour grin. "You do, tough guy. You got the strongest motive to protect the talent."

28

Family Road Trip!

Two months later, we all hit the road. Me, Ma, Pop, Irish Jimmy, and Gooch. My contribution to all this was basically as muscle. Mostly I drove around in a very expensive limousine.

Irish Jimmy said a limousine gave the impression of class. Now with me being so powerfully built, he said, "Ma, your son will make the perfect chauffeur. He's over six foot and he looks like a truck."

So whenever we walked into a world-class hotel, the first thing they would do is have me bring in the luggage and check in. Gooch said it was a very solid move because it kept the doubting hotel managers off guard about us.

The other players had more acting to do. My job was easy stuff. Check 'em in and check 'em out. Keep strangers from getting any big ideas.

When it came to Ma, I couldn't believe my eyes and ears. She took to it all and was having a good old time, just chatting up the suckers night and day like this was a vacation.

To back all this up, they had ten different sets of IDs, licenses, credit cards, and bank checks. The credit cards were the sweetest scam I ever saw, obtained from JoJo Weintraub, a disgruntled Jewish postal worker who operated a, shall we say, schmatte business on the side.

Seems the Irish guy met JoJo on a scam and found out he had access to all of the credit cards that passed through his post office. The light went on in the Irish guy's head. So then JoJo's job was to intercept the credit cards. In those days, before it all went online, the scammers had about two months to operate before anyone realized their card numbers were stolen.

The best part of the scheme was there was a dumpy rundown Penny Arcade on 42nd street in Manhattan, where you could reproduce anything you wanted, such as licenses, checks, marriage licenses, you name it. That was the place to have it done.

I was baffled by that. I asked JoJo, "How does the FBI let that place operate?"

His answer was simple. "The fucking feds are too busy chasing the bank robbers. They don't know this joint even exists. This is just a place where parents get their kids fake IDs so their kids can play games here. You know, make believe."

"Make believe, my ass! These documents are some of the best I've ever seen." JoJo smiled at that.

Ma's self-control during all this was a thing of beauty. When she would strut into a lobby, arm-in-arm with her make-believe sons, she always smiled, watching her son and his "brother" work the hotel manager. Then she'd be right in his other ear, telling him what items she needed to make her stay a more comfortable one.

One of her outrageous requests was to ask the manager to cash a check for fifteen hundred dollars. Without question, the Manager would reply, "But of course, Madam." Whenever there was an inquisitive hotel manager, out came the impeccable IDs.

Ma had these managers dizzy with her superb bullshit. It was hard at times even for me to keep a straight face. Ma could talk the ear off a brass monkey, and believe me, with her big smile and disarming rap, she could distract the devil himself. No one ever suspected what was going on. For me it was like watching some hit play off-Broadway.

"How is the action around here?" she would purr.

"Excuse me, madam, what kind of action?"

Ma would take a big drag on her cigarette, smile, and then exhale a cloud of smoke that could choke a horse. "Cards, darling. Cards."

One night, the response she got was better than unusual. "Well, there are card games at the Knights of Columbus on Tuesdays and Sundays, or right next door at the Mosaic Lodge tonight, after nine. But the big action is in the Police Chief's house every night."

"Oh Morris, would you please get the address? I feel like playing."

"Yes, Madam."

It was funny until I heard that. *The police chief's house?* My throat got tight. Sometimes Ma pushed the envelope a bit too far. Rigging a card game at the police chief's house was not something sane people would do, or so I thought.

And by two o'clock that morning, there we were, all sitting somewhere in bum-fuck Idaho in the Police Chief's home, make that *mansion*, watching Ma having a ball entertaining the Chief. Chiefee was a big drunk who wore a size ten hat and slobbered when he spoke. But he had done got himself some serious money from someplace. It was good to be Chiefee.

Irish Jimmy was admiring the paintings. Gooch was after the maid. My old man pretended to read a Mickey Spillane detective book while he cased around. I was almost shitting my pants, but all I could do was watch.

Ma, well, she could work a room like no other person I had ever seen. Even my old man, who never said a good word about anybody unless he was kissing up, seemed impressed with her play.

She had a knack for flair but she was oblivious to danger. The Police Chief and his cronies were taking a beating, and at some late point Ma finally sensed something in the room had changed.

When she felt it was time to leave, she yelled, "Oh God! Morris, please get me some water and my heart pills!"

That really got the suckers' attention. They responded just like she wanted them to. Confusion changed the mood to one of concern. She was a great actress. My old man always said she made his job a lot easier. We made it out of there on tooth skin. I don't think those guys ever knew I was at the table.

After Ma's death-defying performance at the Police Chief's home, we hit every major hotel across the country. Except for the fifteen hundred a pop on the hot checks at each new hotel, everyone was responsible for their own cash. My job was to call the hotel's wine steward and tell him we were going to have a party. I ordered the best and most expensive Champagne available. It was always delivered without question.

Then I would go to the local U.P.S. and have it shipped home. Lucille told me we had over a hundred bottles of wine, Scotch, and Champagne stashed in the garage.

Irish Jimmy always handled the credit cards. Whenever a hotel clerk got too nosey, he'd put him right on the defensive. "Let me speak to the manager!" The poor clerk would shiver and crawl back into the woodwork.

There was something to be said when you had your chauffeur standing by. It always gave those awkward moments an air of opulence. It was just a guy in a suit, but some powerful message got delivered by the sight of him. It worked every damn time.

When we hit 'em, we hit 'em fast and hard, then kept moving. Gooch and the Irishman hit all the high-end fashion shops. Store clerks would fall over one another, rushing to wait on them.

Wherever we went, Ma and Jimmy had easy marks eating out of their hands. They were impeccable together. Gooch, on the other hand, always had too much pussy up his nose. He worked all the hookers and he loved them all.

He'd always say, deaf, dumb, blind, crippled or crazy, he didn't give a rat's ass. I would not want to ask about the rat itself.

After weeks of this, I started to get itchy and got the feeling this ride was over. I told Ma, enough is enough. But when Ma told that to Gooch, he beefed hard about it. All I could say was, "How far do you want to go with this?"

For better or worse, it was a family operation. Without us he had nothing to shoot for, so we eyeballed one another for a minute, then both took steps backward and into the night. Irish Jimmy kissed Ma. I put Ma and Pop into the limousine and drove us back to Brooklyn.

Three crooks who quit while they were ahead. It was a lesson every gambler should learn.

29

Celebrity Mother

Soon after arriving back in New York from that prosperous road trip, Ma the Mouth (that was now her street handle), Irish Jimmy, and Charlie the Pick were picking out some of the best card games around. This earned you real respect in certain circles.

Naturally, when I walked the streets, I had to hear the same rap all day long, all about my mother. Ma was fast becoming a local celebrity.

Seems her favorite little story to tell during a game was, "My son is gonna be a movie star. He's gonna be in a movie with Marlon Brando." It sounded nice even if she didn't believe it. Little did she know how close she was.

When she delivered her rap, she had a cigarette in one hand and a deck of cards in another, blowing smoke in some sucker's ace at the same time. As much as I admired her action, I started to worry that Ma might get busted. Even the best can get busted, sometimes just because some angry bastard rats them out. At her age, any sentence would be tough to serve.

I was on my way to see Ma when I ran into my man Teddy Brown, the local fence. He told me Irish Jimmy brought him some really nice diamonds that he and Ma had smuggled into the country.

I almost flipped when Teddy told me that. Ma smuggling? The skinny I got from Teddy Brown was that Ma stuffed all the diamonds into a big salami sandwich and then just passed through customs with olive oil and black olives dripping from her chin.

She offered the customs officer a bite. He declined. Ma was not to be denied, so she stuck it in his face, "Take a bite it's delicious, I made it myself. It's better than this airplane food. Come on! Manga! Manga!" She even dripped some of the oil on his shirt.

The customs guy refused the bite, so Ma stuck the greasy sandwich back into her knitting bag. Then she pulled out an oil-stained handkerchief and for five minutes tried to convince the customs guy to allow her to clean his shirt.

Irish Jimmy said it was the best piece of work he'd ever seen. A thing of beauty. She was very, very cunning. Oblivious to fear. Jimmy said Ma was always in her own little world of make believe. He told Teddy Brown that Ma could be ready for a big con with a major hit. I was afraid she might go for it.

New Year's Eve was fast approaching. Ma the Mouth, Charlie the Pick, Irish Jimmy, the Hawk, Holly, me and my bride, we all piled into my limousine and headed for Jersey City. As we approached Fat Albert's Mansion, I already knew the Hawk hated Fat Albert, especially after his brother Funzy wacked Gus. So I drove along wondering, *Why the fuck are we going to this gig?*

I didn't have to wait long for the answer. On the way to Fat Albert's, we stopped in Manhattan and picked up Louie the Dome. Seems the Dome was fucking some hot, rich broad, Sylvia, whose husband, Nick, was not only loaded but for some reason was desperate to get into the numbers business.

Problem being the Dome was a pure hitter, he was not a numbers guy at all. So he called the Hawk.

The key to it all was this Nick character from Jersey City, a friend of Fat Albert's wife, Gina. So she invited Silva and her husband, Nick, to the party. Seems the Dome was really hung up on Sylvia, and so he thought her and Gina and the Dome could have a little party of their own.

On the other hand, the Dome figured it would be a good time for the Hawk to meet this millionaire. What better than a New Year's Eve party? It was the perfect cover to avoid suspicion. Then, to add more spice to the event, the Dome tells the Hawk that Fat Albert's wife is a good-looking social butterfly, and that the joint would be cashed up to the max.

It was also a perfect place to operate for Irish Jimmy, Ma the Mouth, and Charlie the Pick. Decked out to the fucking nines, our team strolled into the Fat Man's mansion, a sprawling three-story job nestled into the Jersey countryside. The whole fucking joint reeked of money. I could smell it, Ma could see it, and my Old Man could feel it. Ma's lamps lit up at the sight of all the diamonds. Irish Jimmy was working the room looking for fresh meat. In seconds it was right in front of him.

She was tall, she was sexy and sassy, and she ripped Jimmy with, "Who the hell invited you?"

He smiled. "How long have you been here?"

"Wouldn't you like to know, blue eyes?"

Jimmy laughed. "As long as you're here, is what counts." He quickly guided her to the bar.

Funzy's daughter, a curvy devil, appeared and looked around the room. I'm telling you, the dress she had on left no room for her to breathe. I was still taking in the sight when a tall and good-looking black waiter passed by her—and quickly ran his hand across her ass. No accident. Deliberate move.

Oh, but her daddy, Fat Albert, caught the move. He waddled across the room and pulled her frail body into a corner, then got right into her face. But I guess his daughter decided to double down on her defiance. She pulled away and ran right up to an unsuspecting waiter, shouting, "Happy New Year!"

She planted a big wet one smack on his lips.

Fat Albert watched his daughter from across the room while she finished kissing the waiter and moved toward another one. He slammed his rotund fist into a table, sending his plate to the floor. Everybody pretended they didn't notice.

Lucille moved fast and ushered me into another room. "Not our problem," she whispered. Besides, Ma and Pop were already engaged in a high-stakes poker game.

I heard Ma saying, "My son makes the best marinara sauce in the world. Soon he'll be making some for Marlon Brando."

From the side of my eye, I caught Funzy's daughter floating around the dining room. Every waiter who passed got something erotic from her, like a touch here, a stroke there. They were too surprised and embarrassed to stop her. She was a kid in a candy store.

To make things worse, she twirled over to an unsuspecting busboy and traced her finger along his crotch, right in front of her father. She winked at Daddy.

I have known some women to be as crazy and evil as men can be. This girl was old enough to know her father, know his emotions, his hot buttons. Her openly sexual act and humiliating defiance of him was a direct attack on his sense of self, his world. He exploded with a blood-curdling scream that engulfed the stricken room.

Fat Albert lost all control. He pulled his gun from his waistband and blew the unsuspecting busboy's brains out. Mayhem exploded like shit through a straw, and Fat Albert ran through the room, shooting one waiter after another.

People froze. Women cried. Politicians fled. When the smoke cleared, Fatso had assassinated all five waiters and the lone busboy. Spent and bloodied from his crazed ordeal, he stood in the middle of the room with the smoking gun in his hand.

It was pretty cut and dry. A guilty verdict for Fat Albert. Life in prison, maybe execution.

Not yet, though.

Sylvia, Fat Albert's wife, sprang into action. She called the guard at the front gate. "No one leaves till I say so!" She turned to Fat Albert's cohorts. "Get Albert the fuck out of here! Now!" The two captains finally recovered from the shock and got busy.

She told Billy the Barber to send all the relatives home, since she knew they would never say a word. Frankie the Wasp ran to the parking area and rounded up all the wacked-out politicians and their wives before they could escape, then, as quick as you please, escorted them back into the drawing room.

School was in session.

"Listen. Listen to me if you want to live. One fucking word about this evening to anyone, you and your whole family and your family's family would be dead, dead, dead!"

On the third dead, me and the Hawk, Louie the Dome, Ma and Pop, and Irish Jimmy all entered the fiasco just in time to hear Billy the Barber say, "You talk, we're gonna gut everyone in this room like pigs."

Everybody seemed to catch the idea. They shuffled away in whispers.

One phone call from the Hawk, and even though it was New Year's Eve, ten minutes later there were five trucks standing by ready to be loaded. What a fucking operation. Meanwhile, me, Lucille, Ma and Pop, and Irish Jimmy all sprang into action helping Billy the Barber's crew.

They were fast, like they had done this enough to get smooth at it. They showed up with enough cleaning supplies to wipe down the Empire State building. Every stick of blood-stained furniture in that room soon did the best disappearing act I ever saw. A lot of stuff, big stuff and little stuff, just went away.

That included rugs, drapes, and whatever else was damaged. Once the site was clean, Frankie the Wasp and his crew dumped the bodies in the Jersey mountains and put the household items in a landfill. By the end of the next day, the Hawk got the skinny that the room was completely cleaned, rebuilt, and furnished like nothing ever happened.

Sylvia assured the inquiring parties that all of the workers were paid and stayed all night and partied hearty till the crack of dawn. When the detectives questioned the nervous politicians, they simply replied a good time was had by all. Once again, the shadow of the Mafia ruled.

Still, Murphy's Law fucks with crooks, too. Sorry to say, all the highly organized work accomplished on that New Year's Eve went right out the fucking window, because one of those so-called wise guys who helped bury the bodies got himself caught robbing a bank. So to save his sorry fucking ass, he told the F.B.I. he knew where those bodies were buried. The stool pigeon knew the Feds wanted Fat Albert so bad, they would give him a deal.

The stoolie showed them the so-called burial site, but oddly enough, the Feds announced there were no bodies found. The stool pigeon walked anyway. His lawyer said, "Hey, a deal is a deal, and that's where they were buried. So someone must've moved them. Then they asked the stoolie where the waiters were shot.

He replied. "I could use some walking around money." He got that too. "Fat Albert shot em," he told them at last. "His daughter was making a big deal out of flirting with them and he couldn't shoot her, so ...."

On that info, the Feds arrested Fat Albert, then when he went before the judge, the D.A. claimed he was a flight risk, and persuaded the judge to keep Fat Albert in jail.

30

A Nation of Squealers

It was a mystery. The F.B.I. really fucked up. No guns, no statements, no available witnesses, no evidence. Not a hair or a drop of blood was ever found at the so-called crime scene. Turned out that "stoolie" who revealed where the bodies would be found was just a truck driver and part time criminal looking for a break. He had no fucking idea what went on that night.

So Fat Albert went free. But that didn't help him much. When the Judge dismissed the case, Fat Albert got so excited, he up and died of a heart attack, right there on the fucking spot.

After dodging all the bullets in his life, it was the old widow-maker that got him. Last I heard, Slick Sylvia was running for City Council.

* * *

This was all too much like Billy Blue Eyes, who was the first wise guy I ever knew who ratted. I didn't realize it at the time, but this rising nation of squealers marked the turning point of the entire Mafia era in New York. Yes, it was a criminal organization, but it held solid structure in the neighborhoods and the businesses, and if you removed all that structure, something else would absolutely rush in to fill it. People were starting to enjoy a sense of freedom from Mafia influence, but they didn't pay attention to what was replacing that power structure. The value of loyalty no longer existed there.

Until those days, ratting was basically unheard of. If the Mafia was the Catholic religion, ratting someone out would be called a mortal sin. When you died, you would go straight to hell with the other rats. I know this picture affected a lot of wise guys, I mean deep down in places where no one could see, maybe not even them.

They weren't saying much, at least while I was around. The papers ran the Billy Blue Eyes story every day, hoping to get another wise guy to roll over.

Then the head of the F.B.I. ran stories with captions that read, "Come forward and the F.B.I. will take care of you and your families. We can get you out from under the scourge of the Mafia. Live like a human being again!" The Feds repeated this over and over.

"We can get you a job! Live clean and enjoy the rest of your days with your loved ones!" Big announcements appeared on all the TVs.

"We will put you in our Witness Protection Program." I'm telling you, these stories were starting to rock the boat. Especially the word "our." It was the key word because it gave a sort of ownership feel. To a lot of the so-called goombahs, especially the ones with the IQs of around fifty or so, the word "our" became very appealing, a very catchy tune.

The F.B.I. used the words "we" and "our," over and over. *We will protect you.*

"OUR PROGRAM, OUR PROTECTION, OUR IDEA, OUR WORD, OUR STRENGTH, OUR COUNTRY."

Over time, with enough repetition, the propaganda had its desired effect. Things started to wobble in the neighborhood.

We began to hear about wise guys rolling over. In my belly, I knew things were starting to loosen up in the ranks of the so-called wise guys. This was a turning point in my life and the lives of most of us in the neighborhood.

The old ways were no longer working.

No one was saying anything about the issue, but goombahs who were once well-hidden in the woodwork all of a sudden came out and started turning state's evidence. I remember Gus preaching to me, "Remember, when termites start to eat at the foundation of a building, eventually it has to fall."

That was Gus' philosophy about what a stool pigeon can do to an organization. I knew he was right, and I was sick inside.

Confusion was gripping the hood, deceit loomed large, and the once-organized streets got uneasy with feelings of mistrust. I saw a variety of street players who were starting to weaken. And pretty soon, out of nowhere, official statements started coming from disgruntled mobsters. It was amazing how much they could rationalize about knuckling under to the feds.

"You want to be in a position to determine your own fate." I heard that one coming from Tony Dags, who I always considered a make-believe tough guy anyway.

So I asked him what he meant by that. The Hawk was sitting with us at the lounge, so when I asked the question with him sitting right there, it gave me some leverage. But Dags sneered at me. "You know, for just a kid, you ask a lot of fucking questions."

"Dags, I was just confused about what's going on in the neighborhood, that's all."

The half-assed mobster reluctantly answered, "You always have to put yourself in position to win."

The Hawk snapped back at him, "At whose cost, Tony? At whose cost?"

The make-believe mobster's face turned red. He said simply, "A man should do what he can do."

All of a sudden, I realized what this marshmallow was talking about. *Let's make a deal, pal.* This cat-and-mouse game was headed in one direction. Disaster.

With the Hawk at my side. I decided to go after this. "Look Dags, there is only one rule on the street, and you know what that is. You keep your fucking mouth shut."

That got interrupted when the Hawk tapped me on the shoulder. The look he had on his face made me feel like I was about to take a six-minute death sentence in an ice bath.

"What's up?"

"Swivel Tooth just phoned me and said Irish Jimmy, Ma, and Gooch were arrested by the Safe and Loft Squad."

"Do you think Harry the Hat will bail my mamma out?" The Hawk just smiled. "No problem. I remember Harry when he was just a shoeshine boy."

Three days and a carton of cigarettes later, Ma convinced some little-league D.A. that she was innocent of any wrongdoing. Ma said she told the young D.A., "How could you arrest a woman who's known you and your family all your lives?"

Of course, some irate detective shouted out, "Hey lady, what does all that bullshit have to do with this case?"

Ma laughed when she told me about it. I can picture her telling them, "I was wiping this kid's ass while you and your police squad were still swimming around in your father's balls, Detective. That's what it has to do with this case. I was helping this boy all his life. I took him shopping. Now how do you expect this man to be able to buy things for his sweetheart if I didn't teach him? And by the way, Sunday is Mother's Day."

Oh, she actually talked like that, all right. Most of the time, it worked, too. She was a living demonstration of bullshit's power to baffle.

31

Dealing with a Charm School Veteran

Ma and me finally walked out of the 61st Precinct, right smack into the wicked smile of Swivel Tooth. He just had to goad her, "Don't go too far, Ma. Your cohort Gooch is getting ready to roll over."

"You're barking up the wrong tree, Sonny," Ma replied. "I'm nothing but a poker player, pure and simple. Got that?"

Swivel Tooth grinned then touched his pistol.

I held up my hand. "You mess with my ma, my man, and I got something for you. Remember, Swivel Tooth, bullets fly both ways."

That backed him off, but threatening to shoot a cop never makes you any friends. People who love the cops hate you for making the threat, while people who hate the cops also hate you for not going through with it.

It was an expensive confrontation. I knew I was in deep shit. So quick as I could get there, I ran to the Black Kitten.

Inside, the Hawk stood next to the jukebox looking out the window. I walked over to him and straight off I told him what I said to Swivel Tooth.

He shook his head. "You know, that wasn't the smartest thing to do, mother or no mother." Then he went to the phone booth, closed the door, and picked up the phone.

I watched him talking for awhile, then he hung up and got out. "Swivel Tooth wants to see you."

That sent a cold chill up my spine, but I got the Hawk's message loud and clear. He had just put his own weight behind the request.

All the way to Swivel Tooth's house, I got the willies bad. I was glad to have my derringer tucked into my concealed holster.

I paused at the door, took a deep breath, then knocked. Swivel Tooth appeared, and once I stepped through the door, I felt relieved right away. He looked tired and worn out. This man was not spoiling for a fight.

Behind him, the room was devoid of a woman's touch. Sheets and socks lay all rumpled up in the corners, putting out a distinct odor. The grey curtains used to be white. The furniture didn't look cheap, it just looked worn out. It all gave off this overwhelming sense of loneliness. At that moment, I didn't know why, but I actually felt sorry for him.

This was not a home. It was more like a hideout. It was a prisoner's version of a bachelor pad.

Swivel Tooth peeled off his coat, exposing a shoulder holster that housed a 44-magnum. When he took off the holster, he did something strange. He threw it across the room in disgust.

He looked at his forty-four while he rubbed his shoulder. "That fucking holster is killing me."

"Maybe get a smaller gun?"

"Fuck you. I need it for guys like you."

Then he walked over to the refrigerator, took out a quart of milk, ripped off the top and drank. He burped and walked over to a cabinet where he pulled out a bottle of whiskey and took a slug of that. Then another, then another.

So I had to ask, "Why the milk?"

He gave me this sheepish grin. "The whiskey is for me. The milk, my mother once told me it would help grow hair on my chest. Now what the hell do you want?"

I just said it straight out. "The thing with Ma, I lost my head and shot off my mouth. You know it was Ma, and I got a little nervous."

"Why don't you go back to school, do some fucking thing? Move to Alaska. Go live in the fucking suburbs. Go eat a fucking mackerel, kid. Take a fucking hike and get off the streets. You will definitely live longer."

The phone rang. He yelled, "What the fuck?" Then pulled at the receiver. "Yeah! What is it? Yeah. Yeah! I know all about it."

He slammed down the phone receiver. "Your ma is in serious trouble. Gooch just cut a deal with the D.A."

"Oh shit. Shit. But.. but.. thanks, thanks a lot for the tip off. And about the other thing, I'm sorry."

"I heard you the first time. Now get outta here, I gotta take a piss." Maybe that's how they teach you to say goodbye at whatever charm school he attended.

* * *

Later, it took a few drinks and the smooth sounds of jazz in the darkened barroom in Harlem to give me back the feeling of serenity. It was the right place for it. A gorgeous black waitress made her way through the crowded bar. Then I spotted Gooch. She strolled over to him and smiled when he whispered something in her ear.

I knew I'd find this piece of shit here in the Ace of Clubs because it was Harlem's hottest night club. A minute later the bronze beauty slinked away and into the smoke and din.

Gooch just sat there, so taken with her that he never saw me slip into his booth. I pulled an ice pick and placed it at his ear while I whispered, "If you rat on my ma, you're a dead man. There is nowhere you can go. I will always find you."

He was smart enough not to try to twist out of the way. I slipped the tip of the ice pick into his ear. "Feel that, scumbag?"

Funny thing, sometimes you stick a rat in the ear and no blood comes out. So I stuck him in his other ear to make sure he got my message.

Trial day, Gooch showed up wearing ear plugs. He told the D.A. he changed his mind because he couldn't hear a thing.

32

Maggie - Who Gave Us All the Crabs

The crowded subway train rocked back and forth while it plowed along, and everyone aboard the cramped cars struggled for a breath of fresh air. However, me, Irish Jimmy, and his buddy Petey Rags Palermo, all just grinned and took the stifling heat. Rags had promised us it would be well worth it.

Rags was an aggressive businessman, so with him, you had a pretty good shot of landing something real. But you never knew. Nobody would be signing any contracts.

Charley Spinach, a droopy-eyed shrimp of a dude, slid up close to Rags and handed him the racing form. Another Rags wanna-be called Spike Green blew his bulbous nose and the sound echoed in the overheated train.

For me, the happiness was wearing off. This was starting to feel like just another packed subway ride in Brooklyn. I was thinking Jimmy better have a fucking good reason for dragging me along with this group of degenerates.

Meanwhile Rags' large nose, far too big for his small face, stayed dug into the racing form.

Charley Spinach snapped, "Rags, the genius over there, your pal Spike Green, says he's got a good one in the fifth."

Rags waved him off. "The only thing Spike ever gave away in his miserable life was that slope-nose broad, Maggie Martino. Remember her?"

Charley laughed. "Yeah! The one who gave us all the crabs!"

The train came to another screeching halt, sending people, racing forms, briefcases, and newspapers up into the air. But everyone had a higher mission. They all broke for the opening doors when the train pulled in. Hundreds spilled onto the platform while Rags shouted, "Hurry guys or we'll miss the fucking Daily Double!"

I watched this quirky little fat man and his cohorts trying to map out the Daily Double, then turned to Irish Jimmy. "Okay Professor, what's on your mind?"

Jimmy just smiled. Like a dick.

"Come on Jimmy, give. I know you."

"That kid, Rags. He wants me to rob his old man."

"He wants you to do *what*? Come on Jimmy, that's not your style."

"I know that. That's why I want you to do it. I want you to meet him."

"Oh, you want me to do it?"

"Yes. I need your opinion."

"Okay. Robbing his old man is one thing, whatever problems they have. But this guy knows who I am. And that's a whole other story. Hey—he also knows you. Jimmy, he knows too much."

"Salerno, this is a three-million-dollar score."

Three ... million ... dollars ....

Right then Rags came running over, like one of those little rich dogs you see on Park Avenue. "South American is a fuckin' cinch in the first."

I had to laugh at his sincerity. He really believed what he said. Then I had a thought: maybe his old man was as bad as mine. So I decided to go along, for now.

I looked at Rags. "How much do you want to go for?"

"Whatever it takes to make a couple of grand."

I liked his style. Rags looked me over, waiting. I felt his anxiety.

"Okay, let's do it."

Rags collected the money and went straight for the betting window. We followed along while he shouted back to us, "Okay, here's what we'll do."

He kept his eyes riveted to the racing form while he walked. "There's ten horses in the second race. It's impossible to pick a winner." His enthusiasm was infectious.

"So we'll take South American in the first race, and wheel him on top of everything in the second race."

We all looked at him as if to say, "What the fuck are you talking about?"

"Believe me, guys, that second race is a pig race. Anything can win it."

I giggled at this little rag picker. He had charm. He also carried an easy, convincing attitude that you had to love.

So once again I got sucked in and went along for the ride. With the three million on my mind.

I was watching this little rag man and his cronies, tickets in hand, pushing their way through the dense crowd and onto the racetrack. The little rag man got very philosophical and shouted, "I love Belmont! It's so beautiful this time of year!"

One by one, the horses made their way onto the track. Rags shouted, "Oh! Yeah! Look at dem beauties! Ain't they great? I love 'em."

I asked him, "Rags, are you nervous?"

"How would you like to sniff my underwear?" This was gangster talk for "no."

I stood there smiling while I watched South American win and do her job. Rags sighed. "Ain't she a beautiful filly?"

We all sat there bullshitting about the second race when the Announcer shouted, *They're off!*

I stood back and watched this funny little fat man with his cigar rolling in his mouth and I wondered why he wanted to rob his old man. Was it just the three million?

My thoughts were shattered by the announcement, *"It's The Creed on the outside and The Factor on the inside! They're neck and neck for the lead!*

There was a long pause. Then, *"And here comes Brightrock with a rush!* Irish Jimmy and Rags started hugging.

"We won! We won! We won!" Rags screamed like a kid. "Do you think he got up? Do you think he got there? Did we win? Salerno, did he get there? Whadda you think? Did we get the nose?"

I laughed out loud and told him, "He got there, all right! He got there! Brightrock got there!" We had just hit the Daily Double, with the longest shot in the race.

"We hit it! Unbelievable! We hit it!"

A little later, the glaring heat of the day drove people into the shade, and thank God, Belmont Park has a lotta trees. We could still find one for a private huddle while Rags meticulously counted the money. Finished, he looked up smiling.

"Eighteen grand. That's six apiece."

Irish Jimmy nodded, looking like somebody died.

Rags shouted, "Oh, what's the matter?"

"I'm still five thousand short."

"Here, Jimmy, take my end and give it to my old man. He'll take it." We drove in silence and nobody said more about it, but I thought that was a hell of a move. A classy move.

When he made the offer, Rags never blinked an eye. I was getting to like this little fellow.

33

Big Mouthing Again

I watched a late model Cadillac roll up. A horn blasted, then a short, fat guy stepped out looking every bit the part of a wise guy. Rags shouted, "Pull over, that's my old man!" He jumped out with Irish Jimmy in tow.

His old man pointed to his truck. "You expect me to put antiques worth thousands of dollars into that piece of shit?"

Rags stood there speechless. Irish Jimmy jumped in. "Pete, here's what I owe you." Pete eyed Jimmy for a second, then took the cash and riffed the bills in unison.

"You're short. What happened to the rest?"

"I'm sorry, Pop."

"Answer me! Where's Dominick?"

Rags couldn't find his voice. His old man ripped into him.

"That useless, good-for-nothing brother of yours is late, the same as you!" Rags just hung his head.

The old man snorted, "Ah, he's probably off somewhere playing with his prick, just like he always does."

It was just then when Rags' brother came flying down the street on his bicycle. He pulled up into the yard and jumped off. But his old man grabbed him by the neck and bellowed, "Where the fuck have you been?"

Rags stood there while his old man shook his brother again and again. "Answer me when I talk to you!"

Frustrated by his son's silence, he knocked him to the ground. Irish Jimmy went to help the fallen cyclist. But the old man hollered, "Clean out this garbage can you call a truck. You hear me, Rags?"

Rags nodded. "Also, I want my name taken off this fucking truck of yours. It's a disgrace."

"You, get up and meet me inside." The despot turned and walked into the Antique shop.

Rags went to his brother. "Dom, you know how he is."

"So why were you late?"

"I had to help Pop."

"Yeah?"

"This morning, Mama hit him in the head with the skillet."

"What for?"

"She caught him with that young thing he's been running around with."

"How the hell she do that?"

"She waited by the Nineteenth Hole and watched them leave together. Then when he came down to breakfast this morning, she whacked him right across the head with the hot skillet. Pop went down screaming. Eggs flying all over the kitchen. I almost pissed my pants. Pop got a dozen stitches.

"Rags, I was so fucking happy watching him squirming around the floor like the pig he is. You know the way he treats Mama and the girls, right? No respect. Matter of fact, I'd like to take his fucking money and dump him somewhere into the street where he belongs."

"What did you say?"

"You heard me. Your fucking ears don't flap over. Let's rob this no-good motherfucker and dump his ass into the fucking street where he belongs."

Rags stared at his brother. "But Dom, you can't just rob the old man."

Dom snapped back, "Then let's kill him."

"Whoa! Now Dominick. We can't just kill him."

"Right. Then let's just rob him."

"No, Dominick. No. We can't do that either."

Dominick pointed to me and Irish Jimmy. "Well then, why not ask them to do it?"

Rags shot me a look. My mouth seemed to respond all by itself. "Why the fuck not!"

I couldn't believe what I just said. Me big-mouthing again, like I was the master of the scheme, getting myself caught up in this emotional scam.

The problem with his father was that I hated that fucking bully from the moment I laid eyes on him. He reminded me so much of my old man. Also, I liked Rags and his brother. So I stepped back, thought about the three million, and went along for the ride.

Irish Jimmy nervously paced the floor in the back of the Royal Coffee shop when Rags and Dom came bouncing through the door. They were a comical team for sure. I grinned at the wimpy bookkeeper, watching him checking out the coffee shop. Jimmy said, "Look at them. They think this is some kind of a fucking game."

"Take it easy, Jimmy. To them it's about getting even. I get it, I get this."

"They don't give a fuck about the money."

"No, Jimmy. They never did. It was you, always talking about the money. I think to them it's some kind of adventure. You know like a James Bond thing. Once and for all, to them it's about getting even with that prick they have for a father."

Dominick slid into the booth next to me and cautiously looked around. "I hope there are no bugs in this joint."

Jimmy coughed and wiped his brow, giving Dominick the evil eye.

I was loving every minute of this caper. Once Dominick was finally satisfied, he pulled out a book from his pocket and announced, "The blueprints." He whispered in his best spy voice, "Okay, fellows, here's the layout ...."

Jimmy pulled out his handkerchief and wiped his nervous brow. I could see he was getting ready to explode.

Dominick went on, "This is it in detail, guys. This is good. This is really good. Now listen carefully, one wall is lined with storage vaults loaded with high-priced furs. Up against the other wall are three double-door safes that go from floor to ceiling, got that? They're also jammed with a stockpile of fancy fur coats that were never claimed. Lost and found kind of a thing."

Irish Jimmy interrupted, "Come on! Get to the fucking meat!" Dominick's cock-eyed eyeball focused on Jimmy. I think.

Dominick replied, "My learned friend, you're just going to have to be patient. I know all about you. You're very impetuous."

When he said that, I almost shit my pants. Jimmy sat there fuming cause he knew this kind of caper was way out of his league.

"You know my Pop's place is all very original. We both helped him build this little fortress of his, all by ourselves. My Pop hates banks, especially the way he does business. You know, in the middle of the night. See this safe? It's really a cool idea to have a fuckin' safe, right? But you just listen and you'll find out how creative my father can be."

He pointed at the safe the way a happy child points at a rat. "This safe is for his important papers. Here's the rub: when you reach inside, you will find a *tiny* button underneath the lip. You guys got that? Press it, and next to his desk the floor opens up like a clam. A hidden floor safe pops up to the surface. Good, right? That was Rags' idea. He's really good at that stuff. The first safe with the papers is for the suckers."

Dom pointed, "That little baby there holds all the really good stuff, like cash, diamonds, Twinkies. Whatever else my old man thinks is valuable. Now all you guys have to do is get the combination from him. Bingo! You guys will be *right* where you want to be—in my old man's money. Remember this was Rags' idea. He designed that whole fucking mausoleum."

I replied, "That's beautiful."

And it was.

34

Three Million Reasons

Jimmy jumped up in frustration and cleared the table with one violent sweep of his arm, scattering coffee cups and sugar bowls across the marbled floor. "I don't think you guys know what the fuck you're talking about. Your old man is too smart to keep all that money in his house. Why would he do that?"

"Wait," I replied, "You better slow the fuck down, pal."

"We're not pals, Salerno. Wake up! This sounds like a fucking fairytale."

"Their old man does business with a lotta Mob guys."

Rags cut in. "Hey, hey, my old man ain't connected, he's just a wise guy's lackey, is what he is."

Jimmy eyed Rags like he smelled bad. "You know, Rags, I never heard of anyone wanting to rob their old man as bad as you guys do."

Rags took a moment for a big sigh. "Okay, Jimmy. If you're afraid to do this, I'll get someone else. It's just that simple."

"I'm not afraid, I just don't believe you two."

I cut Jimmy off cold. "I believe them."

"What, you believe these sick fucks?"

"Yes. And Jimmy, I'm going to do this with or without you."

"Hey Salerno, remember I put you wise on this caper. What I say goes. This is my gig, remember that."

Rags jumped in. He was sharp. "Jimmy, this is *my* caper, not yours! What I say goes. When I came to you, I thought this is what you do, but I can see you're just a con man. If you want out, you can keep walking."

Jimmy stood there. Rags glared at him. Jimmy dropped his eyes, walked into the phone booth, and picked up the phone.

Rags turned to me and whispered, "Salerno, can we trust this guy? He looks fucking nervous. Is he always like that?"

"He's okay. It's possible that he's okay."

"My old man's always heeled. You guys got to be sharp on this one. One mistake and this whole fucking caper is dust."

"I got this. Take a hike and we'll meet you here Sunday night."

Dom cut in, "And I don't care what you do to him! Kick his fucking ass, for all I care."

"Jesus Christ, Dominick. You stay home Sunday and take care of your mom."

Jimmy came out of the phone booth and moved next to me. "I heard that, kid."

"Yeah, he doesn't mean nothing. He's just excited. Remember he hates his old man."

"Yeah, that don't mean shit to me, but there is something that bugs me about this score. I can't put my finger on it."

"Come on, Jimmy, knock it off. We just got lucky. I have three million reasons to like this score."

"You could be right, but I know one thing for sure."

"What's that?"

"When we're done, we gotta put that whole fucking family away."

"Whatta you, nuts?"

"Aw, yeah. This whole fucking caper is nuts. You're nuts, I'm nuts, that family is nuts, and those sick fucking brothers are in bad shape. Sooner or later, they'll give us up to the cops. Think of that? They'll do it the same way they gave up their old man."

Irish Jimmy leaned in real close the way he did when he got serious. "Salerno, you know how easy it is for the cops to back-track this caper? You bet your sweet ass those two will be in custody in a hot flash. Think. You wanna live to spend the money, or do twenty years in Sing-Sing? That's two hundred and fifty-six months. Give or take a few days …."

* * *

The drive home that night was hard. I kept hearing Jimmy's words, "Whatta you, nuts? You don't rob a guy's father!"

He was right, of course. I knew that. But the thought kept rolling around in my mind, how his pop was nothing but a fucking bully, just like my old man. And I hated bullies.

Okay, there *was* a three-million-dollar score at stake, money just sitting up there, doing nothing. I don't think we need to call in the shrinks for this one, do we? There were three million reasons to do this.

I finally got home and pulled into my driveway.

My wife's car was not there. Inside, all was dark and quiet while I walked through the house. Big note on the fridge: "Gone to Bear Mountain with my mother and kids for the weekend."

Was this some kind of reprieve? A chance for me to think it all over one more time?

I reached into the cabinet and got myself a bottle of scotch, took a couple of fast slugs, and sat down. *Okay, Salerno, what are you going to do?"*

This was a wild score, but on the other hand, oh, the money was great. *Salerno, it's just a family thing.*

After a couple more shots of scotch, I thought, *suppose these two get cold feet and change their minds, or tell someone what they are planning to do? I'll take his family troubles right into the clink with me.* My mind was bouncing all over my head.

Then I got this weird gut feeling to get in my car and drive up to Bear Mountain. The desire to do it was strong, whether I could have explained it or not. I put my forty-five in my belt, jumped into my car, and drove to Dags' Lounge. I picked up Jimmy and told him, "We have to do this now. Tonight."

What's the fuckin rush?"

"Jimmy, I'm not asking your permission. Either you get into the car now, or you can take a walk. No hard feelings."

"Hey. Okay. Okay, then. I'll be right back. I got to pick something up."

"No, Jimmy, get into the fucking car. I got enough firepower tucked right here in my belt." Jimmy shot me a look that could kill. "Come on, take it or leave it. I'm on my way."

Jimmy got into the car without another word. He stayed quiet all the way to Rags' apartment.

I knocked at Rags' apartment door. He opened right up, which was nice. He looked me up and down. "What's up?"

"Rags. We're gonna do this. Now. *Right* now. Tonight!"

Rags lit up at that. Whole new face. "It's about time we knocked off that fat bastard! Let's do it." He ran to the car and jumped into the front seat, ready to go, but he also cautioned us. "Remember, the old man's heeled."

Jimmy pulled out a snub-nosed revolver. "Your old man makes one wrong move and I'll blow his head off. Then we won't have to worry about him anymore."

Jimmy pointed to me. "Let's go." I saw the pistol in Jimmy's hand and knew right then he was a loose cannon and there was going to be trouble. So I snatched it away from him.

"One forty-five on this job is enough." I was having a real hard time thinking I was going to have to kill all those people. But I dismissed that thought, hoping something would happen to prevent that.

In a funny way, I was getting to like these little guys. They were game, and I saw no fear in their eyes whatsoever. After all, for them, this was just getting even time. They were hitting their old man right in the belly, right where he lived. But I also knew Jimmy was a novice at pulling a stick-up and he was spoiling for the excuse to put a bullet in somebody's head, no matter what. That made him a serious liability.

Then I thought maybe I needed a bullet in mine for even being here. Something inside me was telling me to stop, but I just kept going. It wasn't the cash. I knew it wasn't the cash. Maybe the need for an adrenalin fix?

More like that.

After we left the New York thruway, I could feel the bite in the air while we turned onto a country road. I made the drive with mixed emotions; fear and greed played with my imagination.

It was Rags who snapped me out of my daydream.

"That's my old man's car!"

I looked while he drove right on by. "You sure that's him?"

"Yeah. That's him and his dame."

We watched the rotund bully and his youthful companion move on into the house. Rags asked me, "What do we do now?"

"Simple," I said, because why not. "Watch me." I bundled up, blinded by the falling snow, and pulled the spare tire from the trunk. I made my way down the desolate driveway rolling the tire. The dense cloud cover made it feel like dusk while I approached the house. Finally, I got to the door and rang the bell. After a minute I heard a husky voice from above.

"Whatta you want?"

I looked up but saw nothing in the heavy snow fall. Which was a smart move on somebody's part. I shouted, "Can you help me?" No reply. "I got a flat tire?"

"Service station about a mile down the road."

"Mister, I got a bum foot!"

"That's too fucking bad. Now take a walk."

What a prick, I thought. Just like my old man. I turned and rolled the tire into the darkness. Rags greeted me and showed me where the car was. We could see the entire fucking spread from the mountainside.

Rags asked, "Whatta we gonna do now?"

"We sit and wait. It's still early."

So we watched and waited and waited some more. Two fucking hours in the cold before Rags saw his old man's Lincoln pull out of the driveway. It was a long, grey job. We watched and waited a while to see if he was coming back.

Finally, I said, "Let's go break into the house before they come back."

Rags shook his head. "All the windows and doors are alarmed."

"You sure?"

Rags smiled. "Tight as a drum."

Jimmy finally spoke, "You know, you are a funny, funny, fucking man. I'm going to have a look around. Wait here, I'll be right back."

Things were changing so fast with this score that I felt out of control. So fast, we failed to notice when the old man and his companion returned. I'll never know how they got back inside without us spotting them. And even still, I couldn't stop the quicksand that was sucking me down. Three million pounds of force. It didn't take Jimmy long. He was all excited when he got to the car.

"I think I found a way in." Off Rags' doubtful look, he said, "Save the looks. Now listen, you just might learn something. There's a vent way above the kitchen window. Is it alarmed?"

"I don't know. I never installed one that high up. But there's a ladder in the garage."

"Do you think you can get that fat ass of yours into that vent?"

"I don't know, wise-ass, but I'm gonna try."

Minutes later, I watched the determined Rag Man squeeze himself into the vent. Halfway in, he got stuck.

At least there was no alarm. So I scooted up the ladder and pushed him right on through. After that, all I heard was dishes breaking and Rags making these grunting sounds. A minute later he opened up and let us in.

35

Another Robbery, Another Show

"So now, pal, you'll be telling me what I need to know. I'm talking about all dose pretty safes you got all lined up. You know." I used a fake Irish brogue to disguise my voice. It didn't have to fool anyone into thinking I was Irish, just keep them from going, "Salerno, is that you?"

"Who sent you?" asked the old man.

"Bronco Bill the Sailor, lad. You know what he tole me? He tole me you have all those sweet combinations all tucked away in that fine brain of yours."

"Fuck you, laddie."

"I like your humor ole man! Now you know that pretty little lassie you got? Well you know, lad, she could find a way to fall down dose lovely sets of stairs you got."

"Fuck you and fuck her. Who sent you?"

I replied, "You mean you don't care what happens to your lassie?" I knew at that moment I had my hands full with this old bull.

His dame screamed at him, "Fuck me? Hey, fuck *you*, you pig! Watch this! You, the guy with the fake brogue. I can tell you the combinations myself. If I do, what's my end?"

I looked at Pete, "Laddie, now tell me, please. She's lying. Right? Mate? Now Laddie, don't be fuckin with me, just do as I say. If not, I'll be putting me number ten up your fuckin arse."

"I'm warning you, don't hurt her."

I jammed my forty-five into his ear. "Just do it before I blow your fucking brains out. Den dey will be all over the nice fucking floor."

"Look, Mr. Fake Irish Man, you kill me, and you'll never get this safe open. Now, tell me who sent you?"

Jimmy entered the room with his face covered by a pillowcase. "Your sons and the rest of your whole fucking family, you self-satisfied scumbag." Jimmy pulled a switch blade and opened it.

"If you don't open up, I'll slice off one of her tits, little man, then I'll fry her nipple with eggs and feed it to you on a platter. You got that, fatso?"

"Okay, okay, hold it, I'll open up, leave her out of it."

My eye caught Rags moving around the room. He was out of sight but watching and listening to every detail. He waved for me to come to him.

"This is weird. I never saw my old man relent. Never." We watched as the broken mobster expertly spun the dial.

When the tumblers fell into place and we heard that magic click, we were all smiles. Old man Pete pressed down on the handle, and asked us again, "Which son?"

Rags stepped out of the shadows. "Me, Pop!"

I stood there speechless while father and son confronted one another in complete silence. No screaming, no sounds, nothing. The staring contest was something you would see in a movie. God knows what went through their minds at that moment. Just as his old man was getting ready to reach inside the safe, Rags quickly reached over and yanked his father away. The rest of us saw why: sitting on the shelf inside the safe, big as life, was a sawed-off shotgun.

Jimmy grinned. "You're a pretty tricky guy for an old dude. Yeah, pretty fuckin' tricky." By then, I had already realized I wasn't going to kill anyone, especially Rags.

But he was frazzled and apprehensive. Rags picked up the big gun and Jimmy snapped. "Let me have that."

I jumped in, "I got this!" Then I pointed the big gun at the safe. "Okay lad, now please, no more tricks. Just hit the fuckin' button."

Old man Pete stood mesmerized. "You … you didn't have to do this."

"Pop, you left me no choice." Rags moved to the safe and reached in and hit the button. It was like something out of the Arabian Knights. The floor opened up. We watched in amazement while a giant six-foot safe emerged.

Jimmy walked over. "This is the best-looking setup I've ever seen."

The old man looked stunned. Jimmy chuckled, "See, if you treated your family better, this wouldn't be happening. Now open this puppy."

I watched the old mobster hobble along, finally reaching his prized possession. I could see it in his eyes, he was getting ready to bolt. Jimmy nudged him. "Come on, Pops, the party is over."

Old Pete spun the dials. The door swung open. Irish Jimmy pulled the old man backward, exposing the contents.

In my fake brogue, I shouted, "Be Jesus! Look, it's a bloody fortune!" While everyone was engrossed with the booty, Pete slid next to the exposed safe and reached in. Rags ran over and kicked his old man in the hand. "Pop, what the fuck are you doing?"

Rags reached into the safe and pulled out a forty-five. Jimmy yelled out, "Old man, try any more tricky shit like that, it will be your last move!"

Inside the safe, I swear it was like looking at the diamond exchange. The jewelry, the money, everything glistened like the head of a sweaty bald man. The safe was at least two feet deep, stuffed and stacked with hundred-dollar bills. I stood there speechless, and for me that was a lot.

Irish Jimmy was in a trance. Rags was smiling from ear to ear. But old Pete let out a scream of outrage and frustration. The sound snapped me back to reality.

Irish Jimmy pushed Pete to the floor. "Shut the fuck up!" Then he tossed Rags a garbage bag. "Rags, you do the honors. I'm sure you have been waiting a long time to do this."

"You got that right."

The old man sat there motionless, watching his son happily fill the garbage bags with loot, one after another. Then Rags noticed the safe had a false bottom. He immediately felt around and saw a catch. He pressed it, then winked at his old man.

The bottom of the safe lifted out. Rags reached in and pulled out several bank bags filled with coins. I ripped one open and my eyes almost fell out.

Rags snapped, "Oh! My God! He looked at his dad. "Pop, these coins, are they from that bank robbery?" The old man looked away in disgust.

"Pop, I *knew* you were in on that burglary! You fucking penny-pinching prick. I wish Mama was here to see all this."

Pete Senior sat there terrified while his whole world was dismantled before his eyes. Irish Jimmy nudged him. "Let's go, fatso. On your feet."

The old man now looked very weary. He stumbled into the wall and fell. Jimmy kicked him.

Rags shouted, "That's enough! You don't have the right to do that!"

But Jimmy was unimpressed. He retorted, "Shut the fuck up," and pulled out his snub-nose. I stepped in and planted a right hand into his underbelly. That dropped him to the ground.

Rags frowned, "That prick was gonna take me out."

Still using my fake brogue. I said, "I know, laddie, let's get your old man upstairs." My mind was racing, wondering what the fuck was I going to do next. I couldn't kill them, but Irish Jimmy didn't seem to have any problem with the idea. So me and Rags tied up Jimmy, filled up my trunk with all the goodies, then duct-taped the old man to the toilet bowl.

We carried out our pissed-off Irish cohort and put him into the back seat. Rags got behind the wheel and off we went into the freezing night.

36

The Beginning of the End

We all drove in silence until Rags opened up, "Look, my old man will never say a word to the cops. He's too tough. And besides all the stuff we took was hot. Every cent."

"Yeah," I agreed, "but now we gotta worry about who he knows. Somebody who might want to help him get revenge."

The heavy snow and slippery road made for slow going. Rags was quiet, I was quiet, and so was Jimmy. Suddenly a police car appeared behind us and put on its lights. There was no way to outrun the cop, so Rags had to pull over.

Rags muttered from the side of his mouth, "What should I do?"

"Just be cool and see what the trooper wants."

I quickly untied Jimmy while we pulled to a stop. The trooper approached our car.

Rags was super cool. "What's up, officer?" We could have been all right. We could have talked our way past all of it. But at that moment good old Irish Jimmy got sugar in his draws and bolted out of the car and ran off into the night. On foot, into that frozen bitch of a night. Two degrees below zero is fuckin cold any place, especially in the cellar of a state troopers' barracks.

The instant Irish Jimmy took off, the troopers were on us like pickpockets. Rags kept enough of his cool to tell the trooper that we had just finished having dinner with his dad. I thought this was a good move, a lie wrapped up in a little piece of the truth.

Another Trooper walked over carrying a double-barreled shotgun. "Okay, boys! Come on outta there nice and easy."

But Jimmy wasn't turning himself in for anything. Somewhere in all the confusion, he actually managed to slip away into the darkness while three of the biggest state troopers I have ever seen swarmed us. The rest started to search the car. The next thing I heard was a loud, "Yahoo!"

Then for some strange reason they slapped us in cuffs and leg irons and drove us back to Pete's house and confronted us with Pete's father.

"Where is your friend, the Irish guy?" Pete's old man demanded. Then he turned to his son. "Where is that piece of shit?"

No reply.

"Officers, he raped my woman." He turned to Rags. "You son of a bitch, you bring these people to my home?" He stood there glaring at me sitting in the cellar. "Pally, you surely fucked up this time."

"Maybe so," I told him, "but all I saw you doing was carrying away the bank bags yelling, 'Yahoo, Yahoo!'"

Pete's old man laughed at that one. "It ain't me you have to worry about. You robbed the wrong man. That old coot Jimmy ripped the fucking toilet bowl right out of the floor and called us. City slicker, you're lucky you're still here. I know that old crook. I bet he's already got a contract on you and his fuckin' son. Oh, by the way, who was the lad that ran away?"

I knew right then Rags hadn't said a word, otherwise the guy wouldn't be asking me. It was good to see I had been right about trusting the Rag Man. So I answered in my fake brogue, just for the hell of it, "Laddie, he was just some poor hitch-hiker we picked up along the way. Never saw the poor soul in me life."

"Okay, wop. Now before I kick your ass all over this fucking cellar, tell me, how did you get his son to go along?"

"That's for me to know and for you to find out." I smiled, watching the big bald guy get pissed. He took off his gun and tossed it to his partner, a neighborhood guy I recognized as someone named Clancy. Then he was the one grinning.

"Clancy," he said, "it's time I taught this greaseball a thing or two." All six-foot-six and two hundred and fifty pounds of him came lumbering toward me. I knew my only chance was my right hand. We moved around the cellar together, both carefully looking for an opening. Finally, not seeing one, I fell to my knees slobbering like a scared pig.

"Please don't hit me, please! Please!"

The big bald guy bellowed out, "Clancy, take a look at this wop, he's a sissy after all! He only knows how to beat up on old men. Look at him, Clancy, he can't stand the pain! Oh, Jesus, wait till I tell the boys at Kelly's what we got here."

He relaxed just enough so, when he walked over to me, I rolled over onto my feet, crouched, and threw a solid right hand into his stomach. I couldn't believe how soft he was.

He dropped like a brick. A guy that size. I stood there looking at the fallen giant and couldn't believe what just happened. Then out of the darkness Clancy came rushing at me like a wounded bull.

I stepped aside as he charged, then threw a cross-body block across his center. He also went down hard. There I was, a suspected felon in a damp cellar with no leg irons on, and two troopers out like a light.

Not a good position to be in. In a matter of seconds, the rest of the outraged troopers proceeded to subdue me, the "crazed suspect." That's the way the Daily News reported it. The headlines read, "CRAZED SUSPECT ATTACKS TROOPERS".

They conveniently forgot to mention the best part of the story, that being the fact that I was in a ball and chain at the time. Three days later, I caught a break. Unbeknownst to me, Swivel Tooth saw the report on his police teletype. He went to see the Hawk right away.

The Hawk went to see his buddy Frankie the Wop, Garbage King of Bay Ridge. Then Frankie went to see Louie the bail bondsman. The way I heard it was Frankie the Wop had to put up a couple of his garbage trucks as collateral; but as simple as that, I was out.

So I hit the street not knowing about my benefactors. I was all the way out in God's country, wondering how the hell did all this happen? I knew my old man would never get me out.

Frankie the Wop approached, riding in a limo. He saw the confusion in my face. "Relax, kid. The Hawk said to say hello."

Still, no matter what he said, there was no way I was getting into that limo until I knew what the fuck was going on. "Okay, you got some change? I need to make a call." I did and found out all was cool. That was fine, but all the way back to Brooklyn, Frankie never shut the fuck up.

He told me the whole neighborhood was buzzing about the robbery. All the wise guys in Bay Ridge were wondering how this all came down. "You know kid, the fact dat you guys robbed his own old man didn't set too well with some people, but there are others who hate old Pete." Then he went on and on about the fact that Pete was a pimp and a double-dealing scumbag and, most of all, he had no respect.

The Wop looked at me. "You know the news reported there was only twenty thousand recovered from the robbery?"

"That's so much bullshit, Frankie. We walked out of there with a ton, millions for sure. They took it all. Every penny. Those fucking troopers got rich."

Hearing that, Frankie the Wop went silent. He drove me to the Black Kitten without saying another word. All he kept doing was chewing his tobacco and spitting into a cup the rest of the trip.

Standing there smoking heavily in the chilly night was a tall guy from the hood known as Black Al. He greeted Frankie then gave me the once-over. "Frankie, he's only a kid."

"Yeah, but he had the balls to rob Pete the Pimp." That seemed to be good enough.

Once inside, the Hawk greeted me with open arms. It was like when a debutante has a coming out party. All the Hawk's friends were on hand to greet me, including Swivel Tooth, which threw me for a loop.

The crowning event of the evening was when Mr. Clean walked through the door. Swivel Tooth smiled. "Brother, it's been a while. How you doing?"

The Hawk just grinned. "I heard you're going into the diamond business."

When I heard that, my belly sunk. Then I took a good look at these two crooks and I finally caught the resemblance. They both had the same crooked teeth. What a fucking round robin this was gonna be. My fucking diamonds, my fucking money, my fucking gold was now in their pockets.

I was in a no-fucking-win situation. What was I gonna say after they bailed me out? "Okay guys, where's my end?" This whole game smelled and had the stench of the Hawk's style all over it. With the Hawk acting as my brilliant savior, all the while he was stealing my fucking money.

No one in the world would question the Hawk. They were all too damn scared. And the Hawk was supposed to be my friend. I had to ask myself, *how the hell does all this work?"*

My fucking head was spinning. If I didn't handle it right, I was sure to get clipped. The Hawk waved me over to see Swivel Tooth. I knew he didn't like cops, but this cop and the Hawk were cut from the same cloth, so I had to be cool and play the game.

I walked over smiling. Swivel Tooth flashed his evil smile and said, "Salerno, I want you to meet my kid brother." I took a look and said. "Mack, no hard feelings?"

He ripped, "Not as long as the Hawk lives."

I smiled at that and replied, "Long live the Hawk!"

The script had changed, thanks to my robbery and my diamonds. I could see that this was going to be a masterpiece put on by the best street urchin there ever was. The Hawk, in the end, would wind up with the treasure. There was no doubt about it.

Old Eagle Eye just stood there laughing at the whole scene with his lone eye riveted on mine. I felt his glare, but what the fuck did he care? He had a pocket full of fresh cash, my cash.

I just had to live with that. But I knew this much, Swivel Tooth and his brother were way out of their league on this one.

Then I said to The Hawk. "Could you get the kid, Rags, out of jail? He's a square shooter. Never opened his mouth. Ask Mr. Clean."

The Hawk studied me a moment, then chuckled. "You like this kid?"

"Yeah, I do. He's a good guy."

Then he ripped into me. "You know that's why you got caught?"

"I know, but he's a good kid. That's why I didn't clip him."

"Good kid my ass! On a job like this, you don't have time to make friends, either you clip em or you don't. Do the job, period. You got that? Not take him to heist his old man! So now you want me to bail him out? What for?"

"He saved my ass!"

"Salerno, you're not listening to me. As soon as you walked in the fucking door you were supposed to kill the son of a bitch. Then after the old man opened the safes, bang, bang, bang, all dead. End of story. Now you got a whole different scenario going on. You take the fucking money and you go home. Now you got nothing but troubles, all because you wanted this kid to be your friend."

"Well, maybe you don't know how I feel. Maybe you never had a friend."

"You're goddam right, and I don't need any fucking friends like that kid. I just got finished telling you, in this business having friends gets you killed."

I pointed to Swivel Tooth and his brother. "Then why are they here?"

The Hawk laughed. "They're not my friends. The diamonds you stole were snatched at the scene."

"What about the rest of the stuff?"

"That you will have to ask them."

"Funny how this all worked out. Everyone's getting a piece but me. If I'm not your friend, then why the hell am I here?"

He laughed. "There's a big difference. You, I love!"

37

Riches to Rags

Rags stayed in jail, and I figured for the time being that was the safest place for him to be. His old man was shooting his mouth off about how our days were numbered, like we were never going to make it to trial. The Hawk said the old man could easily hire himself a couple of hard-hitting low-lifes to do the job. He had the money and he knew a lot of them.

So I laid low too, never telling anyone where I was going or what time I would be there. I would just show up everywhere unannounced. It was a strange situation.

I went to Louie the Lip to see how I could get Rags out of that shithole. The Lip told me to go see Rags' mother, and that she would need to supply the deed to the house to get him out.

That sounded like a million-to-one shot, but when I got there, I told Dominick what Louie the Lip needed. To my surprise, the guy actually knew where all the paperwork was. I didn't know Dominick's mother owned the house. Seems when his grandfather passed, he left it to his mother, meaning that fat fuck had been living large on his wife's dime.

Watching Louie the Lip fill out the papers for Rags' release got me to thinking. "Dominick, do you think your old man would hire someone to hurt Rags?"

"No, he's just a bully around me. But if I were you, I would watch my ass. The guy is a sore loser, and he just lost a lot."

I looked at Dominick and thought this family stuff was hard to figure. Son against father, mother against father. Who could tell what went on with those people?

So I had to be ready for anything. Like Dominick said, I could be left holding the bag on this deal. Then I got to thinking if the old man dropped the charges against his son, that meant the fix was in. Because *somebody* had to take the hit. The next likely candidate would be me. And I would be up the river without a fucking paddle.

All they had to say was me and Irish Jimmy forced Dominick to rob his old man. For the first time, reality hit. I could go to jail for a long time. I told myself over and over that I knew Rags, and he would never sell me out.

I hoped.

* * *

Eight o'clock in the morning was very early for the Hawk to be presented with my troubles, but at the moment he was my man and he had my cash. At least he still loved me.

I hoped.

I didn't really know who to trust. Even though the Hawk said what he said, I figured I should still keep my eye on him, because who knew, but maybe the old man could get to him, too? People get funny when it comes to big money. Paranoia was starting to fog my thinking.

The Hawk came limping through the door. I pointed to his leg. "The leg, what's going on?"

"Gout. Other than that, why the wake-up call?"

"Do you think it's possible to go see the old man and find out what he's going to do?"

I swear the Hawk was the best mover I ever knew. I no sooner made the suggestion when, bad foot and all, he said, "let's go to see the old goat."

In a blink of an eye we were at old man Pietro's door. Funny thing happened when he opened up, he almost fell over from the shock. The Hawk walked in like it was his place. I could see there was history between these two.

I caught a glimpse of Rags and his mom. They were completely in awe watching the Hawk's entrance. I gotta tell ya, he was so gracious with his free and easy style that I knew it had to be completely disarming to a guy like old Pete.

The Hawk approached, smiling, "Pietro! Long time no see." Pete Senior was eyeballing me right from the start. I know he was thinking that I walked in with the Hawk and his son looking to get myself off the hook. I guessed he would do the same thing if he were in my spot. When me and the Hawk went to see Rags about talking to his old man, he never wavered for a minute. He said, "Sure, let's see what he has to say." Then the clincher was, "I'll make sure my mom is home. She'll keep the old man in line." I had to ask, "Does she still have her frying pan?"

She eyed her husband of thirty years. "I don't want my son to go to jail."

"Yeah, so you bring this bunch of gangsters into my home?"

"Pietro! You seem to forget this is my home, too. So get off of that soap box of yours, you old goat. Now listen for once in your life!"

He nodded, then the Hawk told him, "If you don't help my son, so help me God, I'll tell that Mr. D.A. friend of yours. Yes, that bastard, I'll tell him all about the Tommy Oddo case. So help me God, I will."

Wow! That got his attention quick! The old man bellowed out, "Hey, fuck you and your threats!"

Pete's wife smiled. "Pietro, no threats. I'll tell the D.A. how you bought off Judge Rinaldi and how you bullied him right here in this kitchen and then pushed him in the corner. I heard you. And Pietro, you know I got a good memory."

The little man walked away. "You got shit for brains."

"Mm-hm, but my memory is still sharp." She smiled, then waved her finger in his face. "Remember your words to your friend the Judge at three o'clock in the morning? Remember that? And remember what you told him?"

Pete just stood there speechless.

"No? Well, I'll refresh your memory. You said, 'Your Honor, a man should do what he can do.' Then you got into his face and you said, 'Now my friend, I have to do what I have to do.' And like a real tough guy, you blasted him. You bum, you set up your own goombah—godfather to our son Dominick! You bastard, I saw you give the judge that hundred grand. My son is *not* going to no jail!"

Then a weird thing happened, and all of a sudden old Pete started smiling. He looked like he was satisfied with something, but I didn't know what, yet.

Chewing on his cigar, he smiled at his wife, "I'll let your son off the hook on one condition."

She glared at him, waiting. Now this was between them.

"I'm in a good mood today, so you take your no-good son and leave my house."

She laughed. "Mister Don Juan, you seem to forget this is still my father's house. Now you take that secretary of yours and go back upstate where you belong."

Pete just glared at her, so she snapped, "You better be careful, old man. Sooner or later she's gonna give you a dose of syphilis."

Pete waved her off. "Syphilis my ass."

"Those kind always do."

This thing had become a family feud, and here I was smack in the middle. I leaned over to the Hawk and whispered, "This is better than a movie."

She kept on ripping into him. "Do you really think I'm that stupid?" No answer.

The Hawk got up, went to a cabinet, and poured a glass of wine for her. "Here, you look like you need this."

She gulped it down and went on, "Everyone knows what she is to you. I walk the streets and women stare at me. Now you want to put our son in prison? What kind of man are you? Have you no shame?"

He stared straight at her. "You've shamed me for thirty years."

More uncomfortable silence. We sat watching and waiting.

"Pietro, I have been a good wife to you all these years. I gave you five beautiful children, and I raised them all."

"You gave me shit! You're dead inside! You don't know how to make me feel like a man. You're as cold as ice! Loving you is like fucking a corpse."

At that point the "movie" was more than a little uncomfortable. I got up and said, "Pete, we're not here for this."

Pietro yelled, "Shut the fuck up and remember where you are!" He turned to his wife. "Waiting on me and bearing my children was the price you paid for your comfort."

"You're a bully, Pietro. That's what you've always been and you made your son hate you. But this time, you do as I say or I will be visiting you and my son in the same prison."

Pete sat still looking at his wife like he'd never seen her before. Finally, he sighed and said, "Okay, you win. No jail for our son." Then he pointed at me. "But this other son of a bitch, I'm gonna bury."

But Rags put up his hand. "Either Salerno and I walk together or no deal."

There was so much going on that I almost forgot why the fuck we came here in the first place.

The old man pointed to the door. "Okay fine with me. Now take your gangster friends and get the fuck out of this house."

His wife said, "Pete, be very careful what you say and do."

As he left, the Hawk said, "Pietro, you and your wife are both remarkable to watch."

An elegant remark, I thought. Then, the next day, all hell broke loose. The old man turned into a gutless wonder and went to the police to complain about the men who went to his house and tried to convince him to drop all the charges against his son.

The Hawk, with his uncanny senses, flew the coop quick. Swivel Tooth had called to warn him he was going to be getting some company. When the detectives came looking, he was nowhere to be found.

When Rags and his ma heard the news, Dominick said she called the old man the worst kind of a stool pigeon God had ever created then cracked Pete over the head with an iron skillet, screaming, "How could you rat on your own wife and son?" The old man needed forty stitches for that one. Still, he wasn't backing down this time.

The worst part of the whole ordeal was Dominick had to wait for his father to get stitched up for the D.A. to get the news, like a school kid stuck in the principal's office waiting for his punishment.

When the D.A. was finally told about our little visit, he remanded our bail and put us into the Raymond Street jail, a real shithole, to say the least. A week later, the Hawk got a bondsman from the neighborhood, Louie the Lip, to step up for us and get my bail reinstated. Unfortunately for Rags, he had to stay in that rat trap. The D.A. felt that Rags had "too much rabbit in him."

The Judge asked the D.A. what he meant by that. "Too much rabbit?" The D.A. replied, "It means I feel he will go hopping off into the sunset."

The irate Judge replied, "What you feel is not enough. I need facts. You got that, Counselor?"

That pissed off the D.A., who went to his notes. "Your Honor, in 1959, Mr. Pete Scandella, Junior, absconded from the country of Argentina to avoid prosecution to a criminal charge."

Frankie Babe, the resident neighborhood lawyer, jumped up. "Your Honor, that charge has been vacated! Since when is running nude on the beach a criminal charge?"

Frankie brought the release papers to the Judge, who studied them. "I see Mr. Scandella has been exonerated of that charge. But the fact still remains he was running on the beach nude and the fact still remains Mr. Scandella did jump bail."

Frankie pleaded with the Judge, "Your Honor, he was only one of *twenty-seven* college kids who were all running naked. All they did was get on a plane and go home."

"Request denied. Mr. Scandella is to be remanded to Raymond Street jail."

I felt the strain of the streets starting to pull me under, sucking me into some big giant hole. Even though I was fortunate enough to be out on bail, day by day I was realizing I couldn't see where any of this was going. How could I fight the case? The cops wound up pocketing the money I robbed, and I was looking at some hard time.

Lucille was wondering what was going on, but I didn't know what to tell her. For the first time in my life I was lost. On this one, I didn't know how to handle it.

I decided to go over to the Black Kitten and maybe forget about things for a while. When I walked in, my insides jumped. Standing there was the Hawk!

I grinned. "You're back!"

The one-eyed warrior smiled right back at me. "I got some good news for you. I got us a politician who can pull the right strings."

I was dumbfounded. At that moment, it felt really good to have the Hawk on my side, I figured maybe I could beat this rap. He took me to see attorney Abe Josephs, who dropped the bomb on me.

"For fifty grand, you'll get two years. Sorry, no walking papers on this rap. This case is too hot. They don't like it when New York mobsters come into their town."

Josephs told me a conviction and a couple of years would keep everyone happy. At the time, it sounded like a real break. I thought I was looking at many years in the hole. I was happy, I knew Rags would be happy, and my wife would be happy as well! At least until she found out how much she would sacrifice in all this. At first, I ran out of the Black Kitten into the streets screaming, "Yeah, baby! Yeah!"

Then it hit me. Fifty grand. Fifty thousand dollars in cash.

That stopped me in my tracks.

I quickly sold my house with a super low price and got twenty grand liquid out of it, then put my wife and kids in an apartment in the projects. The misery of doing that made the rest of it all too real. Then I headed for the Black Kitten to see the Hawk to find out if there was anything else I could do.

When I walked in, he met me at the door and we walked over to the jukebox. He took out a quarter and played his favorite song "Norman, Norman my love." Usually, when he played that song, I knew something was up.

This time we stood there listening to the music until all of a sudden, this big grin came over his face while he reached into his pocket and took out an envelope and handed it to me. It was bulky; I was almost afraid to open it.

He smiled at me. "Open it, you're a good kid." I took a quick look. Holy shit. Thirty Big Ones. The other thirty thousand to go with the twenty from our house.

What a fast turn of events! I was so stoked, it was the best moment of my life. I could not believe that I had the fifty grand. Fifty fucking grand! Defense money, just like that!

The Hawk handed me a slip of paper. "Here's the politician's address." I slipped it into my pocket and zoomed out into the street.

Of course, I had to tell Rags. Package in hand, I hurried over to his house. But his old man met me at the door.

"Whatta you want?"

I stood there frozen. My feet felt like they weighed a hundred pounds apiece. "Is Rags home?"

Before he could answer, his wife pushed him aside and let me through the door. "I got it."

She walked me into the kitchen, then when we were alone in there, she handed me a package. She winked and smiled at me, "Here's a present from my husband." It was the cash, all the cash I had been looking for. She had no idea the Hawk was helping me, too. Fifty thousand dollars.

I ran out of that house with a hundred grand in my knapsack! How about that? She got the old man to put up the cash! I've seen a lot of things, but this was the best.

The guy that I robbed just put up the money to pay off the connection to squash the case. One for the books!

I ran around the corner to my ma's place. No one was home, so I just ran upstairs and stuffed the twenty grand in her girdles. Because who'd ever look there, right?

I ran back to the Black Kitten, reached into my knapsack and handed the Hawk his package of cash. I grinned and said, "I gotta go see Mrs. Josephs. I'll tell you everything later."

He stepped in front of me. "Slow down kid, what happened?"

"You're never gonna believe what just happened!"

"Try me."

"Old man Pete put up the fifty grand."

The Hawk's eye started flinching. I could see he was having a hard time digesting the news.

"Seriously! His wife got him to spring for the cash. I swear on my mother's eyes. She had the cash all packed and waiting. You fucking believe that?"

38

A New Life

I met Abe's wife for dinner at the Tavern on the Green, a fancy restaurant in Central Park. I scanned the room and there she was, seated at the bar. She was a knockout, and a red-headed knockout to boot. I watched her lips touch the smooth glass and immediately got jealous.

I slid up to her and said, "Mrs. Josephs?"

She turned quickly and gave me a smile. What a smile. I returned my imitation of the same smile and said, "I have something for you."

She answered with her lips licking the glass. "I bet you do, sonny boy." Women have always been kind to me. I don't know why, exactly.

She kept smiling. "My condo is just across the street. It fronts the park and the view from there is spectacular. I'm sure you'll like it."

"I'm sure I will."

After making all my deposits, I left the redhead smiling with the reassurance that her husband, "the Honorable Councilman," would have everything put into place. And after the night I had with that red-headed devil, I felt I was running just ahead of the jaws of the street. Because the streets are like a bunch of ten-headed alligators. They are always snapping at you, trying to pull you in and drag you down.

Right now, I was laughing at the streets and my fears about getting pulled in were gone. It felt as if I was moving in the right direction, proving that how you feel doesn't always have anything to do with how you are. And what was happening on the streets sent me right to the "tombs" to see Rags.

I walked into the visiting room and sitting there was this dirty little bundle of energy, shuffling a deck of cards. "Salerno, come here. I got a great trick to show you." I took one look at this guy and thought, *this guy has a clear fucking head.* Here was a guy eating potato soup and corn bread and all he cared about was showing me a card trick, even though he hadn't heard anything about the good news yet. I loved this kid.

"Rags, it looks like we're going to be okay."

"Did you bring me some cigars?"

"Rags, did you hear what I just said?"

"Yeah, but I'm dying for a cigar. My commissary day is a week away."

So I made sure he had a great week with cigars. Then I ran all the way back to the Black Kitten, took one look at the Hawk's mug, and knew there was trouble.

"What?"

He finally spit it out. "Before Abe Josephs was able to do his deed, the Widow Maker nailed him. That red-headed devil. She turned on me and gave the fifty large to Abe. But Abe was the only connection to the money, so the fifty thousand went for a walk on the wild side and they both disappeared."

What did that mean? It meant that the money was for my freedom. That money was my proof that I could beat the streets. And the money was long gone.

So potato soup and corn bread, here we come.

39

Learning How to Sing-Sing

1-2-9-4-8-9, that was me! My new name, even though it was only a number. As far as I was concerned, being renamed with a number wasn't bad, in a funny kind of way. Even though you were in the can among two thousand cons, it didn't matter, because when your number was blasted over the loudspeaker, no one knew who the fuck was 1-2-9-4-8-9. So in that respect it was like being private in public. I liked that.

Anyway, after we heard how the judge sentenced a child molester who happened to be the fire chief to five years of probation, I had said to Rags, "This judge sounds like he gives people a break. So maybe we got a chance?"

Some fucking chance. When it was my turn in the barrel, I got seven and a half years for armed robbery.

Then he had the balls to ask, "Do you have anything to say?" As if words were going to help me at that point. But he asked, and I had that *chutzpa* thing going, for better or worse.

"Your Honor, how is it that a man who just molested two six-year-old girls only gets sentenced to five years of probation, but I get seven and a half years year for robbing a guy who has been molesting his family his whole life?"

"Bailiff! Remove this man from my courtroom!"

"Your Honor! Tell me this guy I robbed, if I'd a fucked him in the ass like your fire chief did with those kids, I would've got a slap on the hand and you'd have sent me home like you did with him? You know, the fire chief?"

Spittle erupted from the judge's mouth and he pounded his gavel. "Remove this *thing* from my courtroom!"

"Your Honor! Why are you getting so pissed off? It was you who asked me if I had something to say."

"Remove him *now*, Bailiff!" In the blink of an eye, five Bailiffs swooped down on me. Nevertheless, I got the last word in. "Your Honor, I heard the fire chief was your brother-in-law. Is that right?"

Sure it was. Sometimes the streets and the courts operate by the same rules.

* * *

And poof! I'm sitting in the county jail cell awaiting transfer to Sing-Sing Prison. The county cell was dark, damp, and smelled of stale cigarettes and fear. My sentence magically expanded, back in that courtroom, and now I had seven and a half *to fifteen* years to pass behind bars.

In New York State, you earn good time at the rate of a day for a day. That meant if I could keep my nose clean, I might see the parole board in around five years. I thought to myself, *That's only sixty months.* Put like that, the worst I'll do is one hundred and twenty months. Then they'll throw me out and put me on parole.

I was feeling fairly optimistic until I had to hear a couple of old black outlaws singing all night long. "In my prison cell I sit, with my fingers dipped in shit, and the rats are playing ping pong with my balls." It was a happy little melody with lyrics by a psychopath.

You know how a tune can get stuck in your head? Like if you ever went to Disneyland and took the *It's A Small World* ride, and then that fucking ditty ran through your brain for the next six months? It was like that, only no happy children from all over the world. Just miserable cons from all over the country. My time in lockup was beginning with music class.

Finally, one of those singing outlaws blurted out to the other, "When those white troopers come for you, you know you're never gonna make it back to Texas alive. You know that, right?"

"Maybe so, brother, but all I did was shoot that bitch in her big, beautiful ass."

"What for?"

"She told me she wanted me to make love to her the modern way."

"The modern way? What'd she mean by that?"

"I tell you, she shoved my face into her big ass and said suck on this. So I went right to my dresser and got my pistol and shot that bitch, and said suck on that."

"My friend, you can't do that to a white woman in Texas and expect to get away with it."

"I know, brother, that's why I took a hike."

These are the conversations that surround you in such a place. You get educated about crap like that whether you want to or not.

See, the thing about prison is the noise. You can be the toughest guy on the cellblock and never worry about being assaulted. But if you want a little peace, you're going to have to bust out. The more you wish you could just get a few minutes to hear yourself think, the more you realize how far down you've sunk.

But while I lay there in the darkness, thinking about the day, all of a sudden Swivel Tooth himself appeared on the other side of the bars. I couldn't believe my eyes. Swivel Tooth the cop, for sure!

"Mack, Mack! What the fuck are you doing here?"

"I came up to see my brother. His kids are going to college thanks to you and your friends. I heard the judge gave you the max."

"Yeah! He told me mobsters from Brooklyn should never come to his town. Little does he know how corrupt his town is."

He smiled. "Look, I got a present for you. Me, the Hawk, and my bro are giving you twenty-five big ones."

Hearing that I jumped up. "Mack, thanks! Please bring the cash to my mother. She'll dish it out to my wife. By the way, tell your brother we had so much stuff after we cleaned out old man Pete, we stashed a couple of bank bags behind a big bush in his back yard. Ask him not to forget me."

"Salerno, when you get to Sing-Sing, I want you to look up an old friend of mine. He stays there in a place called the Fire House and his name is 'Dutchie'. He's a good guy. Tell him I said hello."

40

The Sing-Sing Blues

Sing-Sing prison is located in Ossining, New York. If you are ever going to commit a crime, get caught, and find yourself sentenced to Sing-Sing, try to make sure you get sentenced in the fall of the year. The ride to Sing-Sing in the pig wagon is simply gorgeous. It didn't bother me at all that I was sentenced on Friday the thirteenth, because oddly enough, I felt I was enjoying a streak of good fortune.

Here's the way I processed the information in my optimism factory: the street was a drug and that drug had been killing me. At least now I was off the street completely. This had the possibility of being the beginning of a new life, a better life. I determined to make the best of it.

It was the kind of a week you can only dream about. Me being from Brooklyn, it was a thing of honor to be known as a born thief who gets sentenced to Sing-Sing. It was like getting elected to the Hall of Fame in street circles and prison yards. One of the alums there was Willie Sutton, the "gentlemen bank robber" who claimed to be the first bank robber to ever present a note. Willie never hollered, "Stick 'em up!" He was the essence of cool, like Steve McQueen.

Then there was Frankie Blough, the Long Island serial killer, who was the last person to be executed there. A long line of mobsters cut their teeth in Sing-Sing. For a guy with my background, it was not bad company, if you turned the world upside down and looked at it that way. Not at all.

I realize this sounds very odd if you're not from Brooklyn. Don't worry about it. That just means you're not from Brooklyn.

When I stepped off the bus, the sunset was marvelous. I could feel the fresh air pinching my cheeks. I was really taken when I saw Sing-Sing close up. I thought, *boy what a nice looking joint for a prison.* The gun towers seemed like they belonged on a fortress from Camelot. King Arthur and those guys.

I wonder where all the knights are?

I didn't have long to wait. Standing in front of me was a "knight," and his whiskey-scarred nose was pointed straight at my eyes. He poked me with his stick and shouted, "Stop daydreaming, wop, and get a move on. You're gonna make me late, and I don't like to be late! You got that?"

He shouted to the driver, "You were late!"

I answered before I had time to think. "The plane was delayed in Saint Louis." Suddenly a pain in the side of my knee sent me straight to the concrete. The Hall of Fame hack leaned over me and screamed, "Crack wise with me again, motherfucker, and you'll eat this club."

I gave him a nervous grin, then quickly got to my feet. He growled, "Wop, for as long as you're here, you only speak when spoken to. You keep your shirt buttoned up, your lip buttoned up, or you get fucked up! Got that?"

All right, so cracking wise with these Olympians was not going to get me a free ticket to this year's Sugar Bowl. From the frustrated look on this hack's weather-beaten grill, I realized all that stuff you see about jokester cons in the prison movies is mostly bullshit.

This was the Major Leagues, baby. No games. The hacks there were a constant reminder of who was carrying the ball.

Just before they walked me into Sing-Sing, I turned and took a last look at the free world as I had known it. I shuffled along making sure I kept pace because they warned us we would get the bat across the side of the leg if we didn't. And I knew the hack with the bat was waiting for someone, anyone to break the cadence.

But once inside, it was a sight to see. Nothing but cells of steel.Everything was painted a pale yellow, very soothing to the naked eye, but of course it was accompanied by an odor. Odor. We need a stronger word. Stink, stench, the smell of death. Nope. None of that captures it.

It must have taken at least two thousand cons two thousand years of shitting and farting and being scared to death to accomplish such an aroma. I came to learn that no matter where you went, it always smelled like a slow fart from the Grim Reaper.

The State of New York could have sent me home right then, and believe me, they would have never heard from me again. But instead I had to face the journey, and it was set to be a classic.

In minutes, I was naked as a jay bird while some make-believe doctor started checking out my asshole. I'm telling you it wasn't like any prostate exam that I ever had. This was just getting a finger jammed up your ass by a dude that was enjoying every minute of it. He smiled, I smiled and farted.

Then when the good Doctor got a peek at my wanger, he grinned, cupped my sack, and barked out, "Oh my, this one only has one nut! But a clean asshole. Next!"

We were informed of the drill: *You move only when you are told to. You breathe when told to. You smile when told to. You never take a shit unless somebody in a guard uniform tells you to.*

Last but not least, we were herded into a huge shower room a hundred inmates strong. When I started to wash I got that uneasy feeling that I was being sized up. I stood watching a hundred men all showering at the same time. A whole variety of dicks. But you had to be careful where your eyes were looking or you might seem interested and set off a reaction.

If you dropped the soap, you never bent over, because that was an invitation, *check this out, pal*. A naked asshole is a wonderful invitation to a loved-starved con. I thought the shower room seemed like a gay man's paradise. In the back of my mind, the "fingers dipped in shit" ditty was replaced by the tune, "Getting to know you, getting to know all about you ...."

Shaving was an adventure. A one-sided razor was offered, hanging on a chain, and fifty cons lined up to use it. If you were lucky, the blade held out until it was your turn. If not, you shaved anyway and cut the shit out of your face.

For the next two weeks, I was kept in isolation for evaluation, known as "Keep Lock." That meant they wanted to see what was going on in your fucking brain. Keep Lock was very confining. You never got out to mingle with the population until you were cleared by the shrink. In the meantime, all you could do, twenty-four/seven, was count the bolts on the walls of the cell and round out your day by jerking off.

My meeting with the shrink was very productive. Mr. Green was his name and fucking around with the brain was his game. After my I.Q. results, he said. "Salerno, I don't know what the hell you're doing in here."

"What is that supposed to mean?"

"You, my friend, have a one hundred and ten I.Q."

"Okay ...."

"You have an I.Q. the same as a general in the army. You, my friend, are going to have a hard time in here."

"I still don't know what that means."

"I means the average I.Q. in here is seventy-five, at best. Seventy-five."

"Okay, Doc, so how does that affect me?"

"It doesn't, as long as you don't try to outsmart one of these dummies. Remember what I just told you and some day it might save your life. By the way, never look any one of these cons in his eye. It will spook them for sure. Always drop your eyes the second you are confronted. It goes a long way in here, because there's nowhere to run and very little you can do to protect yourself."

I went back to the cell and looked at my new home: a toilet, a bed, and a sink. Just like Porky Pig always said, "That's all, folks!"

Lights out came fast, no toothbrush, no pencil, no paper, no books and no toilet paper. Once the lights went out, that was it. The cell was locked tight until the next morning. No exceptions, so if you got sick or had a heart attack at night, you were fucked, end of story.

Wouldn't you know it, five minutes into my journey of love the fucking guard passed by taking the night count and caught me jerking off. He shouted out, "What the fuck are you doing?"

I just responded, "Seven and a half to fifteen." That night was the loneliest of my life.

Five a.m. sharp, the boombox P.A. system screamed out that we all had fifteen minutes to wash, make our beds, and get dressed. I never had to worry about getting dressed because I always slept with my clothes on.

It was imperative to be ready when the cells were unlocked because the guard on the morning shift would hotfoot it up the tier and scream, "If you're not outside of your cell standing for the count, you better be sick or dead, and I shit you not!"

I thought what a wonderful way to wake up, while I stood by my cell at attention. But when the guy next to me didn't come out, I got nervous. It seemed as though the inmate was just trying to hold off the inevitable. The irate guard zoomed up the tier yelling, "1-2-9-4-8-7, front and center!"

Seconds passed, but no one showed. I wanted so desperately to sneak a peek, but I was scared to move. This guy was taking a terrible risk by holding up the routine of six hundred cons and their playmates.

Next, the head keeper came scurrying up the tier bellowing, "1-2-9-4-8-7! You better be dead in that bed." Just then I heard a small voice singing over the head keeper's voice.

"Any day now, any day now, I shall be released ...." I strained to hear, then again I caught the small voice singing, *"Any Day Now."* The voice got louder and louder, until the whole tier could hear him singing.

When the frustrated hack reached the inmate's cell, all I saw was the spittle flying off the head keeper's lips. "I say again, you better be dead, and I shit you not!"

Just then inmate number 1-2-9-4-8-7 came running out of his cell and did a picture-perfect swan dive off the upper tier. Six hundred cons and twelve hundred pair of eyes just stood and stared, watching him in flight.

The sound a body makes falling to their death, it's something you don't forget. Like the smell of death itself, like the melody to *It's a Small World After All.*

Compassion? Ha. The irate guard leaned over the tier and said, "Jesus, look at the mess he's made." Mumbling while he passed me by, "Son of a bitch! Son of a bitch! That stupid fuck had to go and do something like this on *my* shift? Goddamn him! My fishing trip, damn it! Now I'll be late for sure."

I was just glad inmate number 1-2-9-4-8-7 didn't die in vain. At least he made that prick late for his fishing trip.

41

After that show, six hundred cons entered the mess hall in deep thought. An uncomfortable feeling hung in the air. The guards had made sure every con took a good look when they passed the unfortunate jumper.

The head honcho, pipe in his teeth, lectured us while we entered the chow hall. "Gentleman, that's what happens when you are late for the count on my shift." He looked around the room. "Do you all follow my drift? Now enjoy your breakfast. You gentleman got lucky today because our chef Leroy Green has made you his fresh corn bread, collard greens, and grits. Now isn't that a healthy way to start off the day?"

I sat there wondering what fucking game was he watching. Maybe I shouldn't have laughed out loud and asked him.

For the next two weeks I was in isolation once again. No more corn bread. No more showers, no earphones, no pencils or paper. Nothing but you, your dick, and your brain.

Isolation tests the mind a dozen ways. And if you are claustrophobic, you are truly fucked, unless you get yourself a fucking job. I supposed all this isolation was some sort of test to see who could stand isolation and who could not, but I'm not sure what good the information did anybody.

But I guess by the end of two weeks, the officials knew what they got with an inmate. Other than that, they really didn't give a shit. To them, their work was just a fucking job, a paycheck, and after twenty years, a pension. As long as they knew what kind of con they had to deal with, that was good enough for them. Most hacks retire at fifty if they live that long.

Sing-Sing was the receiving center for all the East Coast criminals. Once in keep lock, you spoke to no one, and no one spoke to you. That's isolation to the max. We all walked to the mess hall in silence and ate in silence. Completely unnatural for a guy like me.

Hard as it was for me to keep my trap shut, I knew if I made a sound, lumps was trumps, as they say. Just then a career criminal named Nicky Salerno, no relation, dropped his dentures on the way to the mess hall.

"My teeth! My fucking teeth!"

Then came a sharp crunching sound. Some huge inmate with a bad sense of humor deliberately stepped on Nicky's dentures. I gotta tell you, what happened next shocked the shit outta me. Nicky Salerno went after this guy like he just beat up his kid sister.

The guy he attacked wasted no time. He slashed, blood flew, Nicky slashed, more blood flew. The big guy went down, Nicky went down. And the fucked-up prison guard just stood there while those two lay there, bled out, and died.

This was all before breakfast.

* * *

The second time I went to see the shrink at Sing-Sing, I received my first shot at a new life. I knew it was long overdue. By the time I walked into his office, I was really ready for some serious talk. Two weeks of Keep Lock had gotten on my nerves.

But Doctor Green wasn't there. It was a new guy. I took one look at this character and got a bad premonition. I could almost hear my inner voice telling me, *nothing good can come from this guy.* He was the very image of a strict disciplinarian. Actually, he looked like Ichabod Crane from "The Legend of Sleepy Hollow," my ma's favorite bedtime story. Back then, it was her way of scaring the shit out of me to keep me in my bed.

There I was, looking at old Ichabod, only this time he was alive and had the face of a man who just realized you farted. I wished Mom could've seen the guy. Better yet, I wished he was over at her house, since she loved to talk about him so much.

After the initial shock, I sat. What are you gonna do? He observed.

I looked him in the eye. He observed some more.

I decided to sit perfectly still. He continued to observe.

I changed my mind and looked around. Not a word. He observed.

So I was sitting there trying to be supercool, but I was sharp enough to know that if I came up funny, this guy could send me to the nuthouse in a hot flash. It would be dangerous to take chances with my new storybook boogie man.

The staring contest played itself out when he pulled out a folder and started to read. He grinned. "I see from this report that you come from a pretty good family."

"Depends what you call pretty good."

"All right, so now tell me, why are you here?"

"Short version or long story?"

"I'm here all day long, so whatever turns you on. Let's have it."

Okay, that was in my face in sort of a good way. I relate to hard talk better than polite bullshit. So I figured, maybe I could deal with this guy after all.

So I got loose. "Doc, I got caught. Simple as that. That's all there is. No one but *me* put me in here."

He stopped for a second. Like a guy with a fly on his nose. "Well okay. Good. I'd say that's a healthy start."

Boom.

"Yeah! Doc, I always knew this time was going to come. I just wish it hadn't happened when it did."

"Why was this robbery so special?"

"Oh, Doc. It was a life-changing score."

"I hear that all the time."

"Even so, a lotta money went south, Doc. A lotta money."

Fuck. The instant that came out, I knew I had pushed him too far. It was like a frozen blast of air went through the room.

"Did you ever stop and think that you could've caught a bullet or killed someone?"

"Doc, to tell you the truth, I never thought about that."

Once again, everything came to a quick stop. He got that fly-on-the-nose look again for a second or two, then he went, "Would you mind if I gave you an I.Q. test?"

"I just took one for Dr. Green."

"I see that, but I want one for myself. I like to start fresh."

My calendar was free for the afternoon, so we did the test. Moments after he got his results, he had this grin.

"Not only do you have a solid I.Q., but you also score very high on the ability to reason and solve problems. *That*, my friend, is an important element in dealing with these people. It can be a very hard thing to do. My point being, that's what you *must* learn how to do in here. You are not on the street. In Sing-Sing, different elements always seem to rise up and bite you in the ass. That's why your ability to reason is the thing that can save you in here. It can keep you alive so you get another chance to try life on the outside."

I didn't know if I was supposed to respond, or agree, or what, but he kept going anyway. "One other thing, before you get a big head, sometimes people with high I.Q.s don't fare so well in life. They don't use that great ability to reason. They waste it."

"If I'm so fucking smart, then how the hell did I wind up in here?"

"Ding! Good question. Look how smart you are already. Next thing is, keep your smart thoughts to yourself. You have to be careful not to expose these men for what they are. Stupid people hate it when you point out that you're smarter than they are."

"But what am I actually supposed to do?"

"For starters, no bullshit sessions with these cons. You fuck around with them, you use your brain to make them look bad, you'll have nothing but trouble. For you, your best survival tool is your ability to schmooze. It could save you, if you do it right. You comprehend that, Salerno?"

I just smiled. Sometimes you say less. See? I was learning.

"Sing-Sing is loaded with gnarled veterans. They have endless ways to hurt or kill you. But you have one built-in advantage, Inmate Salerno. You like to talk, you need to talk. Well, under their culture, you're a guy who's *expected* to do all the talking, because you just got here. Sort of like letting them all see who you are, working your way in."

"So you're telling me to just keep it real and be myself?"

"Jesus. No. I am not. Honesty can get you killed. You're not Mr. Pimp-in-the-box anymore. You have to learn how to call yourself your own best friend, because you're all you got in here."

Once again, I wasn't sure if we were just supposed to sit and think about this in silence or if I was expected to make some reply. Dr. Ichabod sat there observing and drinking his coffee, but I could see the wheels turning in his bony head.

"Inmates and guards in here are all under the gun, every day. Most try to be funny in some sarcastic way, if they can. Helps to lighten up tension. Guards, especially, are a very nervous bunch. They never know when they're going to get it in the back. Try to look at things from their point of view."

Then he stood up, like we were all done. "So! Mister Pimp-in-the-box, it was wonderful talking to you today. Anytime you need me, I'm here."

A breather. "Thanks, Doc." I got to my feet and started to leave, having already learned enough to know there was no point in pointing out to him that I never pimped anybody.

SO far, the session had been easy. Way too easy. I should have known.

Ichabod Crane picked up an invisible sword and shoved it into me. "One other thing, I just got word today that your wife Lucille had your son Charlie committed to King's County mental hospital for observation. That's all we know about it."

42

Pimp in the Box

It hit me in the belly like a dose of food poisoning. I stood planted. "What happened? Why the hell would she do that?"

"Mothers do strange things when they lose their husbands, Salerno. Again, that's all the information we have. I know this much, though, the mother has complete jurisdiction over her children. That's the law. If I were you, I'd just let a lot of issues slide."

"Why is that, Doc?"

"Because in here, you will live a lot longer. You follow my drift, Mr. Pimp-in-the-box?"

Again with the pimp thing. I was beginning to suspect this guy was not a fan.

"Salerno, if you were a real father to your children, you wouldn't be in this position, and maybe your son wouldn't be where he is today. I know you understand everything we talked about. If I get an update on your son, I'll let you know."

All right, the shrink's observations rang true. Ichabod called me out. In fact, he impressed the shit outta me with some hard, straight talk. I thought, right then, *I'd better plan my game and play it right. First thing, I gotta find out what happened to my kid."*

Prison got real for me then. The frustration of helplessness had me in iron chains. There could only be one game to survival in this shithouse, and that was the mind game.

My own thoughts were all I had, like movies replaying on loops, I constantly reviewed things in my mind.

I used my imagination to prepare, thinking about getting released into the prison population. I knew that out there, I would always have to be looking for the Edge with a capital "E." Schmooze it up and play the Edge of any opportunity.

Never revealing the Edge is how I will survive in this toilet! I hope ....

Sing-Sing was the premiere receiving center for all the Eastern prisons. Evaluating prisoners was what Sing-Sing was really all about. Once they decided who you were, then they sent you to the prison that suited your personality.

My thoughts were running wild, *where do I fit in in this joint?* The answer to that was an empty cell. I had my thoughts and I had the steel bolts that kept this bird cage together, always waiting to be counted again.

I could hear old Iron Eyes skipping along the tier. You could tell it was him. Funny, the things your mind focuses on when you are in a solitary confinement.

This time he shouted, "Open up! "1-2-9-4-8-9!" Hearing that, my insides started to race. Iron Eyes entered my cell. "Your presence is wanted by the Kitchen Keeper."

I must have had a blank look on my face.

"Son! I guess you got yourself some connections in here, because you just got here and already Mr. Sour wants to see you."

"How come, sir?" I could see he liked me calling him sir, and going under his authority suited him fine. Of course, in reality, I wished he had a bent dick.

"If Mr. Sour is calling for you, it has to be for a god-damned good reason. Because that pain in the ass don't call for nobody!" Iron Eyes glared at me. "Don't tell the grumpy bastard I said that."

Then we hotfooted it over to Sour's office. When we walked in, I saw Mr. Sour the Kitchen Keeper sitting and eyeballing a report.

He stood up. To my surprise, he was a tall, thick-boned Polish-looking guy with a nice warm smile. The friendly face seemed unusual for this place.

"Salerno, I have been looking over your complete record. It's very interesting. Now, they call me the Kitchen Keeper, and that's because I run the butcher shop."

BINGO! The butcher shop. I knew why I was there.

"How would you like a job in the butcher shop?"

I laughed. "What's the pay?"

The big man smiled at that, which was good. "I like a man with a sense of humor. Thirty-five cents an hour, take it or leave it!"

"Wow. Can I spend it all in one place?"

"You never see a dime until you leave this place, along with a kick in the ass."

I laughed at that. This was going okay so far. "Got it, Mr. Sour."

"Pete is good enough."

"Got it, Pete. Now that sounds like a solid offer."

He shrugged. "See you tomorrow morning, six a.m. sharp. And Salerno, a word of caution. You just got one of the best jobs in this institution. When word gets out, you are going to take a lot of heat."

"From who? What kind of heat?"

"Street heat, the kind you're used to, only in here it's a lot different. More intensified. Remember, be careful who you do business with."

"Why are you telling me this?"

He grinned. "I don't want my new butcher stabbed. So be cool."

"I'm cool, see you in the a.m." That night I laid in my cell thinking about what had happened. Man, what a score, working in the butcher shop!

Or was it? The little speech the Kitchen Keeper ran by me was a red flag if ever I saw one. Be careful of this, be careful of that. Be careful of who? Like my old man would say, where's the meat?

When Mr. Foster walked by for the night count, he hollered, "1-2-9-4-8-9! When I'm counting, your feet must be on the fucking floor!"

His nasty voice invaded my slumbering brain and startled me. "Yes sir, Mister Foster!" I jumped to my feet, but Foster eyeballed me long and hard. Then he did a strange thing; he leaned into the bars and whispered, "Salerno, how in the hell did you get that gig? For Christ sake, your dick don't even stink yet, and you jump in here and get the best goddamn job this joint has to offer?" I leaned into the bars. "I'm a butcher, so when I got here people listened to my rap." His tiny eyes widened, looking for more, so I gave it to him. "I told the shrink I could save the State a ton of money if I slaughtered the pigs."

Foster took a long pull at his hairy ear. "No shit."

"You got it as I know it, now that's between us." I doubted whether old Foster ever listened to anyone more than two seconds in his whole life, but right then I had the Edge. His response was perfect. Just as I hoped.

"You know, Salerno, a good pork roast every once in a while goes a long way with me."

My eyes narrowed at that request, like I was just then getting an idea. "Mister Foster, it's funny you should say that, because standing here, that's just what I was thinking about. I didn't want to bring it up and maybe insult you."

He flashed a grin. "I can see you and me are gonna get along just fine, if you know what I mean?"

"I was thinking along those same lines. Sir."

"Aw yeah! You and me gonna have a good ol' time together, especially if once and a while you slip me a bottle of Tequila."

His puffy eyes narrowed. "Jose Cuervo in the skinny bottle. The one that has the worm swimming in it." He cleared his throat then moved on.

Watching him skipping along past the other cells, I thought *if I'm going to hang out in this jungle I might as well enjoy the ride, because you never know how long life is going to last.*

Especially in a sewer like Sing-Sing Prison.

43

How Much Wood Can the Woodchuck Suck?

But by far the biggest challenge to life in that jungle was the resident hacks, also called "trustees." Old Foster and the rest of the cloned hacks who ran that joint were always willing to endure humiliation from the warden and his staff to have their little piece of authority.

For them, riding shotgun every day and watching these prisoners was better than being out in the cold. I could see these make-believe cops for sure didn't have an opinion or a take on anything else but this prison. That was good to know. Their ignorance and their tiny bubble of a life gave me an Edge.

News traveled fast in the joint. One day earlier, no one in the world knew I existed. Today I was a real somebody. Just like being in Hollywood, where everyone has a schtick. The butcher's job was mine. I laughed while I thought, *Be cool, butcher boy, and maybe you can survive the jungle after all.*

* * *

5:00 a.m. sharp. The idiot box on the P.A. system started screaming, invading my sleep. I hit the sink to get ready for my morning whore bath in the fresh cold water, which was very stimulating, very invigorating, and mostly humiliating to endure.

Foster had a good time telling me how the brown bar of soap they gave each of us was really good for the complexion. "It's good for dry skin! Keeps you smooth and soft. Just like a baby's ass."

His mockery wasn't enough to weigh me down, though. This was the first morning since I arrived at Sing-Sing that I was looking forward to the day. I started walking toward the mess hall with the other cons, and all you could hear was the scuffling of feet that made this trip three times a day, seven days a week.

I finally was marching to their silent cadence when out of the rat pack emerged a toothless wonder, veteran of the Sing-Sing wars. I grinned when this gnarled old sewer rat approached me. What trouble could he cause?

"Salerno!" he wheezed. "Woodchuck is the name, gossip is my game." Gossip. That made sense. Everybody needed an Edge in there. So he claimed gossip for his realm. Otherwise he would just be another shriveled-up prune of a con.

"Woodchuck, my man, what can I do for you on this fine Spring morning?"

He flashed a set of hardened gums. "Son, it's not what you can do for me, it's what I can do for you."

"Just what is it that can you do for me?" But before he could respond, Foster approached us, so I said, "I'll see ya in the big yard."

I wasn't quick enough. Foster screamed. "Salerno, no talking in line!" So that put an end to that.

After spending weeks doing solitary time in Keep Lock, my first walk in the sun was glorious. There I was in Sing-Sing, with its manicured lawns and flowered gardens standing in stark contrast to the people who accompanied them. The view was breathtaking from on top of the hill fronting the Hudson River. The river current was mesmerizing. I had never stopped to consider how beautiful the Hudson River really was.

Looking down at the foot of the river, I saw volumes of glistening, rolled-up barbed wire. The razor coils reached six feet high into the sunlight, a constant reminder of where you were, just in case you forgot.

Still, the crisp air was refreshing. I realized the view, the mist, the seagulls, all gave a strong sense of the freedom beckoning from only a few yards away. That thought gave me chills right up my fucking spine.

Then I looked at two cons reading the Daily News. One con yelled to the other, "Lefty, look! Isn't that your old lady?"

"Where?"

"Right there! Isn't that her?"

Sure enough, there was a picture of his wife and another guy walking hand and hand on opening day at Belmont Racetrack. "Lefty, what the fuck is that all about?"

Lefty was cool. "I'm here, she's there, I'm doing life and she's living life. Fuck it. Let's get to the big yard." At least nobody could tell Lefty he was in denial about things.

It was pretty hard to deny much of anything there. Every time an inmate looked down the winding road toward the big yard, he remembered exactly where the fuck he was. That was sure true for me. But as I walked down the road, I passed a quaint-looking building done up like a little red firehouse. It was a sight straight from a storybook, and it blew my mind to see something as beautiful as that in this environment.

I gaped while I approached the front of the "firehouse," waiting for something like maybe a big red fire truck to come roaring out. Then someone whispered from behind me and I realized that I knew the fucking voice. Woodchuck.

"That's where all them mafia dudes hang out. It's off limits to everyone. You all need a pass to go inside that place, except me."

I played the Edge by acting like I admired his toothless ass. "Woodchuck! You walk around here like you own the joint!"

He chuckled. "Son, I been here fifty-two years. Don't need no pass." He waved his arm. "See all this scenery? Sompin' else, ain't it? Well, I been the gardener here for some forty years, more or less. Seen 'em all. Willie Sutton, Capone, Lucky Luciano, Joe the Boss, Joey Gallo from Brooklyn and the big man Albert "A." All them stars come see me, sooner or later. You will too."

Woodchuck shot me a look. "I heard you're the new butcher boy. We never get butcher boys in here."

I smiled and tried to draw out his hustle to see what he was up to. "You got that right, Woodchuck man. There's some gossip for you, right there."

He flashed his gums again, then spit a wad of tobacco juice. "Butcher boy, you're still a kid, so tell me—how the hell did you get the best gig in this joint?"

I shook my head. "Woodchuck, that's for me to know and for you to find out." But I grinned at him. "Then you'll have another piece of gossip to trade."

"You better sober up, new guy. You gonna have a lot of people coming at you, looking for meat."

"Uh-huh. Like you, Woodchuck?"

"Butcher Boy, you're lucky I'm even talking to you. Nothing moves around this joint without me knowing what's going on. You got that?"

I dropped the smile. "Look, pal, first off my name is Salerno. You don't call me Butcher Boy. Got that? Second, I don't give a rat's ass who the fuck you are and what the fuck you do. Or the mother that made you. So take your fucking attitudes, and stick 'em up your degenerated ass. I have never responded well to tough-guy threats from toothless little dudes who assure me I'm going to come see them. It makes me want to see Death before I do any such thing."

So I walked on, and the next building that stuck out for me had a huge green door. Nothing else around there was painted that color. It looked out of place. A husky voice pierced my thoughts. "That's the entrance to the Sing-Sing death house. A good place to stay out of."

A very large black man stood smiling at me. He glanced in Woodchuck's direction and said, "You just made yourself an enemy. That little squirt is gonna run right to those mob guys in the firehouse and tell them the way you treated him."

I shrugged him off, but he kept on with it.

"Be careful, that midget pulls a lotta weight with those mobsters."

"What's his story?"

"He supplies those boys with everything they need. Shit like porn magazines, sucks a little cock, even takes it up the ass from time to time."

"Thanks, that's good to know." I stuck out my hand. "Salerno is my name and meat is my game."

"Big Al is the name and being black is my game." He grinned at that one.

"Well Big Al, tell me what goes on in there?"

"You don't know? Man, that's Death House! There you sit for twenty-odd years doing nothing. Most guys die before they ever see the chair."

I got a sick feeling in the pit of my stomach, and it really sunk in where the hell I was.

Then as we approached the two steel buildings all you could hear was the buzz of human voices. The closer we got, the clearer the sounds became. Soon it was a roar. Again with the prison noise.

"What the hell is this place?"

"It's called Wreck Hall, where the elite meet to eat. Let me tell you something before you go into that shit hole. Remember you're a new mickey, so you just can't walk in and sit down anywhere you fucking please. You have to stand at the wall with the rest of the uninvited guests and wait till someone in there invites you to sit your sorry ass down."

"What do you do?"

"I don't go near that shit hole, not my style. I just walk in the big yard and smell the fresh air."

Together, we finally hit the big yard, and to my surprise there was a baseball game in progress. They even had stands with seats in them, just like the ones you sat in at Ebbits Field.

What a contrast. When I looked up the hill to see where I just came from, all I could see were big red buildings that housed the cons. "Big Al, I gotta tell ya, at this point I'm a little fucking dizzy. My first walk on the wild side, here. What a fucking joint."

"If you stay here long enough, you'll get used to the view."

"What does that mean?"

"It means, meat man, that Sing-Sing is still just a fucking prison, period. Don't let all this pretty shit out here turn your head. You're in the Big House now, baby, and from here they will ship you out to places like Attica, Green Haven, or maybe even Dannemora."

Yeah, maybe so, but being afraid to walk into Wreck Hall didn't feel right to me. So instead I made a beeline for the door and went inside.

First impression: they weren't earning any blue-ribbon awards for excellence. The "uniformed prisoner look" didn't play here. Seemed you could wear anything you wanted, hats and do-rags. The bathrooms were unattended, and the hacks were nowhere to be seen.

Big Al was right about the seating. It looked to me like only the high achievers got to sit down. I saw unruly inmates passing contraband right out in the open. Sex was going on all over, but nobody seemed to be coerced into it. Open door stalls left the action right there to be seen, and everyone was having a good ole time. Gamblers of all kinds were filling some pockets while others walked away without saying a word. No sore losers there.

Strange as it may sound, there was an overpowering sense of freedom. Still locked up, but less confined. The biggest impression I got from all this was a buzz in the air, a sense of urgency about everything. Every man in there gave off the sense of having a limited time to get a lot done.

The place was loud, but to my surprise everything ran along in an orderly way. Whites with whites, Puerto Ricans with Puerto Ricans. Blacks with blacks (the word nigger was still in play). Gays with gays (the word "fag" was still in play). Italians with Italians, or wops with wops, since people hardly ever called you Italian. Irish guys with Irish guys (micks with micks), and rednecks with rednecks.

I was amazed by the entire circus, and by the fact that there was not a hack in sight. The code of respect in that place was based in the fear of terrible violence, but it worked as well behind bars as the softer version of the code of respect used to do back in the neighborhood.

These cons had worked out a way to give themselves maximum freedom within the confines of that place. Which meant it worked pretty well most of the time, but that nobody can control everything.

Because I walked into the bathroom and the smell was so bad, I could taste it on my tongue.

44

The Sing-Sing Shuffle

There were six hundred cells to my cell block, but I had to be lucky enough to have a warning bell fastened to the wall right above my fucking cell. It didn't just sound off, it stabbed you in the ears. This of course would be followed by amplified announcements through the P.A. system.

When the bell went off, I opened my eyes and realized it was time to earn. Play the Edge and get some things fixed around there.

Foster didn't waste any time starting in. "My advice for all you so-called late-sleeping purists is this: Relax! Chill! Don't get all worked up over getting up at 5 a.m. It's nothing to worry about. It can't hurt you. It's not like the Surgeon General has to go out and issue a special warning or anything like that. Why would you rather sleep when you can wake up and see me, your savior, your mentor. I'm the best goddamn prison guard of your whole miserable generation, and I *know* you cons want to see Mr. Foster play havoc with all those lazy motherfuckers who keep me from getting my loyal fans dressed and out of your cells on time. *Right?*"

Then Foster changed tune and went back to his natural condition, which was ballistic with bulging neck veins. "I am opening the doors now. Any cocksucker who makes me late for my breakfast will feel the full wrath of my territorial rights!"

The cell doors slid open, and after that all you heard was the Sing-Sing shuffle. But even though nobody hung back,

Foster continued shouting. "You think that's bad, making me late? No, of course you don't, because all it does for you scumbags is liven up the game. It makes everything seem fresh and exciting again."

Then, a hollow voice from below filled the cell block with another opinion. "Foster, who the fuck writes your material?"

Foster leaned over the railing, looked around, then shouted, "What's your number?"

The voice from below bellowed loudly, "Butterfield Eight, Motherfucker."

The entire cell block went deathly quiet. Seconds passed. Then the place erupted into a medley of screams and maniacal laughter.

To my surprise, Foster stayed cool. I didn't think he had it in him. He just stood there chewing his pipe, waiting for all of us to have our laugh. Then he yelled into the microphone, "You all have *two* minutes to zero hour!"

In the blink of an eye everything went back to business as usual, but he didn't go for any payback. That was it. And I realized if that was all he was going to do, Foster must actually have a little sense of humor.

I thought, *I can work with that.* It was a fucking great moment. I actually felt like I was happy. I saw an Edge.

* * *

On the way to the mess, Foster pulled me from the main line and guided me right into the officers' mess. "Salerno! These are my associates."

Having me in his grasp seemed to be special for him. For what, I didn't know at the moment, but I was sure he had something up his sleeve. I could see the urgency in his face when he bit down on his pipe and announced, "Boys, here he is, and he's all mine."

When I heard that, I didn't know what to think. *He's mine? What the fuck?* This guy is talking about ownership?

So what would my Edge be in this? Then it hit me, I could have it made in this shit hole. The thing to do was to play the dumb guinea until I found out why there was all this heat over a fucking butcher job.

Foster pushed me into a corner. "Salerno, this wise bunch I just introduced you to are the guys who run this prison. Nothing goes on without them knowing. You can do good time if you do what I tell you. If not, you will just do bad time. And my guinea wop friend, when I'm finished with you, the good Lord himself will not recognize you."

So my Edge was the good wop. "I hear ya, boss, loud and clear."

"Good. Now let's go see Pete. He's a fucking pain in the ass if we're not on time."

"Is Pete with us?"

Foster's face showed an uncharacteristic grin. "Yeah, he's with us."

I knew I was skating on thin ice, but I decided to slip my Edge underneath him and try to flip him over. "Mr. Foster, that ain't good enough for me."

That stopped the old redneck. He frowned. "Why the fuck not? I told you he's with us."

"I have to know what to do with him. If he ain't with us, I'll have to find a way to go around him. I gotta know what the fuck."

The next thing I knew I was on the floor. All I saw was a flash of light. When I opened my eyes, there was a BIG man with "BIG" spelled in all capital letters because that's how BIG he was, and he stood over me with a bat in his hand.

"Newbie, don't fuck with us."

I rubbed my aching head. "Why would I fuck with you guys?" But knew I had gone too far.

"You writing a fucking book, Salerno?"

"No sir, I'm working for the F.B.I."

He shot me a quickie. "You got a lot of wise-ass in you don't you boy?"

"No disrespect. I gotta know what I'm doing."

"You're asking a lotta questions for a newbie."

"And you gave me some fucking headache."

He smiled, "Good. I'm the P.K. and I run this joint. As long as you are with us, it's going to be Mr. Wimple to you."

"Mr. Wimple. Mr. Wimple, all I'm saying is if I'm gonna be a player, I got to know how to move. Otherwise all my talents go out the window."

Wimple thought a moment while he wiped his bulbous nose. "Looking at your record, I see that you were a butcher."

"Yes sir, Mr. Wimple. The best in the 14th Street meat market."

"I also see you are mob affiliated."

I just looked at him and grinned.

"Salerno, wipe that grin off your fucking face or I will wipe it off for you. Now you follow?"

"Yes, Mr. Wimple."

Wimple wasted no time. He ushered me into the butcher shop and took me to see Pete, who got up smiling and said, "I'm sure on the way over the boys gave you an earful."

"Oh, not too bad, sir." I looked around the shop, it was an impressive layout. "This is a first-class operation."

Wimple took me into the cooler, and to my surprise it was filled with hindquarters of beef. I thought, *you don't need all this meat to feed this population. Time to find out what's going on ....*

So while Wimple gave me the nickel tour, from the other end of the cooler strolled the head dietician, Mr. Weiner, a Jew. Tall, bald-headed guy, it was strange to see a Jew in the middle of all those rednecks.

The first words out of Wiener's mouth were, "Young man, I hope you can cut meat."

"Does that famous bear still shit in the woods?"

"Another fucking wise-ass I don't need. Foster, get him the fuck out of here now!"

But Mr. Wimple pulled Pete and the irate Weiner off to the side between the hindquarters of beef. I could hear the trio of schemers going round and round. Once the summit was over, they all emerged.

Mr. Wimple came out looking mad. "Salerno, from this moment on, you keep your trap shut." Then he stormed out of the cooler. Wiener walked over and said, "Smart-ass, if it was up to me, you would be in the hole. It seems your skills outweigh your stupidity."

Pete chimed in. "You report to me every day. Look Salerno, I know you're a pro, so I want New York steaks, sirloin steaks, flank steaks, roast beef, all cut to order, wrapped and boxed to perfection."

Wiener glared at me and added, "Wise ass, you fuck this up and I will have you sleeping with the sodomites. Clear?"

"Crystal."

My head was spinning while I walked to the mess hall. These guys had a fucking great thing going on, but I didn't have an angle on it and there was no way to make a fucking nickel.

Sitting on the mess hall floor where it was cool, waiting to go to work, I heard some cons yelling. So I looked up.

The card game was tense. From what I could see, those were some serious players. I asked one of the cons watching, "Donuts, what the fuck is all that screaming about?"

"They're playing bridge. A fucking bridge game. But those are four wackos right there, first class psychopaths. So they can make a scene and get away with it. There's the Russian, that little guy sitting across from Big George. He was just released from the loony bin. Double door security. His partner is Big George, that black baldheaded guy. He could pop open a can of peas with one hand."

Just then, the Russian freaked out and flipped his cards into the air. "George, how many times have I told you not to overbid your fucking hand?"

George just gave him a puppy dog smile. "Well, it looks like I'm going to have to suck my thumb tonight."

When I heard that it got my attention. "What does that mean?"

Big George heard me and grinned. "On that hand, son, I just lost my man. Do you play?"

"A little," I replied, the way you're supposed to. "What are the stakes?"

"Simple. If we win, they suck our cocks. If they win, we suck theirs."

Cock-sucking as a prize? I sat there drilled to the concrete floor. "Uh, what happens if no one wins?"

"In case of a tie," George explained, "we have a circle jerk." The guys laughed at the thought of a circle jerk.

George looked at me. "My man, are you in?"

I had only seen them play a little, but they already revealed they were too unstable to communicate as partners. Plus I had already downplayed my skill at bridge, a game you damn well better know how to play if you pal around with Italian gangsters and their families. These guys didn't know it, but they were marks.

Problem was, they didn't represent easy money. They represented a circle jerk.

Everything familiar to me about a card game ended at that instant and everything went into complete batshit mode. From the corner of my eye, I saw the Russian pick up a giant ladle and dip it into a pot of boiling oil. I just thought he was doing some cooking. In one fluid motion he ran to Big George and dumped the contents on his shiny bald head. *Holy Shit! Boiling oil is part of the game?*

George screamed and I could hear his skin sizzle. But he kept in his place. I would have thought he would run or something. The Russian then screamed at him loud enough to be heard over his cries, "Never ask me to be your partner again!"

That took about two seconds. The hot oil rolled down the aged warrior's body. The guards just stood there and watched the scenario play out. It looked like their sense of don't-fuck-with-it was running pretty high.

Pete stepped over to me waving his hands. "Easy, no sweat, here. Forget that crap. Happens all the time."

But the smell of burning flesh got me sick. George's screams were pathetic. And since it seemed like a lifetime could pass before those guards got any medical help there, I shouted, "Put him in the meat freezer!"

Everyone looked at me like I was crazy.

"The cold will stabilize his system! *Do it!*" I could have also told them I thought it might work because I saw it in a movie, but that would not be playing the Edge.

Pete jumped on it with me and shouted, "Move! Let's go!"

"Get me some tablecloths," I shouted. "Where do they keep them?"

"Why tablecloths?"

"We wet 'em so when we wrap him up, they'll stick to the body and cool it evenly."

Wiener walked over and muttered, "You better know what the fuck you're doing."

You can't play the Edge if you don't stick it out there from time to time, risk getting it chopped off, so to speak. So I just asked him, "You got a better idea, Einstein?"

"You I don't like, Salerno. You got a fast fucking lip." Then he stormed off.

Foster saw it and shook his head at me. "I got to tell you, you didn't make a good impression with Mr. Weiner."

"Mr. Foster, I don't give a damn about his feelings. That poor fucking bastard over there just got French-fried and all Weiner did was look."

"His name is Mister Weiner, to you. And all I can tell you is, it was not a good way to start your day."

Of course that depended on your point of view, whether you looked at it from the angle of the system who liked everything nice and docile and beaten-down, or from the angle of a newbie using the reputation of a joker to grease his path.

45

Grandma's Recipe Saves the Day

Lunch in the officers' mess was a big hit that day. I was in a good mood so I made them Grandma's marinara sauce with spaghetti and meatballs. I'm telling you, they swallowed that stuff like they were starving. While they ate, the topic of the day was Big George and the way he got fried over a card game.

I was cursing them under my breath while I did the cooking, but a young prison guard interrupted my daydream. He looked like he couldn't have been no more than fifteen years old. "Sir, those meatballs were the best things I have ever eaten."

Sir, he calls me sir? I smiled. "Thank you, sir."

"Oh no! Not sir. You can just call me Sylvester. Everyone calls me that."

Not sir? I can just call him Sylvester? My mind starts singing, Edge, Edge, Edge .... I grinned. "Okay, Sylvester, thank you. Now what can I do for you?"

He was very shy for a prison guard, thin and frail. I wondered what the fuck he was doing in this place.

"Could you give me your recipe? I know my mom would love to have it."

Jesus Christ, a real human being. "Sylvester, I'll tell you my grandmother's recipe right now. Got a paper and pencil?"

"Right here."

"Okay, here we go. You get one pound of chopped meat, two eggs, cheese, the Italian kind I'm saying, you understand, salt and pepper, breadcrumbs, and fresh basil. Got that? Good. Then dump it all in a bowl and mix up the meat with all the ingredients until you get everything nice and sticky. Then roll 'em and dump 'em into your tomato sauce and cook 'em for a half hour.

"P.S., Sylvester, give your mom the secret: *never* fry or bake 'em ahead of time. Put 'em in raw. She's gonna be tempted to pre-cook 'em but she's got to resist the urge. Got that?"

Mr. Wimple walked into the kitchen like a bad smell. Sylvester spotted him. "Gotta go, that's my dad. Thanks for the recipe."

His dad. Wimple. Okay.

Wimple talked with his son, then walked over to me. "I'll need twenty steaks. Bring them to my office, asap. Also, my son told me he's going to make meatballs, so add a couple of pounds of chopped meat."

Later Mr. Weiner came swaggering into the kitchen. Word was out. "Wise ass, make me a batch of meatballs. I want them ready when I leave."

But I turned and walked away from him like I was a free agent with a pocket full of cash. I still had some leverage. As I walked into the cooler, I heard, "Don't you ever walk away from me like that again."

But he didn't follow me. He didn't push the issue. It has never ceased to amaze me how much a good skill can keep you from having to suck up to assholes.

That night, Mr. Foster and I delivered the homemade meatballs. Then we strolled into Wiener's office, and to my surprise the room was an eclectic version of art deco, and in the corner sat Weiner getting a blow job. The young inmate doing the number on him saw me but continued tight with his work. So I just backed out. Weiner was none the wiser.

On the way out, I gave Mr. Foster the package of meatballs and told him, "Give these to Sylvester. Mr. Weiner was too busy getting his dick sucked."

That night I sat on my bed a long time, wondering what the fuck kind of guys were running the joint. It seemed to me like they were stealing with both hands on this meat scam. Nobody wanted to recognize the fact that as the butcher, I had keys to the vault. The was an Edge to be developed there, I was certain.

But I also thought, *Salerno, you gotta be careful, you could get caught in a shit storm. There's too many players in on this. It's gonna blow up sooner or later.*

Foster came by screaming, "Gentlemen! When I come by to make the night count, you had better have two feet on the floor. This is my last announcement on this matter. I shit you not!"

I heard his feet shuffling closer. When they stopped outside my cell I looked up and there he was, all smiles. "Two feet means both of them." I slid off my bed onto the floor, but the move exposed my naked body.

"Salerno, gimme a break. You wanna be a poster child? Fine. I'll arrange it. Next time put some clothes on. I got good news for you. The medics brought Big George to a SAC base just down the road. They put him in one of those machines they use for pilots who get burned up. Guess what? He lived. Not bad, Salerno, thinking on your feet like that."

But then he leaned closer to the bars, so nobody else could hear, and finally got real about things. "Tomorrow, I'll bring my truck around to the back of the butcher shop. Fill it up. Here's the list."

He handed me a sheet of paper.

"I'll be there three-thirty sharp, right before the four o'clock count. What you do is make damn sure you got it filled up *before* my shift ends."

I stood there in the nude and asked, "What happened to the Russian?"

"Christ, would you please put something on?"

I laughed. "You're not funny like Weiner, are you?"

"Not at all, it's just that when I'm having a conversation with you and there you are dangling around it's a little hard to concentrate."

"Yeah, Mr. Foster, I understand. If you were standing there naked smoking that pipe of yours, it would be pretty hard for me to concentrate, too."

Foster laughed the way you do when nothing's funny.

"By the way, your new wakeup call is three a.m. You'll be cooking meals in addition to your butcher work."

I was trying to get my head around this news when he added, "They sent the Russian to Dannemora. Box A. He'll love it there. Plenty of crazies to keep him company."

46

Pouring Time Down a Bottomless Well

Hard work moves time forward. The months were really moving fast for me, the mornings, the lunches, the dinners. Before I knew it, three hundred and sixty-five days flew by.

The first year.

One day Pete showed, as usual, and happily escorted me into the butcher shop. "Salerno, it's all yours. Here's a list of things for you to do, but today you have to double the order."

I looked at the page. "Pete, this is some list."

He just walked off. After a while I saw why the list was so long. There was a hell of a conspiracy going on. Serious money was changing hands, and the taxpayers were picking up the bill.

I finally got the picture. I saw how they were robbing the taxpayers blind. Mr. Wiener was the key, because he did all the ordering.

Pete regarded me as the happy idiot of this bunch, because he got fat on the plan while I worked for lunch money. It was Pete who signed for all the beef that came through the prison. If the shit ever hit the fan, he would be held responsible.

But by that point, I had seen enough of Pete to know that in this chess game he never really knew what the fuck was going on. He thought he was doing all right on his end, but he didn't really get it. This little group was making a serious killing.

Loose lips sink ships, however, and there was a lot of bickering going on. That meant there was a lot of dangerous information that could leak. For instance, Wiener and Lt. Bender owned a supermarket in the town of Ossining, where the entire meat supply was unknowingly supplied by the taxpayers of the State of New York.

I was finally getting the picture about my rapid rise up the ranks in prison life. When I showed up there, it had made it a lot easier for them to fine-tune their scam. They loved the fact that I was a butcher because they had full control of me.

Free butcher. No wonder I got the royal treatment. This was the missing information the other inmates sensed. In spades.

Foster loved waking me up at three a.m. By that, I mean he mostly loved the way I cut meat. He would watch me and say, "Salerno, you should have been a surgeon."

The officers' mess was jumping, and there was Foster holding court about his wonderful find, like I was a draft choice who somehow got overlooked. I served him his bacon and eggs, then whispered, "The company I used to work for had better bacon than this shit you're eating."

He gave me a sly look while he continued stuffing his face. I left and went into the cooler. Didn't take too long for Foster to follow me.

"What was that you said?"

"You mean about the bacon?"

"*Yes*, the bacon!"

"First off, I noticed that the companies Wiener is buying from suck."

"How do you know that?"

"Mr. Foster, I worked for the best meat company on the East coast. All I have to do is call my old boss from Wexlor Meats and you'll get the best for less. You got my drift?"

Foster sucked heavily on his pipe. "I'll be right back."

Foster must have made a quick u-turn because as soon as

I started to cut some flank steaks, he walked up with Mr. Wiener.

"Tell him what you just told me."

"Tell him what?"

"The bacon, the meat company, and all that."

"Oh! Well, I was just talking about the possibility that if I called my old boss, I could get you guys a better deal. But I was just talking out loud."

Foster's face dropped. "What do you mean, you was only talking?"

"I was just saying what could be if things were different, but you guys are all set. I mean, I know about institutions, we used to supply a lot of hospitals and city jails."

Weiner didn't know the name of the game. He was eyeballing me like a hawk. "What city jails did you do business with?"

"I always dealt with Harry Bloomstein, the head dietitian at the Raymond Street jail, and Mark Steel over at Rikers Island."

I could see it in his eyes—he knew who they were. He was all business. One false move and I would be history, but God help me, there was a scheme to develop here.

Wiener looked suspicious. "Tell me how you know what companies I deal with?"

"Easy, I see the names on the boxes. I know all those companies. And I don't know what you're paying, but I bet you guys would do a *lot* better if you dealt with my old boss."

"Why are you so interested in helping us out?"

"I'm not! I only mentioned to Mr. Foster about the fatty bacon he was eating and now all this happened. I was just talking about the fatty bacon, that's all. I mean I know my job. I know about these things."

"What 'things' are you talking about?" Weiner demanded.

Time to push the Edge. "Look, I cut meat all day long for you. Can't you see I know my stuff? Oh yeah, I meant to tell you, the way you have me cutting your steaks is wrong. You could make them go a lot farther if you let me do things my way. You should think about that."

Make the meat go farther—they didn't have to think too long about that. Shortly after the evening count, I was ushered from my cell into Wiener's office. There, to my surprise, sat the Warden. A tall man, well-groomed, he was fat and sassy, drinking whiskey with a milk chaser. He loomed large in this group of penny pinchers. Lieutenant Bender was in another corner rubbing his scarred scalp.

When Bender looked at me, a smile crossed his face. Weiner was busy making drinks but never took his eyes off me, either. Mr. Foster was serving the warden a dish filled with nuts.

I realized I was surrounded by a bunch of wheeling and dealing rednecks who had somehow put this scheme together. That in itself intrigued the shit outta me.

I won't say Warden Williams was a huge man, but in fact he wore a size nine hat and had the hands of a basketball player. All the while he was scoping me out, he was also squeezing a walnut. Finally, he cracked the nut open. He threw the shells on Wiener's desk then carefully ate the seed.

Wiener wasn't too happy about the mess, but it showed everybody who was the boss in the room. I loved it. Even being in jail, I loved a good scheme, and this was one was great.

I wished the Hawk could have seen all this. He'd have been proud of me, because I now had the attention of The Man. Warden Williams saw my smile as I acknowledged who he was.

He grinned. "Boy, you fuck with me, you will spend the rest of your time on the coal gang." Then he leaned closer. I could smell the whiskey on his breath, and it smelled damn good.

"Tell me now, boy, how would you like that?"

"You know, Warden, I can't knock nothing I never tried."

He froze for a moment, then burst out laughing. That caused him to spit nuts and whiskey all over Wiener's desk.

Williams bellowed, "Boy, I like your style! Mr. Weiner, give this boy a man's drink!"

Mr. Wiener went to the bar, poured three fingers, and dutifully handed it to me. I smiled at him and shot it down before he could take it back. Oh man, did it feel good sliding down my throat. My brain buzzed while watching the warden rumble over to the bar. I got curious when he picked up the ice pick. A second later, he violently slammed the ice pick into the desk.

Unfortunately, Weiner wasn't fast enough. He looked at his left hand—it was pinned to the desk. He started gasping like a drowning man.

"Son, don't you ever cross me."

That fuckin' move brought the redneck-infested freak show to a halt. All eyes were on Wiener's crucified hand.

Foster was bug-eyed and breathing heavy, but he finally removed the ice pick from Wiener's hand. To my surprise. There was only a pin hole with a small amount of blood.

Williams laughed. "Don't worry son, you'll live. Now that we understand one another, let's get down to business."

Another three fingers of whiskey went down. He made a one-eighty, then looked me in the eye.

"Salerno, tell me how you are going to make things better for me."

"For us, sir?"

"There is no 'us' in this equation. There is only me and my belly, but I never eat alone."

"Let me show you, Warden. I can if you get me an outside line."

He picked up his phone and said, "Sally! Please get me an outside line." Williams had this smirk all over his mug. Something seemed to be going his way.

He hit the phone's speaker button. "Son, you don't mind if we all listen?"

"Be my guest, Warden. Just sit back and listen."

I looked at Williams a moment and then spoke in a very low, quiet voice. "Warden, if I place this call, you stand to make yourself a lot of money. I'm not interested in the fucking money. Got that? I need you to help me get my son out of Kings County Hospital. My angry, pissed-off wife had my son committed, Warden. He's only seven."

The phone rang. "You're on, son"

When I heard an answer, I spoke right up. "Solly, it's me, Salerno!"

"What? I thought you were buried in Sing-Sing!"

"I am. Long story short, right now I want you to say hello to Warden Williams."

"What? Hello. Uh. Warden."

The warden got on and said, "This boy of yours here just told me you could make my life easier if I did business with you?"

"Yes! I see now. You got that right, Warden, and if you listen to Salerno, he will make it happen for you. He was the best butcher I ever had. It's a damn shame you got him."

"I got him because he had too many mobsters up his nose."

"Maybe so, Warden, but you listen to him, he'll make you a lot of money. He's an earner.

Williams laughed. "My friend, that remains to be seen."

"Warden, you should listen to me on this one. Just let him go over the books. He'll get everything straightened out for you. He's a wiz with numbers, and most of all, number scams." He can spot one a mile away."

"We'll see about that, too. I'll be giving you a call. Nice talking to you."

Williams hung up and looked at Wiener. "Wrap up that hand of yours. You don't want to get it infected. Also, get me all the order slips for the past year and give them to the kid."

Wiener just stood there, stunned. He looked to me like his motor skills were sputtering.

Williams shouted, "Wiener, did you hear me?"

"Yes, sir! I'll get them for you asap."

"*Not* a-fucking-sap! Right now! Foster, go with him. I want those slips on my desk earlier today!"

It was a long night in my cell with those books. But it seemed like every time I came up for air, good old Mr. Foster was at my cell leaning on the bars. Finally, he came out and asked, "What's up? The warden told me to keep an eye on you."

I looked up from the book pile. "I gotta say, Mr. Foster, this Wiener is making a fortune. I've checked and cross-checked everything. He's stealing from the crooks who are stealing from the state. He's got his own little deals going on with all the jobbers he's doing business with. Very nice indeed. On top of that, it's for sure that he's skimming off the top and then splitting the profits with the companies he deals with."

I lowered my voice before I went on. This was not information for Woodchuck's gossip line. "Mr. Foster, looking at the whole picture, I can already see this is only the tip of the iceberg. I didn't even get to the inventory on all the beef. Wait until Warden Williams hears about this. He's gonna need a couple of stiff ones."

"Son of a bitch, Salerno. You sure about this?"

"Yes, sir. These figures don't lie. It's all here in black and white."

Foster just turned away and waddled off. "Goddamn that man. Goddamn him."

47

Squealing on Crooked Cops

I was still asleep in my steel crib when Mr. Foster shouted. "Rise and Shine. Rise and shine!" I opened my eyes, and the first thing I saw was the Warden's big head. He smiled at me, so I said, "Warden, you got yourself a partner, and a good one. Mr. Wiener has Pete signing in for all the beef that comes through. Guess what? Pete doesn't even have a clue where all the beef is going."

The warden got this very serious look in his eye. "What does that all mean?"

"Well, from what I've seen so far, your pal is paying these companies a lot of money for their products. That tells me he's doing business with them."

"What kind of business?"

"I'm sure he's got side deals going on with every one of them. Simply put, Warden, if they want his business they have to dance to his tune. If not, he goes elsewhere, simple. You get the picture?"

"Sounds interesting, but I want you to explain this to me like I was a six-year-old."

"Okay look, Warden, it's simple. A box of bacon should cost ten bucks. The jobber charges the state fifteen bucks. In turn the state sends your pal Mr. Wiener the extra five.

Williams exploded, "Stop calling him my pal!"

"Wait, Warden, it gets better. For every pound of meat you buy for the State, your pal is putting at least a buck a pound into his pocket."

"Salerno, I'm not going to tell you again. Stop calling him my pal."

"You do the math. If he puts four hindquarters on the scale which should weigh eight hundred pounds, he puts down seven hundred pounds. So now your pal puts a hundred pounds of beef into his pocket. Did your pal tell you about that part?"

"That son of a bitch has been fucking me right along!" He turned to Foster. "Get rid of the kid, asap."

"What? But Warden, I'm your man!"

He looked at me. "Sorry son, but you just became the boy who knows too much."

I just sat there in my cell knowing I had overplayed my hand. The warden stood there and I could see he was in deep thought. Then he spit it out. "Salerno, this incident never happened today. Do I make myself clear?"

"Loud and clear, sir." The big man turned to leave then stopped and asked me, "That son of yours. What's his story?"

"Yeah, Warden, yeah, well …."

"Lets go, spit it out, I don't have all day."

"My wife, she had my son committed to the nut house."

"The nut house? What for?"

"Nothing, Warden. He's not nuts, she just can't handle him. Warden, he deserves better than that. He's only seven."

"Knock that shit off, you already told me that once before. You know, he's getting a bad deal only because his daddy isn't there to watch his little ass."

Williams turned to Mr. Foster. "Get what's-his-name the shrink! Crane."

Foster replied. "Yeah, I'll get him to take care of this."

"1-2-9-4-8-9, report to the reception room!" I looked up at the loudspeaker. "You know, Mr. Foster, I'm gonna miss that bitch box."

Warden Williams entered the reception room. "Salerno, I'm sending you to Attica with all the bleeding hearts. It's a tough prison so watch yourself."

Mr. Foster asked, "Warden, what should I put in his folder?"

"Just put down he was strong-arming a bunch of niggers. They'll believe that."

"Yeah, those fleabags in Attica are going to love that.

Make sure you put a lot of leg irons on him like he's been a bad, bad man. That'll look good." He turned to me. "Nothing personal in all this."

"Yes, but Warden—my kid. Don't forget me."

"You shut up with that shit."

Sitting there alone waiting to be transferred, everything finally sunk in. They put enough leg irons on me to sink a fucking ship.

48

Attica. What an amazing place. At first glance, you would never think this was an infamous prison. It had a clean and relaxing look which was very disarming, especially with all the sculptured lawns that surrounded the prison, lined with red roses and daffodils. A beautiful lie.

Shattering the mood was a six-foot-six, two hundred thirty-pound prison guard. "My name is Captain Novell. Welcome to Attica, the best feeding prison in the world. The rules are very simple. Keep your shirt buttoned up, your lip buttoned up, or you get fucked up." That was the same thing they said to me at Sing-Sing. I had to wonder if these guys compared notes. Did they all go to the same conventions?

Once the outer doors were opened, I was startled. Attica was a prison within a prison. Attica itself is surrounded by high walls with hundreds of yards of those well-kept lawns and gardens.

There were four yards: A, B, C, and D, all joined up to "Times Square," a fifty-foot round cylinder connecting the four yards. One had to pass into the "Times Square cylinder," as it was called, to be able to get into another yard.

Eye contact was nonexistent out in the yard. Blacks on one side, whites on the other. Armed guards walked the roof tops, keeping a constant vigil on the cons below. If I wanted to talk to a black prisoner, I had to get permission from one of the guards lurking above.

I looked at the lost souls shuffling about, and there was a chill in the air that went right through me. I started thinking *Man, I really did not sign up for this when I took the local mobsters for my role models.*

There were five hundred prisoners in that yard, yet you could hear a pin drop. The warden's policies had done the impossible, silencing a prison full of cons. I had never been around this sort of isolation. I have a big fucking mouth and I like to talk to people.

As I walked, deep in thought, I could feel a thousand eyes burning into my back. Then a loud P.A. speaker blasted out, "1-8-5-9-2, report to Times Square immediately."

Then it hit me, *that's my number.* Anxiety and fear gripped my body at the same time. Something bad or unpleasant was going to happen, especially given the urgent way my number was blasted out on the P.A. system.

When I reached Times Square, standing there like a supernatural being, like a god, was the six-foot-six Captain Novell. Tall and black, I had just learned that behind his back he was called the African Cyclone.

"1-8-5-9-2, stop daydreaming, when you hear your number called, you get your sorry ass up here." His intense, beady eyes became slits. "You got that, Salerno?"

"Yes, sir."

"Captain to you"

He towered over me, so when I finally looked up all I could see were the insides of his nostrils.

"Yes, Captain."

"Salerno, you report to Jim Parker. He runs the pig farm." He looked down at me with an expression of suspicion. "Salerno, do you have any rabbit in you?"

"No, Captain. Not that I know of."

His opinion of my response was unfavorable. "Listen to me, Mr. Smart-ass, you're going to work outside these walls. So one day if you decide to hop off, remember when they catch you—and make no mistakes, they will …."

I shot him a smirk.

"Oh, yes they will, wise-ass, and I will be the last thing you'll ever see. You understand me? Don't answer, just listen. *Especially* don't decide to run on the weekends. Remember that. I don't like coming here on the weekends.

* * *

Soon it was so early in the morning it was the middle of the night. First day on the pig farm.

"Salerno, you can call me Mr. Clark, or Big Jim, so let's get something straight right now. Going to work on the pig farm is no joke. This is no over-the-wall cake walk. You gotta feed these suckers three times a day, and these six hundred-pound sows, hogs, and piglets eat every fucking thing they can. Including your arm. I wanted you here so you can slaughter these pigs for us. The warden at Sing-Sing is an old friend, and he told me you were the best man for the job. That's why you're here.

"Now remember, city boy, these pigs have the ability to convert inedible food into a meal. Do you consider yourself inedible?"

I sat there thinking, *This guy never shuts the fuck up.*

Big Jim pulled the truck next to the prison wall and backed up, then walked around to the back and opened up a hatch. He pulled out a huge round tube. He took one end of the tube over to the wall of the prison and what looked like a night deposit box. He put his key into the box and turned it. Seemed to me a big tube like that couldn't fit.

I asked. "Big Jim, how are you gonna get that tube into that hole?"

"Son, this is not a regular hole. This tube is the best material for telescoping because it's pliable, so when they remove the inside flash weld, the tube just slides into the vat and locks into place. All you do is hit the button, then all the waste from the prison is pumped into the truck. This is the morning meal for the hogs."

The upside of the hog farm job was that I was not working inside the prison at all. The downside was, I smelled like I came straight from hog heaven.

Plus, I had to get up every morning to report to the Kitchen Keeper, Mr. Gillett, also known as the Avocado King. Rumor had it that Mr. Gillett had a whole fucking valley of avocado trees paid for by the state, while the state never tasted so much as a single one of them.

Another scam the taxpayers were paying for. I shook my head. I definitely chose the wrong vocation.

Mr. Gillett was a bald-headed, angry man, pure and simple. So when I approached him every morning, he would yell things at me like, "Salerno, when you come into my kitchen you had better have had a bath."

Personal hygiene standards are a good thing. So every morning I took my sink bath and then reported for duty. I walked right on past him and straight to the huge vat, a hundred-gallon puppy filled with the garbage of the day. One day, I got curious so I climbed up the ladder, opened the vat, and looked inside. To my surprise it was empty.

I noticed the tube on the bottom was wide enough for a man to slide into, and then into the truck, and then straight into the pig pens. Mr. Gillett screamed out, "Salerno, what the fuck are you doing up there?"

"Mr. Clark told me to clean the vat." I was bullshitting a mile a minute.

"Get down from there before you fall on your ass!"

My mind was racing now. My heart was pounding so hard I thought it was going to explode. I had just discovered a way out of that joint!

I immediately went on sick call, got two aspirins, and returned to my cell. All night long, I struggled with this new-found discovery. Questions kept swimming around in my head. *What do I do? Where do I start with this? If I break out, where do I go?*

I wondered if I should just use this information as a safety valve. Maybe it would make the time go by faster, knowing I could get out of this hellhole anytime really I wanted to.

I tossed and turned all night long. The tension twisted me up inside to the point that I felt a pain in my stomach like getting stabbed. Something was definitely wrong, more than the tension of a possible escape route. My insides hurt so bad I thought I was going to die. I rolled around the floor. When I threw up, it smelled something awful. I was sweating hard. My head got so hot I felt like I was ready to pass out.

I got on my knees and stuck my head into the toilet bowl trying to cool off. Then I rolled onto the cold floor and just laid there moaning.

I tried to get up, but I had pissed myself, and in the darkness, I slipped on the wet floor. Finally, I couldn't take it anymore and screamed, "Motherfuckers! Somebody help me!" The inmate locked up next to me was called Iron Eyes Deluca. He whispered, "Salerno, what's up?"

"My stomach. I'm burning up."

"Man, you are fucked. You gotta wait till the morning. These cocksuckers will never open up. You could die in there; they don't give a fuck! Wait! Maybe you got one shot. They have Jewish services in the morning. Put your towel on the bars. The hack on the night shift goes around checking. Services are at four am. Salerno, are you a Jew?"

I am today, I thought. "Shit yeah! I'm as Jewish as they come."

"Good. That might save you."

Seemed like an eternity before any help arrived. I doubled up and somehow fell asleep. It lasted maybe a few minutes before somebody started banging on the bars to my cell.

"1-8-5-9-2! Let's get going. I don't have all day." It was none other than my old buddy, the Captain himself, the African Cyclone, looking all sharp as a daisy and as fresh as a rose. "Salerno, I didn't know you were of the Jewish persuasion."

"On my mother's side, Cap, on my mother's side."

"It's Captain or Mister Novell. We are not buddies, only my friends can call me Cap. Now get your ass moving."

"I'm on it, Mister Novell. I'm ready." Somehow by the grace of God I managed to pull myself together and then scooted out the door. The African Cyclone slammed the door so hard, I'm sure he woke up the whole fucking cell block. On the way to the synagogue all we heard from the pissed-off peanut gallery was "Hey Cyclone, next time you gotta make a little more noise?" Or "Why don't you go back where you came from!" Or just, "Your mama, Cyclone!"

The best I managed to catch was, "Cyclone, you know what they call a nigger in a tree? A branch manager!" That remark got to the big guy. He walked over to the switchboard and opened every light in the cell block.

The moaning and cursing of the sleepy inmates filled the place. Cap walked me to the synagogue, then turned to me and demanded, "Salerno, do you even know what goes on in a synagogue?"

I was in so much pain I just wanted to scream. "Captain, I was on my way to the officers' mess but on my way, I was tripped up by a blind man. What's a blind man doing in here?" My bullshit made him pause just long enough for me to duck into the synagogue and leave that Goy behind.

'Standing there to greet us was the rabbi. He opened his arms to greet me, but I collapsed into his.

When I awoke, standing there smiling and drinking an ice-cold beer was the doctor, Buttonhole Schwartz. Buttonhole was the best one-eyed, half-drunk surgeon we had, and by the grace of God, he just happened to stop by at that moment to see his old pal, the rabbi.

I looked down to see what had been done to me, and I had a two-inch scar where they took my appendix out. That scar was a beautiful thing to see. Cyclone snapped, "Doctor, I would appreciate it if you would not drink in the hospital. I don't know what kind of a place you're running here?"

Buttonhole finished his beer, burped, and opened another one. "Officer, when I'm here, this is my hospital, I'm sure I've earned the right to drink a beer." He eyed the Cyclone. "There will be no handcuffs restricting this man. He almost died. He needs some peace and quiet."

Boy did I.

He looked around the room. "Please roll him over to the window so he can get some sunlight."

"Wow, what a view," I said out loud. I could see all the action going on in the yard.

The pain was almost gone, nothing more than the sting of post-op surgery was left, and it wasn't nearly so bad as the pain that put me there. Seemed that this beer drinker had some sort of a heart.

49

Wallkill State

I was rudely awakened yet again by the African Cyclone, this time shouting, "Salerno! Pack it up! You are being transferred to Wallkill State Prison at first light."

"Wallkill? Where is that?"

"You'll find that out when you get there."

So come morning, the African Cyclone and I drove for two hours in stark silence. Once again, they put enough leg irons on me to sink a ship. The difference was this time we traveled alone in a car together.

I thought it was real charming being chained to the floor of the vehicle. "Captain, what happens if I have to take a piss?"

"Go right ahead." Maybe this man had a diploma from charm school, but I never saw it.

Wallkill State Prison looked to me like an old golf and country club. What is it about great lawns on houses of horror? Wallkill was located in the heart of a green and serene valley.

We drove up a long and swirling drive from the road to the prison entrance. On the way up, I saw a swimming pool, tennis courts, and an outdoor gym. I whistled, "What a layout ...."

"Scumbag, I don't remember giving you permission to speak."

I felt like answering, *Scumbag, I don't remember you telling me I needed it*, but I had learned a thing or two.

When we got to the top of the road, the Cyclone pulled up and stopped, scowling while he unlocked my chains. I stepped out and tried to stand but fell to the ground. My legs were so cramped, I couldn't move. I tried to get up but my legs wouldn't cooperate. So the Cyclone kicked me in the ass, screaming. "Get the fuck up!"

But one of the Wallkill guards yelled out, "Hey! I don't think that was necessary!"

A guard didn't think kicking me was necessary. Imagine that.

"It's necessary according to me! He's still *my* prisoner. But hey, if you want this piece of shit, take him. He's all yours."

The Cyclone walked toward the entrance of the facility, where he was met by a strong-looking Marine. Short haircut, clean shaven, excellent physique.

Both men studied each other until I waddled up, leg irons and all. The Marine asked, "What's with all the iron?" The Cyclone handed him a folder.

"Read that. Meanwhile, you can have him, my compliments, chains and all." He handed the guard his cuff keys.

I could see the guard didn't appreciate the Cyclone's attitude. He reached down and unlocked the leg irons and handcuffs. "Mr. Novell, please don't forget to take these with you. We won't be needing them."

Minutes later, I was sitting alone in the office of the principal keeper, called the P.K., enjoying a few rare moments of perfect silence. Not a voice to be heard. The principal keeper is the true muscle of the prison, with the warden being more of a figurehead. That message was reinforced by all the dead game on the walls: moose heads, deer heads, and a couple of bear claws. One sheep's head seemed to be staring me dead in the eyes. If we were back in the neighborhood, I would clock him for eyeballing me like that.

The silence was broken when the P.K. walked in and pulled out a chair. "So, Salerno, you hunt?"

That caught me completely off guard. I was prepared to be threatened, called names, and maybe mocked by him. I was all set to listen to him assure me I was a bag of shit who threw his freedom away and did not deserve any better treatment. So his gentle question grabbed me like a fishhook. It took me a second to find my words.

"Well, I'm not a hunter, I guess, but once I went with a bunch of guys from the neighborhood. They let me come because I am a butcher and I can cook, so I got the invite."

"Did you go?"

"Oh yeah, yeah. Let me tell you, these guys don't invite anyone on their hunting trips. Nobody. It's a sacred thing to them."

Another odd thing: the P.K. was actually listening. So I went on, "Anyway, on the first morning I was cooking bacon for the boys, when out of nowhere came this big fucking bear. He must of smelled the bacon 'cause he came a running, full on, snorting away. So I shot him."

"Oh, you shot him? You just shot him? What kind of a gun?"

"A beauty. A World War II German Mouser. Not only that, I was the only one to snag anything for the whole fucking trip. They were pissed because these guys are pros and they expect a lot of themselves. I mean, their campsite was a thing of beauty."

"Where did you hunt?"

"Way up in the Delaware mountains. One of the mob guys from the neighborhood owned some property, so we all went."

"I would like to ask you a question: what the hell are you doing in here?"

I smiled like you do when nothing is funny. "I got caught with my hand in the cookie jar."

"You know, when Warden Wilder asked me to look into bringing you here, I really had my doubts. The reason being this is your third prison in less than two years. That makes me wonder: what makes you so mobile?"

I just looked at the P.K. "I wish I had an answer. I guess when Sing-Sing was done with me they sent me on to Attica. Once I finally got to Attica, my appendix burst. A guard we called the African Cyclone told the Warden that the Muslim trouble-makers and I were thick as thieves. Like he thinks an Italian Jew is gonna picnic with a bunch of Muslims."

"Who is this African Cyclone?

"The Captain, that officer you met outside. He drove me here."

"All right then, Salerno, I can tell you he's not why you're here. You're here because you got skills. We need you to teach these inmates how to cut meat. Far as I'm concerned, what went on in Attica has nothing to do with you being here. You were not transferred as punishment. I ordered those chains taken off of you first thing because Wallkill is a minimum-security prison. You can walk away anytime you please."

My eyes went wide. I couldn't help it.

"You're here on an honor system. No locks on your door. Your room is not considered a cell, it's more of an atmosphere. We also have a swimming pool, tennis courts, handball courts, and a full gymnasium. You play basketball?"

"No, Mr. Walden. Horses are my game. Can I get racing forms sent here?"

He chuckled. Not a huge chuckle, but it was better than a smack in the face. "Sorry, gambling's not allowed. Now, tomorrow you report to Moishe, the civilian who runs our kitchen. I can tell you this much, Moishe is a very good man, but at times he's a bit cantankerous. So be kind to him. Moishe does not have your experience with the butcher knife, either. So treat him well. You got that?"

"Yes, sir."

"When I say 'treat him well' I mean *don't* try to teach him."

"No teaching of Moishe. No sir."

Next, I was ushered to the cell block. Whoa! It wasn't like the cell blocks in Attica at all. All the doors were made of wood, and each door sported a window. The walls were painted a soft brown, giving the dormitory a homey feel. For a prison.

All the rooms featured a bed, a closet, and a sink, plus each had its own window. You could actually open or close the fucking window in your cell. How about that?

Then it hit me, *where's the toilet?* I turned to the guard. "What happened to the commode?"

He smiled. "7-7-6-7, it's at the end of the hallway right next to the showers, all in the same room, just like home."

"How do I take a leak at night?"

"Just open your door and walk down the hall and take your piss, like you were at home."

"The doors to these rooms, can you lock them?"

"No dice, sorry to say."

He saw the frown on my face. "You have a problem with that?"

"Well, yeah. Anyone can walk into my room. I mean at night when I'm asleep."

"We have a strict rule at Wallkill: no one is allowed into your room at any time. Only if *you* invite them in. You understand that?"

"I do, but what the fuck happens if someone comes in anyway, in spite of the rules, while I'm asleep?"

"Every man here knows he will be sent to solitary, and then shipped out. What we have is called the honor system. You understand that? Are we clear?"

I answered, "Yes, sir," but I wanted to say, *are you fucking kidding? The Honor System? How many of these motherfuckers have any honor?*

This joint was so relaxed, it felt too loose. Honor system, my ass. At least there was a guard at the end of the hall. That was the vantage point. In order to pass into the cell block, you had to go by him.

That at least kept you somewhat safe from the wacky population while you slept. The only problem was there were still ninety-nine inmates in that block who had access to your room at night and access to you.

I had already spent too much time in places like Attica to let my defenses down around a bunch of cons. For me, the setup was nerve-racking.

Then I noticed the doors opened out, so there was no way you could rig up some sort of barricade for protection at night.

They'd thought of that one already.

50

Sleeping With the Sharks

I don't know if I actually slept that night with one eye open, but it felt like it. I could hear inmates shuffling back and forth going to the crapper. It was supposed to feel casual, but it felt like sleeping while sharks circled around.

In the morning, I realized if I could get a piece of rope long enough for the job, I could tie one end around the inside doorknob and the other to the leg of the bed. Some strong guy could still get in if he wanted to bad enough, but he could never do it without waking me up first. That way, I could at least cancel out the sneak-up effect.

The breakfast bell was actually sort of soothing when it announced time for chow. I jumped up, got dressed, and was out the door in five minutes. But once I got outside my room, I stood there all alone.

Not another inmate in sight. You know how in the old Western movies some guy always says, "It's quiet ... too quiet."

Slowly, other inmates began to emerge from their rooms. No rush, every con was only half-dressed, some were still in slippers, others in pajamas, some just in their shorts. I felt like I just joined the circus. What kind of headcount was this?

Some young kid who locked up next to me stepped out and made eye contact. He smiled. "Hi, I'm Thomas."

"Yeah, Thomas. Salerno. From Brooklyn."

"I heard that's a good place to live. Someday I'm going to go there. I'm from here in Wallkill. I live in the town."

I looked at this kid; he was like a precious stone. What was he doing in here? A tall blond, thin, with long slender fingers. This guy was not a fighter.

"Thomas, what are you doing in this joint?"

"Oh. Well. My uncle had me arrested."

"For what?"

"I was working on his chicken farm and he told the police that he caught me fucking a chicken."

This kid looked so fucking innocent, when he told me that, I didn't how to respond. I stood speechless. Yes, me. Richie Salerno, Mister Motormouth. No words.

Thomas went on, "You know, you can go to breakfast at any time. You don't have to go at all if you don't want to."

"Just like that?"

"Yes. Just like that."

So off to breakfast we strolled, and it was very cool there, like a restaurant. They even had choices of coffee, tea, or water. While I was sitting with Thomas, I could feel us getting the once-over from the others, but there was no particular segregation by race or by gang membership in this joint.

I had to ask, "Thomas, what was the real deal with you and your uncle? I mean, a chicken?"

"Nah, he made that up. The real thing was, he was always trying to touch me and I didn't like that."

"Did you tell that to the cops?"

"Yeah, but my uncle knows everyone in town. He's been living in Wallkill all his life. The old goat told the police I had pissed in his scotch bottle. Ugly things that you can't prove you didn't do, so who would believe me? He's also the town pastor and the postmaster."

"Holy shit. Why didn't you tell your ma?"

"She's dead."

"What about your dad?"

"My dad is coming home soon. He's a Marine. He will take care of me. He told me and I believe him."

Just as we got up to leave, a skinny black man slid over to us. "They call me Skinny Joe. I'm from A block, across the hall." Then he leaned over and got into my ear. "I have my eye on this kid. You got that?"

I looked at him then. I also noticed three other dudes giving me the once over, so I told him, "Skinny Joe. Salerno from Brooklyn. Skinny Joe, I don't dig your attitude. So whatever you're selling, you better go somewhere else. Nothing here for you but a lotta pain."

The skinny man gave me a shit-eating grin, then got up very slowly and went back to his buddies. I looked around. There wasn't a guard in sight.

I turned to Thomas. "Tell me, what do you do in here?"

"I work in the library. It's okay."

"Thomas, you have to be careful in this joint. I mean, you always have to be hanging out with some guys. You can never be alone."

"Can I hang out with you?"

"Yeah, but you're in the library and I'll be working in the kitchen."

"Can you get me a job with you? I can wash dishes. Or I can serve people!"

"Mm. Yeah … okay. I'll check it out, that's for sure."

When we left the mess hall, Skinny Joe and his cohorts were all in attendance giving me the stink eye. Seems he wasn't the only one with his eye on the kid.

* * *

I walked into Moishe's kitchen for the first time, and it was immaculate. Everything shined. The surfaces glistened. Moishe was a five-foot-five bald Jewish man with a big belly and a full beard. He had a feel of kindness about him, and he approached me smiling. "Salerno! Moishe Weinberg. Pleasure to have you here."

I thought, *wow, what a fucking reception.* "Moishe, thank you. I'm glad to know you, too."

"Good, now let's get down to business." He waltzed me into the butcher shop"

"Moishe, this joint is beautiful."

"Yep. And I got just the job for you."

"Bring it on, that's why I'm here."

"You know we got a pig farm here, the best in the county, beautiful white Landrace pigs. I knew you were coming, so I have 200 hundred pork butts all ready. What should we do with them?"

"Moishe, let me slice them up nice and thin, so you can make pork cutlets. These pork butts will go a long way."

"This is good, Salerno. This is very good, but a lot of work."

"Yes, I'll need another pair of hands.

"Agreed."

"Great. Now Moishe, I know this kid in my cell block, he'll be perfect. Is he okay?"

"I'll call the P.K."

"Thanks, Moishe. Thanks a lot. Would you like me to cut up some pork cutlets for you to take home?"

He laughed. "Strictly kosher! No pork."

My first week working in the kitchen was good. Moishe and young Tommy got along great. At the end of that week, I was busy breaking down a side of beef when P.K. Whalen entered.

"Salerno, tell me what happened in the recreation room the other night?"

"Nothing much, Mr. Whalen. Dykes got frustrated when I asked him to change the channel. He blew his top."

"What for?"

"Mr. Whalen, I don't have any idea what goes on in that guy's head. He just lost it."

"Salerno, I just went through your record. I see a pattern that disturbs me. You seem to have a short fuse. The stuff that you were involved in, in Sing-Sing …."

"What stuff?"

"Seems you were deeply involved in some kind of a racial dispute?"

"No racial dispute, Mr. Whalen, that was a gambling issue, a sore loser so to speak."

"Mm-hm. Then the Attica fiasco makes it seem like you have a nose for trouble. They say you were tight with the Muslim radicals there."

"The Attica thing, Mr. Whalen, I was just a bystander, pure and simple."

"What am I going to do with you?"

"Mr. Whalen, I get what you're saying, but I like it here, I need this shot to make parole. I got a bunch of kids out there, and I plan to play ball with you here."

"Salerno, I got this feeling you're a fix-it man. So the next time you think something needs fixing, I want you to come to me. Don't fix it yourself, or you'll find it doesn't get fixed. That's the only way you're going to survive in here."

"Mr. Whalen, I'm sorry, sir. I really am. And I don't want to get on your bad side, sir. But it sounds like you're describing the life of a snitch. I wouldn't know anything about being a snitch."

"Tell that to your kids. You keep secrets, you'll never make it out of here."

Moishe walked in at just the right time. He called out, "Whalen, I need this beef cut before noon. Cut the bullshit and let Salerno do his job."

I looked at the P.K., smiling. "You told me Moishe was cantankerous."

P.K. did not share my humor. But at least he turned and walked out. I had just dodged a bullet.

* * *

The next three months were golden. I did my job, stayed to myself, and the best thing was, Dykes got transferred to Green Haven Prison. With that episode behind me, I was just about to go stand in the chow line when the P.K. entered my room.

"Salerno, Warden Wallhick wants to see you."

When I heard that, I knew I had to immediately adjust the situation with a new scam. "The warden?"

"Yes, Salerno, the warden here is a civilian from the University of Columbia. Can you listen without agreeing or disagreeing, liking, or disliking, or planning what you'll say when it's your turn?"

"Yes, sir. I can do that."

"And when talking to the warden, can you say what you need to say without bullshitting?"

Of course not. But I could feel my abdomen jumping up and down with anticipation. My whole body sensed an Edge. "Absolutely."

"Do that and you will be in good shape. Fuck around and I will ship you out of here so quick you won't be able to find your asshole."

"Mr. Whalen, when you go to sleep tonight, please take a few minutes and pray for me."

"Salerno, see what I mean about you? Now, was that a wise crack or were you sincere?"

"Oh, I'm as serious as cancer, Mr. Whalen. Thanks."

"Don't thank me. This was not my idea. Personally, I think you are a risk. I read your report many times. So don't fuck with me. I know you got that big I.Q. rolling around in that scheming head of yours."

He turned and walked out the door.

Driving up the road to the Warden's home was a lesson in humility. The P.K. was laying down the law big time.

"Salerno, this is a big responsibility, working outside the prison. Everyone but me likes the idea. Absolutely no contraband goes into that prison. Not a fucking toothpick of any kind. There's a huge responsibility facing you. I'm counting on you to handle it. What worries me is, the warden has a sister and three daughters. You get my drift?"

Yeah, I got his drift, but it was the same as anybody else's drift: stay away from the daughters. What else? Did anybody ever say, "Oh, and there are three daughters living there, so I certainly hope you can grab each one at some point and fuck her eyeballs out."

Maybe to you. No one ever said it to me.

We drove the rest of the way in silence. Then in the distance, I saw a sprawling three-story home surrounded by manicured lawns and old oak trees. We pulled up to a Victorian mansion.

Standing in the driveway was a six-foot man dressed in a white linen suit and wearing a white panama hat. He moved toward the car but I saw right off he was staggering. The P.K. shot me a look. "Salerno, not a word."

"Yes, sir."

The man bellowed in a huge voice, "Mr. Whalen! You brought my discovery! Thank you!"

His "discovery?" Right away I thought, *This guy is a fucking drunk.*

"Warden, this is Richard Salerno."

"Salerno, I want you to know the doctor who took out your appendix is a friend of mine. He told me you make a mean marinara, and son, I do love Italian food. That's why you're here."

I saw the P.K. roll his eyes. "Warden, he's all yours."

"How late can I have him?"

"Ten o'clock is lights out."

"But if I need his services a little later, I'm sure no one will mind. Right?" Warden Wallhick grabbed me by the arm without waiting for the answer. "Let's go, Salerno, we're going shopping!"

The P.K. stepped in front of the Warden. "Remember, Warden, I'm responsible for that inmate."

"I know, Mr. Whalen, and I'm responsible for you and that whole fucking bunch we got down the road. Now, if you will excuse me, I'm getting hungry."

The warden looked at me. "Son, you don't have any rabbit in you. Right?"

"Not a trace, Warden."

* * *

The kitchen was as big as a gymnasium. A double oven went wall to wall, refrigerators and tabletops filled the room. Wooden floors supported a giant marble island filled with every alcoholic drink known to man.

I was slicing up onions when the warden appeared, drink in hand. He winked at me. "Son, if I allow you to drink, you know you cannot ever go into that prison drunk. Right?"

"Oh. Right! Right, Warden."

"See, I hate to drink alone."

"Understandable." I smiled. "Vodka and soda with a piece of lime, if you don't mind."

While Warden Wallhick was happily making me my drink and I was engrossed in chopping up garlic, in walked this red-headed female, a big-assed beauty with a pair of tits that went from here to there. They looked real, too. But when I heard the ear-splitting sound of a wolf howl, that was probably just my imagination.

"Hi, we didn't get a chance to meet. I'm Eunice Hutton Carter, Mr. Wallhicks' sister. I run this house."

I smiled. I couldn't not smile. "Whatever you need, please don't hesitate to ask. How many for dinner tonight?"

"Five of us. Me, the warden, if he makes it to dinnertime, plus his three daughters."

"Yes, ma'am."

While I was busy cooking and the warden was busy drinking and smelling the marinara, I said, "You know, Warden, this is a big place you got here, and it's three stories high. I mean you gotta climb three flights of stairs to get to the top. That's a lotta stairs."

He laughed. "Son, I never get that far."

I thought some more. "Warden, I think you should have an elevator put in this joint. Get some of the bigger guys to come in and do the labor for you."

He snickered. "First off, this is no 'joint,' it's my baby sister's playpen."

He thought some more. "But you know, that might not be a bad idea. So tell me, anything else on your mind?"

"Yes, since you asked. I say a man in your position should also have a butler, a gentlemen's gentleman."

"Mm-hm. So far, I like your style."

While I finished mixing the meatballs, I told him, "Warden, that prison of yours has all the guys you'll ever need to make your life here more comfortable. Get yourself a warden's gang and put 'em to work. Lotta guys would jump at the chance."

"Do you think the state will let me have one?"

"I can tell you this much: the warden in Attica has a warden's gang, and the warden at Sing-Sing has one, too."

He gave me a long look while he took another shot of his favorite Scotch. "My sister would love a housekeeper and a maid. My daughters would, too."

"In that case, I got good news, Warden. There's a kid locked up next to me, his name is Tommy Moats. He would make a great house boy. You know, pick up after you, serve you your drinks, get you what you need."

"Damn it if you didn't give me a great idea. I'll talk to my sister. What about a cook?"

"Cook? Warden, what cook? You got me!"

51

Easy Living

On the following day, a guard came to tell me to get ready to work on the warden's gang; however, when I got there, he didn't seem thrilled to see me, so I started right in, "You know, Warden, I haven't had the opportunity to make you my grandmother's favorite dish."

"Okay wise-ass, let's hear it."

"Lasagna, cooked with crushed meatballs, three cheeses, veggies, and Grandma's most delicious marinara sauce."

"You know, Salerno, you are one of the most interesting characters I have ever met. And for that reason and for that reason alone, you are going to make me your wonderful grandmother's lasagna. Right?"

"Right, Warden!"

I went back to my room feeling pretty good about things and slept like a baby, until I woke up to hear Tommy screaming next door, "No! Please! You're hurting me! Oh, God! *Please.*"

What the fuck??? I stormed out of my room, ran into the hall, only to be met by a solid right hand to the face. Another jammed into my stomach.

I went down hard and rolled across the hallway. Rule number one is get up and do it fast. I jumped to my feet and fired a left hook into the skinny bastard who was attacking me, catching him across his jaw. Right to the turn-off button.

He went down to stay. But then I got a foot planted in my back. It knocked the wind from my sails, and once again I went straight to the floor. I looked up to see a knife coming my way, so I spun away and rolled on the floor until I could get to my feet. All this time, Tommy was crying out, "Please! Please no more!"

Then *here comes the knife* so I dropped to the floor and kicked the feet out from under the attacker. He went down and I kicked him in the face, then ran into Tommy's room. There was Skinny Brown, buried in Tommy's ass. I grabbed him by his shoulders, pulling him out of Tommy's ass. Unfortunately, what with the suction effect and all, out came some of Tommy's innards in the process.

I threw Skinny Brown into the hallway with a kick in the nuts. Then he ran to his cohorts and they all scurried down the hallway. I screamed to the guard, "Stop those motherfuckers!"

But what I saw, I could not believe. The guard opened the gate and let the assailants get away. Apparently, just ending the confrontation was enough for him. Justice wasn't his problem.

* * *

Sticking up for Tommy got me a stint in solitary. By the time another three months passed, I was sitting with my thoughts starting to wobble toward the crazy side of things.

Finally, the hack on the night shift came to the door. "Salerno, you have a visitor."

A visitor? What the fuck was going on? No one knew where I was. A minute later when the ancient cell door opened and light flooded in, I almost passed out from getting stabbed in the eyes by the new brightness. The guard gave me a minute to get my eyes open again, then I was led off to a waiting room.

Another hour or so passed before the door opened. In walked a young man in his twenties, dressed to the nines. Suit and tie, crisp and clean, a great shoeshine.

He put out his hand. "J.J. Hines. I was sent here by Thomas Moat's father."

"What? Tommy?"

His father, the marine? The one who was gonna show up and fix things? I thought Tommy made him up.

"I'm their lawyer. Now I'm yours. I'm here to make sure you are being treated well."

He looked at me. "When was the last time you had a shave?"

For a second, all I could do was eye the guy. Then I went off the wall. "First off, what the fuck happened to Tommy? And second, what about those motherfuckers who opened up his ass, counselor?"

"Have you not had any information at all?"

"Oh yeah, and before I forget, the guard on duty that night. What happened to that piece of shit? He let them in from the other cell block, he had to. Then he let them out again. The no-good cocksucker is responsible for all this!"

I wound up panting and had to sit down. I hadn't worked up that much exertion in months. I was spent.

The lawyer just listened, calm as a cucumber. "Mr. Salerno, my employer wishes for me to assure you Thomas is doing quite well, thanks to you. Instead of suing the Board of Corrections, I made a deal for Tommy's release."

"He's *out*? Tommy's okay and he's actually out?"

"Yes. To answer your question about the prison guard, this is not for public knowledge, very classified and all that, but I think they sent him more or less to Siberia. My advice is to let the issue die."

"Siberia?" This was happening way too fast.

"Now that leaves you."

"Me? What about those scumbag rapists?"

"They have been charged, and they will have their day in court. I'm sorry, but the law is the law. I know you realize that. Now, once again, that leaves you …."

"I heard you the first time. Me. Now when the fuck do I get out of this shit-hole?"

"That I cannot answer. I'm only here to make sure you are being treated properly under the law."

"Counselor, you tell Tommy I'm okay, will you? Thank him and his father for looking out for me. But you know, I do a good thing and here I am, locked up like a dog in double-door security like *I* was the bad guy. What the fuck is that?"

"Mr. Salerno, I'm being paid to check on you every day and make sure you are being treated okay. That I will do."

"Yeah I get that, but *please* do me a favor and go upstairs and talk to the P.K. He can move me out of this shit-hole in a flash."

"I already did. He assured me you will be out of solitary in the morning."

Some people, they just have to save the good news for last.

* * *

The next morning at five o'clock, there I was sitting in the P.K.'s office and smelling like a sewer after not bathing for ninety-one days. When the P.K. arrived, I could smell his cologne before he walked in.

"Salerno, I see you are in need of a shave, a bath, and a new set of clothes. Unfortunately for you, you have to wait until you get to your next stop. I'm not sorry to see you leave. I never wanted you here in the first place. I always knew you were going to be a thorn in my side. I knew you were a wise-ass, I'm in this business a long time, and I can smell them."

That's right, he told me he smells wise-asses like it's something to brag about. Two guards walked in and started to chain me up. When the hammerheads finally finished, I couldn't move. I could barely stand and couldn't walk at all.

"Mr. Whalen, unless you like it wet in here, I would advise you to get me to a fucking toilet. Cause, I gotta take a piss awful bad."

"Salerno, do what you got to do. I'm done with you."

I did, I pissed, and in seconds I could feel the warm piss running down my legs, boy it felt so fucking good, pissing in his immaculate office. I was there surrounded by a warm puddle when two long-armed leathernecks walked in.

Six-footers for sure. They checked me out. Whalen handed them a report, and one leatherneck opened the file and his eyes got wide. Then came the surprise. "You know, Whalen, for what he's done, he should get a fucking medal. Get those fucking chains off him."

Things suddenly got interesting.

Whalen shouted, "As long as he's on my prison property, the chains stay! When you get him to Dannemora you can do what you want."

The two giants flanked me and helped me waddle out the prison gate. They weren't harsh about it, though, and once we all got outside, they smiled.

One said, "Salerno, I'm Horace, and that's my partner Willie. Now let's get this iron off you." By the time that was done, the warden himself came driving down the road. He parked his car and wiggled out.

"Sorry, kid."

I just nodded.

"These guys will take good care of you. Dannemora is a tough joint, so watch yourself."

52

The Funhouse

Turns out Horace and Willie were just two rednecks from Dannemora who were basically waiting for their pensions to catch up with them. It was as simple as that.

Willie was a tall leathery farmer with the hands of a steel worker. Grinning, he handed me a can of chew. "You chew, son?"

"No, Willie, not yet."

"Well, the warden said to take care of you and that's just what we're gonna do."

Horace spit into a cup and said, "Steak. Pussy. Some good chew. Then a nice cold beer."

I replied, "In that order?"

"I tell you, me and Willie, we're going for some of that fancy New York pussy."

I figured that had to be bullshit but decided to play along. "Let's do it, Horace! Let's do it!"

Horace put the pedal to the metal and we were on the way. I was sure this had to be some sort of joke, but they kept on being serious about it. They kept acting like we were really going to do this.

But I was hungry as hell, and my stomach started growling with anticipation when we pulled into the driveway of a big red house with a neon sign flashing, "PUSS'S PLACE."

This joint was a thing of beauty, not just a restaurant, but an old-world whorehouse with all the trimmings. Then Willie handed me a jacket.

"Get that prison shirt off. We wouldn't want to give this place a bad name."

Sure. The coat will make me smell better.

Horace sang out, "Boys, a den of happiness is coming right up!"

No bullshit? This party was actually happening? Turned out these boys wanted to have themselves a good time and they didn't mind if I joined in. That just made it more fun for them, more like they were being bad boys.

I felt like I died and went to heaven.

Willie was moving pretty quick. Horace yelled, "Willie, slow down or your gonna pop your load 'fore we get thar!"

But Willie was joyful. "Horace, I want two this time! I wanna stack 'em one top of another. We got enough cash for that?"

Horace grinned. "We got plenty. Warden said show Salerno a good time, then he slipped me three hundred."

The warden! So that's why he showed up to send me off.

Willie zoomed up the walk, then I hit the bell. When the door opened, I almost passed out from the fresh smell of perfume. Man, it had been a long time since I smelled perfume.

Standing there was a tall brunette with the shape of a zaftig fashion model. Horace smiled. "My, oh my, Miss Puss, you get prettier every damn time I see you."

Miss Puss just smiled. "You boys look like you all need a bath. Especially the young one."

Miss Puss gave me the once over. We locked eyes.

"Willie where did you pick this one up?"

"Wallkill."

"What am I supposed to do with him?"

I spoke up. "Miss Puss, I'm Richie Salerno and all I need is a bath and a little loving, and I will do the rest. I'm so ready."

"Well then, Mister Salerno, let me show you the way to paradise."

Willie grabbed me by the arm. "Now remember, you're on your honor."

Miss Puss smiled. "Willie, don't worry. He'll be too busy. Besides he doesn't look like he has any rabbit in him at all." It seemed like everybody I ran into already knew about that running rabbit phrase.

Miss Puss guided me into her inner sanctum. Gold faucets, marble bathtub, and a commode fit for a king. For a guy in my position, the place was breathtaking. I just stood there smiling, so she said, "Salerno, don't just stand there, get rid of those smelly rags."

I started to undress.

Miss Puss stopped me. "Here, let me help you."

As soon as she touched my skin, my plumbing started to come alive. Then the perfume hit me. The closer she came, the stronger the scent.

You would think my unwashed smell would have turned her away. But Puss lifted off my shirt. Her dainty fingers were now touching all of me. I felt like, I really didn't know what, like I was in a time vacuum. She was a pro, smooth and so wonderfully attentive. Finally, she unbuckled my pants. Of course, I wasn't wearing any drawers, so there was my swollen stick all thick and wide and ready to go.

Puss took a step back. "Oh, you sweet thing. I think instead of calling in one of the girls, I'm gonna do you myself. I don't usually get involved with customers, but just look at that thing."

My Johnson was standing straight as an arrow. It was so hard I thought the skin was going to split. Then she reached for a towel, ran it in hot water, and gave it a squeeze. She wrapped it around my dick and gently rubbed. Then she took me into her warm mouth and let me tell you with some very wonderful strokes she knocked me to my knees. I had no fucking chance. I exploded into her mouth.

Legs weary, I let her guide me into a warm bath. Then as I slid into the hot water, I mumbled, "Lord please let me die here." I wallowed in that perfumed water happier than I had been since I last walked in the outside world.

The next thing, Miss Puss's silky smooth body slid in next to mine. I watched her beautiful breasts being cupped in her hands, then she said, "Here, let Mommy feed you. You look awful hungry. Look, look, how full they are! They need to be sucked." She guided her hardened nipple into my mouth. While I sucked on her, I thought, *Salerno, this is a hundred-thousand-dollar hooker you're working on.* Then I felt her body shake with passion. "Yes," she moaned. "Mommy needs to feed you."

I don't know how long we were in that water, but my fingertips and toes wound up getting waterlogged. She finally stood up and I looked at her luscious black bush.

"Puss, you know it's beautiful, it's a beautiful sight."

Smiling, she lowered herself onto my face. At some point, the warmth, the clean feeling, the satisfaction, all combined to put me soundly asleep.

I dreamed about pussy all night long. I saw myself in every possible sexual situation. But I was rudely awakened from that dream by someone shaking me.

"Wake up, Salerno! Wake up, goddamn it!" Puss was standing over me with deep concern on her features. Seeing that look, I jumped up. "What?"

"Willie is dead, that's what. Dead!"

My half-awake brain started to scramble. "What? How?"

"The old fuck went and had a fucking heart attack! I told him not to do all that coke."

"Son of a bitch!" I shouted, panic filling me. "Now what? Where the hell is Horace?"

"Horace took off last night with a couple of the girls to go gambling. I haven't seen him since, only God knows where he is. Listen to me, Salerno, what the hell do I do with Willie's body?"

Maybe the pressure was cracking me up, but I started to laugh. From my perch, this was a funny deal going on here.

Puss looked at me like I was crazy. "What's so funny?"

I threw my hands into the air and gestured around the room. "This whole situation. Look, Willie's dead, Horace took off with a bunch a hookers, and here I am serving hard time in a whore house. If that ain't funny, you tell me what is."

Puss wasn't into my humor thing, what with the dead guy and all. "Salerno, I got a dead fucking redneck cooling off in the next room. What am I supposed to do with him?"

I thought Puss was only seeing this from her end of the problem. "Him? Fuck him! What about *me*? What am I supposed to do? I can't go home, I can't call the police, and I sure can't stay here."

"So what are we going to do?"

"I'll tell you, we're gonna sit tight until Horace and the dames show up."

"No, Salerno, you don't know Horace. When he has a pocket full of cocaine and a couple of hookers, it could be days. Longer if he hits a couple jackpots."

"Look, Puss, if these guards don't check in with their supervisors, the brass is gonna think something happened. Then all hell will break loose around here."

"What are you talking about? Nobody knows where the fuck you are. Willie never checked in with the prison. Think about it: 'See ya, I'm going to Puss's Place to get laid.' He never did that. Why don't you just keep on going?"

Puss picked up a set of car keys. "Take my car. Keep going south till you hit the thruway."

I looked at Puss and for the first time in my life, I was at a loss for words. Puss broke the silence.

"Salerno, how come you didn't think about that?"

I heard her, but in my mind, I was still backtracking, how the fuck do I get out of this? Just keep on going? South America? Boston? Cuba? Go look up old friends? Go to work on a farm? Call Ma? I didn't know what the fuck to do, I wasn't prepared for this. I was only supposed to take a ride, eat a steak, and get laid.

What the fuck am I gonna do? Maybe call the Hawk? Call Swivel Tooth? Yeah sure. Call Swivel Tooth.

Then I had another thought, if I was good in the joint, I could be out in five years, then I thought *that's only 60 months*. That ain't too bad. My head was spinning. Because if I split now, I'd be running for the rest of my life.

No plans, no money, no nothing. Fuck it! I looked at Puss. "Puss, I better call the prison myself."

"What? Who are you gonna call?"

"The warden, that's who."

"Salerno, you just can't pick up the phone and ask for the warden."

"Okay, then, you call him."

Puss took the phone but looked at me in disbelief. "You sure you want me to make this call?"

"Yeah. I mean, I guess so. I don't know what else to do."

Puss broke into a smile. "Salerno, I got quite a bit of cash stashed. Whatta you say, I got friends in Rio. We could live there with no problems. No jail, no warden. We could live like kings. We drive over the Canadian border, I'll get us both passports. I also got friends in Canada."

Now my head was really spinning. I gestured around the room. "What about all this?"

"Not mine. I work for the warden. This is his gig."

"Good, then you call and ask for him."

I could see Puss was hurt.

"Look, Puss, I got four kids. And my Ma."

We walked to Willie's room. His eyes were wide open. They seemed to be following us around the room. Puss shouted, "Cover him up," so I covered Willie while she dialed.

"Hello, Warden Whipple, please. Just tell him it's Puss. He'll know."

"Warden, hi, it's Puss. Right. I have a situation here …. No, now …. *No,* right now. Willie Sparks has dropped dead. Plus, some other issues that need your attention and *only* your attention here at the house."

Half an hour later, which was agonizing for me, the warden came strolling thru the door and waving a paper in the air. "Salerno? Are you Salerno?"

"That's me in the flesh."

"What the hell are you doing here?"

"Getting laid. What do you think I'm doing?"

"You son of a bitch, you're supposed to be in jail, not in some whorehouse."

"I know, Warden, but your boys told me you wanted us to get laid. So I'm here and Willie is dead in the bed."

"Dead in the bed. What the hell happened?"

"As far as I can see, he shot one hell of a load."

The irate warden turned to Puss, but she was right there with a glass full of bourbon. He slugged it down, then sat and looked up at me. His expression spoke a world of outrage and it was focused on me.

I got a woozy feeling in the pit of my stomach. *This runt, he has the power to do anything.* At that moment, I wished I could reconsider Puss's offer. At this point, it sounded damn good.

So I sat next to the Warden, waiting for some kind of reaction from him. I didn't know what I was about to do, but fortunately Puss handed him another shot of bourbon. The little man gulped it down like he was dying of thirst.

Then Puss did a strange thing. All at once she had a polaroid camera in her hand and then she was snapping pictures of me and the warden.

He saw her and yelped, "What in the world are you doing?"

"Just a little insurance, I like this boy and I wouldn't want to see anything happen to him."

"Come on Puss, what is this, you kidding me or what?

"I wouldn't want anything strange to happen to him. You got that?"

He jumped up. "Puss, I don't believe it. You let this boy get into those steel bloomers of yours? Kiss my French ass, you're stuck on a fucking criminal?"

"Maybe I am. Anyway, you better do what I say."

"Puss," I told her, "you got my address, for sure. Thanks for the ride."

The warden guided me to the door. There was no other direction to go. I didn't have any rabbit in me.

* * *

The twenty-mile drive to Dannemora was interrupted by a black sea of grief and mourning while a major funeral procession wove through their neighborhood. Hassidic Jews were taking advantage of every viewing point, including balconies and lampposts.

I said, "I guess the dead guy must have been a holy man."

"Holy man, my ass. He was the best diamond smuggler there ever was. Don't let that procession fool you. Now tell me, what did you do to Puss? How does any man turn the head of a woman like her?"

"I can't say, Warden. I think it was just a little TLC and a lot of stern worm."

"A lot of what?"

"A lot of—"

"Yeah, never mind."

53

Dannemora Prison

The sight of Dannemora Prison was cold and dreary, foreboding. This wasn't going to be any kind of feel-good incarceration. When me and the warden pulled into the town, all I saw was walls, walls, and more walls. The prison looked like something Hitler would've built. High walls blocked out the sky, while their color scheme of battleship gray made for an eerie portrait.It looked like some kid dug a huge hole into the side of a mountain, and then stuffed it with a prison town.

I quickly learned about the cold there. Dannemora in the middle of the winter always feels about 30 degrees below zero. Early in my stay, when the night hack banged on my cell door at three in the morning, I thought, *Salerno, you could've found yourself a better gig than this.*

"Rise and Shine, city slicker. You gotta milk those cows."

"Officer, I never milked a cow in my life."

"Easy stuff, son. Just pull on those nipples same way you stroke that dick of yours."

Great.

The farm was a half-mile from the prison. The weather was in deep freeze mode, with snow so deep we had to be transferred in snowmobiles. Yeah, just like when you were kids on sleds. But as soon as the cold wind started ripping through me, I didn't feel ready for any of this.

I entered a barn filled with cows, but all I heard were the sounds of Chopin coming from loudspeakers. It wasn't turned up loud, but it was clear. I wondered why.

The cows were beautiful to look at, but the smell of cow shit was hot and overwhelming. Mr. Harrington, the notorious farm boss, stood with me and looked at the long line of cows. "Salerno, when your buckets are full, you walk in the middle of the barn because cows are very finicky. They kick, so be careful."

"Thanks, Boss. I got this. No problem."

No problem, my ass. On my way back to the pasteurizing room, I caught a kick that sent me sprawling across floor.

I came to in the prison hospital and found out I got clocked by Cow Number 1621. Seems like good old #1621 was a known fucking nut case, and this being the last straw for her, they shot her in the head.

How hard did #1621 kick me? A week in the hospital and I couldn't take a dump. Seems the kick to my back ruptured the pipeline to my ass. I was stuck in my prison hospital room when in walked Doctor Do-Good. The sigmoidoscope was his game, meaning he was going to examine my colon by means of a flexible tube that went straight up my ass.

Now get this: you get no anesthesia for this procedure. *It's easy stuff,* is what the doc said. "You can handle this, right?" Funny thing about what you can handle when you don't have a choice in the matter.

Once they stitched me up and I got back out, Mr. Harrington decided I wasn't a good candidate to be around cows, and maybe I would be better off raising chickens. I didn't argue.

Life went on and everything fell into one long, miserable routine. Mr. Harrington had his motives, too, beyond keeping Richie out of danger from marauding cows. He knew twenty-five thousand newborn chickens were already scheduled to come to the farm. Seems Columbia University calls all the shots when it comes to the farm, its animals, and supplies.

Once again, I caught a break by being in a place where my services were needed. Things went along fine and the months dragged by, until one day I came out of the hen house and walked into five prison guards all loitering around the chicken shack. At the corner of the garage was the warden, carrying a clipboard.

"Salerno, last night when I finally went to sleep at two in the morning, there was a $239,000 tractor parked in the garage. You know the garage on top of the hill next to your chickens? You hearing me?"

"Yes, Warden."

"Now tell me, do you know anything about that tractor?"

"Warden, I watched Mr. Harrington put that tractor to sleep last night. Saw it myself. Then he drove me back to the prison."

"Have you seen anybody carrying any feed from this location?"

"Well, yes, Warden. I see officers going into that garage all the time."

"Or maybe a tractor going out?"

My blood got cold fast. Whatever the truth of this might be, it would take no effort from the Warden to put it all on me. For all I knew, the whole thing might be an insurance scam, with me in the middle.

"Warden, maybe I haven't been in here all that long compared to other guys, but you know, I'm getting ready to see the parole board. I am one hundred percent keeping it clean, sir. I'm just your chicken wrangler, that's all."

"Yeah, you are, but you and Mr. Harrington have been together a while."

"Please, Warden, say what's on your mind."

"The fucking tractor is on my mind, Salerno."

"Warden, my story is simple. Mr. Harrington parked the tractor in the garage, and then he drove me back to the prison. What happened after that, I don't know."

"Who has the keys to the garage?"

I reached into my pocket and tossed them to him. "There they are."

"No duplicates?"

"Not that I know of, but you can't really tell."

"You know, Salerno, why is it you're always around when things happen? Your bio shows you, time and time again, involved in shifty things. Why is that?"

"Warden, that I don't know. But I do know this, I'm not involved in anything that could hurt my chances for parole. No way. It wouldn't be worth it."

At that moment, my pulse would have been about right for a sprinter. He let me walk out, but I knew it wasn't over. There I was, anxiously awaiting the parole board, and now this thing was spinning around and tearing through my future like stray bullets. Wardens, tractors, PKs, prison guards, all with the ability to report to the Board of Parole.

Then, on the morning of my parole hearing, who should show up but Mr. Harrington in the fucking flesh. There was no way to know if it was good news or bad.

"I'm Angus Aloysius Harrington, Mr. Johnson. I was ordered here to speak on behalf of inmate Salerno."

Johnson wiped his running nose, sneezed, then glared at Mr. Harrington. "You never sent in your report."

"Struck down with scarlet fever."

Johnson wiped his running nose again. "Mr. Harrington, there was nothing wrong with your tongue."

When I heard that remark, I knew the shit was on, 'cause no living ass on this fucking planet can talk like that to Mr. Harrington and get away with it.

I knew he was going to rip Johnson a new asshole. And I knew right then I never had a Chinaman's chance in hell at getting paroled.

Mr. Harrington stood eyeing Johnson.

"Take a seat. Mr. Harrington."

"I would rather stand."

"I have trouble seeing you."

"There's nothing wrong with your hearing is there?"

Ah, shit. Two minutes into this hearing, and I was already dead in the water. Those two went at it for a solid half hour, debating details of my prison record.

Mr. Harrington finally relented, but before he left, he looked at Mr. Johnson and said, "I have something to say to you. I'm done with you because there is no sense of reality in your mind. You follow? Salerno here is a caring human being and he should be sent home to his children."

Johnson picked up a report and sputtered. "Did you know while Salerno was in Wallkill State prison, he beat four men senseless? He never went to get the guard on duty. Never stopped to think. All he did was to react."

I jumped up once again, not thinking. "Mr. Johnson! There was no time to think! Some poor kid was getting raped!"

Raped is right. Turned out there was a lot of it going around.

54

The Long Wait

Oh man, it was gut-wrenching to sit in that cell and wait for a decision. But I always try to be a positive guy and it seemed like I should dare to hope.

To my surprise, who should appear at my cell but the warden himself.

"Sorry, Salerno, you went and got yourself an R.O., two years reconsideration only. Come back in two. Next time, keep your mouth shut or you'll never win." So much for daring to hope.

* * *

Sixteen months dragged by. Every day there was a pressing prison problem brought to my attention, soaking up time. There is mercy, at least, in keeping busy.

At long last the day arrived when I was standing in front of the Frenchman, my private name for the warden. Being the charmer that he was, he sneered at me and said, "I hear you're having a ball with the other maggots."

I gave him a smooth smile of pasteurized bullshit. "Just doing my time, Warden, just doing my time. How was France?"

"That's none of your fucking business! I called you here because I see you are up for parole, so just a word of advice. You're going to face the same parole officer when the time comes, so keep your fucking mouth shut. I think you got a good shot to get the hell out of here. I'm going to recommend you for release.

"Now I have a lot of work to do. Good luck."

I just turned and walked out. Never said a word. I was too scared. It was like holding a ticking bomb. I had never been able to figure this guy out and it was too late now.

The following week, when it was time to see the parole board, I was scared deep down. Scared the way it is when you sleep but you don't get rest, and you eat but the food tastes bad, and every surface in your life is covered in blades.

I had taken my maximum dose of prison life. I asked for Keep Lock, the only privilege they allowed, so I would never have to leave my cell until I went to see the board. In this case, the isolation was much better than the random fate you had to accept walking around the yard with the other cons.

What a privilege. That was the longest seven days of my life. But the upshot was I made it to the hearing without any more marks against me.

The day of the hearing, I was a nervous wreck, washed out. I really had to push my will to go forward. Every bit of me inside was filled with this terrible dread. It must have showed more than I realized. When I walked into the Parole hearing, the Frenchman eyed me, and when I sat, Mr. Johnson looked at me and asked, "Salerno, are you okay?"

"Yes, sir."

"You look a little nervous."

The Frenchman jumped in. "Mr. Johnson, enough with the small talk. I have a pressing issue I have to attend to, but before I leave, I want this parole board to know that inmate Salerno here has been in my employ many times, and his attitude has been exemplary."

The Frenchman got up then, and get this, on the way out he actually cracked a smile. First time I ever saw that man smile.

Mr. Harrington spoke up, "Mr. Johnson, all I have to say to this board is, send this man home."

Mr. Johnson just sat there reading over the papers before him, and for the life of me I couldn't get a read on him. Finally, he looked up, straight at me. "Do have anything you wish to say to this board?"

"Yes, sir, I do. I'm not one of these guys that makes a quick U-turn and comes right back. I need to be with my kids."

"Speaking of children, how do you plan to cope with the fact that your wife has had two children since you have been incarnated?"

This one hit me hard. Maybe that was the purpose. I stood there wondering what could possibly be the right thing to say to them about that.

"Mr. Salerno. What about it?"

"Well, if she will trust me, I will give it my best shot."

"And if she doesn't want you?"

"Then I will build my life accordingly."

For thirty-six more hours, they kept me in limbo. It was just business as usual, I guess, just another fucking day. But not to a guy that has just done one hundred and twenty-eight months.

Then one of the water boys came strolling down the tier. He stopped at my cell. "Salerno, how about some fresh water?"

"No, thanks."

"Well then, how would you like to go home?"

"Willie, stop breaking my balls."

"Okay, I just thought you would like to know you're leaving on the first of the month."

Willie's voice went straight through to my brain. *"You're going home! First of the month! First of the month!"*

"Willie, how the fuck could you know that?" Oh, I needed it to be true.

"Salerno, when you been in this joint long as I have, then you'll know. You got two weeks to wrap up your business here."

I sat there shaking my head. *There's one for you, Salerno. The fucking burnt-out water boy just gave you the 411 on your life.*

There was, however, a small catch: what the parole board actually said was if I was going to be released on the first of the month, I had to be released into my father's custody. Otherwise, I would have to wait *another* six months, because all of the halfway houses were filled to capacity. Another six months.

I asked Rabbi Katz to place a call to my mom. She told the Rabbi she was very sorry, but my father didn't want me in his home. Rabbi Katz gave me his blessing and said. "Son, this too shall pass."

So will a kidney stone. Tell that to the patient writhing on the floor.

I was on my way to the big yard to see Joey the Blond, just as big and ugly as he ever was. He saw me and yelled out, "Salerno! What's going on with you?"

I said to the Blond, "Joey, my old man will not let me stay in his home, but it's a condition of my parole."

"He said that?"

"Yeah. Told the parole board a big, fat no."

Joey turned to a six-foot chunk of muscle. "Charley Dog here is getting out in the morning. I'll have him go see your old man."

This is one of the many ways inmates can and do reach out to touch someone from inside maximum security. I decided to go back into Keep Lock. I was a fucking nervous wreck.

It took a week of pacing the cell until little Willie the water boy gave me a message from the Blond. "He says all is good. No problem on the home front." Joey's man did his job.

I couldn't help laughing. My old man must have shit a fucking brick when Charley Dog walked into his shop.

Maybe things were starting to go my way? When Solly told the parole officer that he had a job for me working as a butcher, that was the clincher. I was all set. With a week to go, I was actually going to make my parole date.

* * *

It was September when I walked out of Dannemora State Prison, the same year the Mets won the World Series. I took my last look around, and then it was just a short walk to the bus stop. But then I stopped in my tracks. Standing there big as life was Mr. Harrington. I almost shit a brick. Grinning, he handed me an envelope.

"Salerno, here's a little walking around money." No hellos, no good byes, no conversation. He got into his car and left. It felt odd that he cared enough to give me money, but not enough to show me basic courtesy. Go figure. He left like a fart in the wind.

It got a lot more strange when I got onto the bus, sat down, and opened the envelope. Four grand. All in hundred-dollar bills, looking right up at me from their little hiding place down there in that envelope.

I kept my reaction cool because I didn't dare start attracting attention. But inside I had a good laugh. Because I always knew deep down it was Mr. H. who nailed that tractor. I knew because the key to the main gate that hung in my chicken shack was old, but on the day after the tractor disappeared, the key was shiny and new. Nobody thought to question it, and me, I don't have any snitch in me.

The warden had been right all along. He was dead sure it was Mr. Harrington. I smiled all the way back to New York.

55

Sure, You Can Get Out, But Can You *Stay* Out?

Checking in while on parole, trying to play it straight with them. Standing at 40th Street and 8th Avenue, I was a little numb and just looking at the parole building gave me instant butterflies. The people inside that place had the power to yank me at any time.

When I entered the parole office, sitting there was a young guy no older than me. He looked up. "Salerno, I'm John Dewey, your parole officer. Have a seat."

"You any relation to Thomas E. Dewey, the mayor?"

"Yeah, he was my uncle. You're good."

"Johnny, here's the truth. I can't stay in my neighborhood anymore. Too many mobsters. You know, after this dime I just did, it's like I'm a number one draft choice to be a made man in the hood. The problem is you're supposed to be honored if they ask. If you refuse, they take mortal offense. I mean the things these guys do for revenge. I gotta find a good neighborhood. Someplace where no one knows me."

"Oh, hey, if you find a good neighborhood, call me. I'll move there myself. Right now, you're going to live with your parents, right?"

"Yeah. That's where I'm headed today."

"Good. I see you got your old job back. That's good too, so stay loose and I'll see you next week."

"Yeah, okay. Thanks, Johnny."

"One thing. Tell me, Salerno, what is the best steak to eat?"

"Now that's a good one. Next week, I'll bring you a couple. I mean, better to show you than tell you, right? Other than that, the only thing I can tell you is to buy the best steak you can afford."

Then it was done and I was gone. I hustled out of the building, jumped into a cab, and laid back. "Brooklyn. 3805 Avenue P."

As soon as the cabbie hit Flatbush Avenue, I had him drive me around, looking at all the old spots. Ten years. Nothing had changed. All the trees were still there, the broken sidewalks still broken. It even seemed like all the garbage cans were in the same spots.

When the cabby pulled up to my mom's house, my old man was sitting on the stoop, smoking a big Havana. The sight of him there made me feel like I swallowed a bowling ball.

I got out and carefully walked over to him. He gave me one of his standard greetings.

"I want you outta here."

"Don't worry. I don't want to be here either."

"Another thing, don't be sending any more gorillas my way."

"Okay, Pop. Better yet, when Joey the Blond gets out next week, you can tell him that yourself."

I turned and walked into an empty home. Ma had moved out and Pop was there alone. It was such an empty feeling, to be stuck in that place with Charley the Pick.

I ran up to Fat Sam's, where I got the news about him. His wife Millie told me cancer got him. Fat Sam was a good friend. I cried for her. The hits kept on coming.

I tended to sit around by myself, depressed, maybe sucking up an egg cream. One day I opened up a newspaper to the sports pages, but nothing interested me, so I went to the rentals pages. And there it was, bright as day: "Singles."

Looking for single male, one bedroom, no cooking, facility is hot plate only! Must have a job. Call!

I'd say it was half divine providence and half dumb luck. Because my ma always told me there was no such thing as coincidence, it was "just meant to be." And that was true most of the time. No matter what it was this time, I got on the phone. When I hung up, I had myself a new room.

I never went back to my mom's house that night. I didn't want to see my old man or have to deal with him again. I took the train to Manhattan, checked into a nice hotel, had a good meal with three martinis, and fell off.

Bright and early, I went to see Johnny boy. He was all smiles, watching me slide through the door.

"What's up, Salerno?"

"Got a room in Queens. A nice family, a good guy and his wife and four kids. Greeted me like I was their long-lost son."

"How was the neighborhood?"

"Great. All residential homes. I don't see any gangs or mob guys hanging out there. You believe that?"

Turns out plenty of people believed it, the wrong people.

* * *

Getting lost from the neighborhood had been one thing, but disappearing was another. Frankie the Greek, who I grew up with, became a big man while I was away. As kids, we were inseparable. But we weren't kids anymore.

Frankie let it be known that he wanted to see me. The next Sunday morning, when everyone was in church, I met my old pal under the Brooklyn Bridge on the Manhattan side. It was damp, the kind of cold you feel in your feet. Frankie stepped out of his Cadillac, and we hugged and hugged, and he said, "You look great."

"You don't look so bad yourself, Frankie." And because guys like us don't appreciate bullshit, I said, "Frankie, I want to get right to it. I'm done. I saw enough in the last ten years to fill a book."

"Yeah, Salerno, when I didn't hear from you, I figured as much. All I want from you is this: I want to know how Tommy Eyeballs and No Nose Deluca conducted themselves inside."

"Frankie. If I do that, it makes me a stool pigeon. Right?"

Frankie just stood there scratching his beard. So I explained.

"That, pal o' mine, I cannot and will not do. I will tell you this, though, Frankie. The mob as we knew it has changed. It's not the same outfit anymore. Mobsters inside changed the whole landscape of respect. A lot of them turned stoolie and did whatever it took to get through the day. Frankie, I saw it in Sing-Sing, Attica, and Dannemora, all downhill. The problem being nobody knows who to trust anymore. I would never bullshit you."

He tried another angle. "You were in Wallkill, though. So what about Gino G, Potatoes, and Charley Wide Eyes?"

"Forget about it. All I can say is they were an equal disgrace, one and all. Don't bother with names. Fucking cry-babies. One more thing, I crushed Billy Blue's head 'cause he went after a good friend of mine. Frankie, this I will tell you, Billy fell in love with a young blue-eyed blond that got committed to Box A."

Frankie eyed me at that. He was awake now.

"But when Billy Blue supposedly went nuts, I think he was bullshitting. To tell you the truth, I think he faked it just to be with his lover. I'm done, Frankie. Besides, there are a couple of guys in the neighborhood that got made since I been away. I know them. They were little stool pigeons when they were kids. They know that I know that about them, too. So I gotta be careful. I've left the hood behind. Now I'm gonna get up early and cut meat. My wife divorced me and I can't blame my kids for wanting nothing to do with me. I'm gonna try to find myself a good woman."

We said some good-byes, but as I turned and walked away, I had a sense of a bullet hitting me in the back of the head. It was the hardest thing I ever had to do, to turn down a made guy who was also a boyhood pal. I knew I would never see Frankie again. The made guys were my idols once. Walking away, I knew I had turned an invisible corner.

I went to see Ma and tell her what happened between Frankie and me. She was alone in the apartment, standing in the kitchen and stirring a pot of sauce. I thought maybe she might throw a fit and fling hot marinara at me, but when I laid it all out, she didn't crack wise or give me any Ma the Mouth bullshit. Instead her whole face changed into an expression of pure relief. She told me, "Son, things like this are the little miracles in our lives."

56

Heeding the Wise Hooker

Walking up Nostrand Avenue in Brooklyn, I was filled with anticipation, wondering how this was all going to play out. After all, I hadn't seen Lucille or my kids in ten years.

I reached the doorstep of a rundown apartment house and looked up to the window, and there was that beautiful face. It hadn't changed. We locked eyes. I smiled and said, "Lou, how about a cup of coffee?"

She just nodded. I proceeded up the stairs, and with every step I was overwhelmed by the ugliest feeling. It slowed me down while I took the steps one by one, until I reached the top.

My family, existing like this. Living on welfare had to be tough with four kids, and then two more while I was away. I was embarrassed down to the bone, walking into this new world. When I first saw Lucille, I wanted to take her into my arms. But that was an outdated impulse. She wasn't mine anymore. Those days were gone.

My kids just stood there staring at me. For the first time in my life I had no idea how to behave or what to do. It was like I was in a time warp. Nothing moved.

I got flashes of things I had not done. Things fathers do with their wives and kids. Going to the playgrounds, helping them with their homework, going on hikes, having fun at grandma's house.

I knew the warden was right: *I let this happen* .... Finally breaking the uncomfortable silence, there was Lucille's live-in boyfriend. Her taste had not gotten any better. In fact, it seemed to have gotten worse. My heart sunk a few notches at the sound of his voice.

"Remember this, hot shot, you miss one child support payment, I will drop a dime on you so fast it will make your head spin."

Oh man, did that room get quiet. Lucille just stood there. Everything was suddenly very awkward.

Trying to break the uneasiness, I said, "You know, Lucille, since when have you become a collector of cheap trinkets?"

I looked him straight into his drunken eyes. "You got that?" I was overwhelmed with helplessness in the face of all this. I had to do something.

I guess I panicked. I said to her, "Look, Lucille, I'm not here to play any games with you. Please, I want you and the kids to walk out of this shit-house and come with me."

Just then the two kids she had with the drunk guy came running into the room. I nodded to her, "You can bring them, too." But Lucille gave me a long, hard look, and simply said, "I can't. You know I can't. We both know I can't trust you anymore."

And oh, damn it all, she was right. She and her kids made for seven people. I was a broke ex-con, fresh from the joint, having no way to support even a small family, let alone a group that size. Without friends who were made men, I had nothing.

I left feeling crushed but knowing she was right. If she were my daughter, I would want her to kick the jail bird to the curb. And she did.

So I was alone again, a single ex-con living the quiet life out in heavenly Queens. No mobsters, no wannabes, just me.

Before long, I was very lonely, and I felt the absence of a family. But thanks to my landlord, Christopher D. Sullivan and his brood of Irishman, I was made to feel at home as their live-in roomer. They were hearty meat-eaters, too, meaning I was soon sharing in the cooking and generally hanging out with them.

Yeah, things were going smooth, but I was still lonely for the company of a woman who was perhaps not a hooker. I tried being with a prostitute when I got out, and I was embarrassed because I couldn't get it up. Then the hooker told me, "You need to go find yourself a woman to actually be with."

No shit. But I just got out of prison.

I needed a woman I could talk to, a woman I could hold in my arms. Make me feel like a man. I was lost. But I knew I had to suck it up and pull my life together. Lucille severed her life and the kids from me.

After all that, I could only hope to pull my life together with a good job, then maybe get lucky enough to find a woman who was also my friend. That put me back working every day in the 14th Street Meat Market.

Life at that point was hard. The long days and the lonely nights started taking their toll. My only outlet after work was to go to Frank's Restaurant, located right across from Western Meats.

I was generally bushed by the time I got there, so I would just sit and have a drink. I told my friend, Solly, "You know, Solly, I been scared ever since I got paroled. It's like walking into a room full of powder kegs. Every day I wake up, I ain't got nobody. My family kinda disowned me. Not that I can blame them, but somehow it makes it even harder to know my parole officer could yank me back anytime."

But what was Solly going to do? It wasn't his problem and we've all got our own. He was a friend just to sit and listen.

Nothing changed the fact that the following day it was back to the mundane routine cutting. A butcher working in a cold room hour after hour has to be tough and skilled, but the thing about work like that is the long-term exposure to the cold. Somehow the constant deep chill made the loneliness of the city engulf me along with the bite of the air.

Coming to work and going home, the subways felt nearly as cold as the coolers. They radiated the feeling, *no one cares, no one gives a shit. Make a wrong move and that fucking parole officer will have your ass on a bus back to prison.*

By the grace of God, a co-worker came to me, "Salerno, you wanna buy a couple of tickets to my wife's dance?"

"You know I would love to, but I've got nobody to take to any dance."

"No worries," he told me. "You could take my wife's girlfriend. She's a nice gal."

A blind date? Okay. I never did one of those before. But I guessed it would be better than sitting in my flat looking at the walls.

Blind date. What do I do? The questions would not stop rolling around in my head. When the time for the date came, there was even more anticipation while I rode the subway to see her.

The loneliness swimming around in my head had me off my game while I knocked on her door. I didn't know what to expect when she answered.

But when she did, oh, she was gorgeous. A dark-headed beauty with a smile that could melt ice.

"Hi, I'm Ronnie's friend, Richie."

Her smile got bigger. "I'm Jenny."

In that first minute, I was so lonely and starved for affection, I would've done anything she wanted me to do. Lucky for us both she was a normal young woman.

The dance that night was wonderful. Finally, I got her home, and when we reached her door, she looked at me with her beautiful brown eyes, and said, "I had a great time."

It was so simple. So beautiful. This invisible expression of respect, of appreciation for the other person. It got me choked up for a minute. It was awkward but it was wonderful. It was a part of life I hadn't known in a long, long time.

Seemed as if, in the past, I had always been looking for adventure and not really for love. I felt certain this time I was looking for the right thing. A whole new world had opened up to me, and for some reason I wasn't scared anymore.

My first real date turned out as well as that hooker predicted it would. It changed everything. Everything.

All of a sudden, I had a different outlook about the subway, the buses, the cold, and getting up at 3:00 in the morning to go to work. Every day was hard, but knowing that I could call Jenny on her lunch hour gave me a whole new outlook on my life.

It was like carrying a little heater in my pocket.

* * *

Our next years together were the best of my life. I had married my best friend. The problem was my occupation. I was always looking for something else to do. It kept nagging at me. Working in the cooler every day was wearing me down.

I would look at the butchers who had been working for years in those ice boxes, and it was scary. Knuckles bent, backs bent, and most of all, the drinking. A nip here, a nip there, and then stitches here and stitches there, all ending up in a disaster.

I wanted no part of that. The injuries came along so often, the union converted a store front into a full hospital clinic for the butchers' injuries. Sometimes the cuts were so bad, the guy never made it to the hospital at all.

So I was constantly looking, without knowing where to go. The baffling question was frustrating in the extreme: how to start something new, something workable for me.

Watching television one night, I saw *Kojak* and I told my bride regarding his acting, "I can do that."

Then, when we were watching a good movie, I said, "I can also do that!"

I would cry out at every TV show and every film, "I can do that. I can do that! I can do that!" She finally yelled at me, "Shut the hell up and do it!"

Great idea.

Sitting in Frank's Restaurant pondering over what my bride yelled at me, I turned to my cohort, Eddie.

"You know Ed, I think I could act. I think I'm gonna be an actor."

"You're too fucking old."

A young waitress heard the remark and moved to me and whispered, "Mister, you know the big actor, Anthony Quinn?"

"Yeah, I know who he is."

"Well, anything he can do, you can do."

You get that? Bless her for her kindness. Like Ma said, "These are the little miracles in our lives." Once again, there seemed to be no such thing as coincidence. This was just meant to be. Because she had more to say.

"There is an acting school right down the block." That woke me up. I went home that evening and told my wife, "I signed up for an acting class today."

"You did what?"

"You heard me. Time to put up or shut up."

I walked into my first acting class without a clue of what to do. The room was full of wannabe actors. The teacher looked to me like an actor trying to get his message across the best way he knew how, but I really didn't know what to make of all this. I wondered how you teach someone how to act.

Funny, the first words out of the instructor's mouth were, "People, William Shakespeare said, 'To thine own self be true.'" I looked around the room, nothing seemed to register, so I went for it. "Does that mean you never rat on yourself?" Pointless humor. Bad habit. The instructor threw me a hard look.

"The most important thing an actor can achieve is to be still, inside of your own skin. Do that, students, and you will be on your way."

My big mouth got the best of me that first day. "Does that mean less is more?"

"Look, who are you?"

"Salerno."

"Salerno. If you listen, you might be able to learn something."

Good point. My big mouth was definitely a weakness in certain situations. I sat there and never said a word the rest of the day.

I also sat in that class for another ninety-three days, watching this actor teaching these kids the ropes, until the day came for me to waltz out the door singing happily, "See ya in the movies!" It was time to give it a real-world try.

That night, me and my bride made the best acting resume you could ask for from a beginner. It was true and honest. The honesty part was the catch. The resume read,

Experience – ATTICA PRISON: Studied the art of method acting. The art of survival for eight thousand, seven hundred, thirty-six hours.

DANNEMORA STATE PRISON: Studied Improvisation. The skill to be able to adapt to any situation.

Training – One hundred and sixty months. Sing-Sing: three years of comedy training. Sing-Sing, was a joke. Skills: Butcher, Cook, Tailor.

My lovely bride took it to work that day and made copies, then sent them out to every acting agent in the New York Metropolitan area.

Turns out when it comes to agents, if you stick to the real ones, there are not as many of them as you might think.

57

Starring Al Pacino

The only mistake I made was putting my boss's contact number on my resume. Good thing the boss was my friend Solly, because by the end of the workday, there were fifty-five phone messages sitting on his desk. You read that right. Fifty-five.

"Salerno, where do we start?"

I just stood there, totally flabbergasted. "Solly, I have no fucking idea."

"You know Salerno, this is first time I have ever seen you speechless." He smiled at me. "Okay, I'll pick one for you."

He studied the long list then said, "Why don't you start with an advertising agency? You certainly have the gift of gab." He looked some more. "Ah, here's one! Seems to me you have an appointment tomorrow at ten a.m."

I took the shot. The next day, at my first interview, I sat waiting in a hustling advertising agency. It was an otherworldly experience for an ex-con. So many good-looking women were all over the place, I got dizzy. Then a fashionable, short-haired beauty walked up to me.

"Mr. Salerno?"

"Yeah!"

"You have a ten o'clock with Steve. Follow me, please."

As I walked along this office, funny I didn't have any butterflies, the way you do when you look for work. I must say, looking at her wonderful ass helped. I was ushered into his office. It was huge!

A slight, skinny man sat behind a huge desk that was covered with papers. "Salerno!" he called from behind the pile. "I'm Steve Swartz, Managing Editor. I called you because I just loved your resume."

As soon as I heard him speak, I knew he was gay. He studied my resume while he went on, "This method acting you spoke of in Attica, do they have classes?"

"Steve, every waking hour in Attica was a learning experience. Mostly how to survive. You learn the method day by day, it keeps you alive. Get my drift?"

Steve watched me intently for a moment, then did a strange thing. He offered me a stick of chewing gum. I took it, and we both chewed while he studied my resume.

That night me and my bride were in bed talking over the interview. "Honey, he wanted to give me a blow job."

"So what's the big deal? You're no altar boy."

"Yeah, sure. That's all I need is a blow job."

Jenny cracked up. "Come on, big boy, what's a little cock among friends?"

Just then the phone rang. "Hello! is Richard Salerno home?"

"Who's this?"

"My name is Shirley Rich and I'm casting Sidney Lumet's new film. It's called *Serpico*, and it will be starring Al Pacino."

I slammed down the phone.

"So who was it?"

"Some bullshit call from one of the kids from my acting class."

"Did you ask who it was?"

"No, I just think some of those kids from class are breaking my balls."

The phone rang again. "Hello! Mr. Salerno, are you still there?"

"Look lady, I got no time for bullshit."

Jenny yelled, "Wait!" But it was too late. I hung up the phone.

"Why did you hang up so fast?"

"Babe, I gotta get up at 3:00 a.m." But right away, there went the phone again, ringing in my ears. "Son of a bitch!" I went to grab the phone again but this time I was too late. Jenny beat me to the punch. "Hello, who is this, please?"

"Once again. This is Shirley Rich. I'm a casting director and Mr. Salerno was recommended to me by my colleague, Steve Swartz. Is this his home?"

"Yes, it is. This is his wife, Jenny, but my husband is sleeping. He has to get up very early for work."

"Okay, then tell him to meet me at 6:00 a.m. at 600 Madison Avenue. I will be standing in the lobby waiting for him."

Smiling, my bride hung up. "See? It was legit!"

"Come on, Babe, that's a bullshit story. Meet a film casting director in front of a building at 6 a.m.? What kind of crap is that?"

"I believed her."

"Sweetheart, six in the fucking morning?"

"I believed her."

"In the fucking lobby? How about 'meet me in my office?' What happened to that?"

"I believed her."

"You know, sometimes you're so hard-headed."

"I don't care what you think. I believed her." She rolled over and showed me her ass. "I'm tired."

"What about me, now that I'm up?"

"Go to sleep. You're going to need your rest. You have a big day ahead of you."

Never slept a wink that night and 3:00 a.m. always shows up real fast when you can't sleep. Riding the subway with all the drunks and pimps at that ungodly hour was an adventure. Only on this day, I was on my own adventure with last night's phone call still ringing in my head. Should I or shouldn't I listen to Jenny? Was that a bullshit story or not?"

But then, right there in that miserable subway car, knocking me out of my daydream, were three punks standing too close right in front of me. Three wacked-out shit-heads. I could sense them cruising for trouble. My position in the corner seat on the train car made it easy for them to surround me, to cause trouble. Little did they know, at that moment, that they just got on the wrong ride.

One shit-head pulled out a knife and glared at me. "Let's have it," he said.

Their dangerous point of ignorance was that they were fucking around with their little pocketknives up against a butcher who was carrying his own much bigger knife, because he worked best with his favorite cutting tool. Out came my twenty-inch blade.

The train pulled into the stop and they ran out the door.

After that adventure, I walked down 14th street with my mind still struggling. *What should I do about this casting thing?* I would hate getting fucked over for some lousy joke.

Later, I was busy working a line of hindquarters, slicing off flank steaks, when Solly walked up to me. "Salerno, you're in a daze today. You're working these hindquarters like it was your first rodeo. What's up?"

"Yeah, Solly. Do I look that bad?"

"You do. What's on your mind?"

"Long story."

"Okay pal, let's have it."

"Last night, I got a call from a woman who says she's a casting director, casting a big fucking movie called *Serpico*, starring Al Pacino."

"So what's the problem?"

"Solly, I think it was a prank call from the kids in the acting class. The woman said to meet her at 600 Madison Avenue at 6:00 a.m. in the lobby."

"You better take my Caddy. It's parked out front. The keys are in the ignition."

"What? Solly, you think so?"

"Salerno, cut the crap! Madison Avenue is ten minutes from here. Go take a look. Hurry, it's 5:45."

That did it. I ran and jumped into the Caddy, still dressed in my greasy black sailor hat and wearing my bloody apron. I put the pedal to the metal and breezed up Madison Avenue, checking store fronts around the address I was given. My heart was pounding by the time I finally spotted a little old lady standing in the lobby of 600 Madison Avenue. I could not believe my eyes. I parked Solly's Cadillac, stepped out, and I just stood there looking at this lady. I edged closer, and I could see this was a classy woman.

Then I thought, *what the fuck, I must look like a crazy man, dressed in a greasy black sailor hat and a bloody apron.* I raised my hand. "Hi, I'm Richie Salerno."

"Well, it's about time you got here. I said 6:00 a.m. Can you act?"

"Can you?"

"I'm Shirly Rich. Follow me." So off to her office we went.

"Sit."

I sat and waited in my white, blood-stained apron. An hour went by. Then in came a bunch of character actors, one after another. I looked at them and they looked at me and gave me a wide berth. No one dared to sit near me. The blood on my apron was starting to smell, and to boot, it was hot and stuffy in that room. I was frustrated and just starting to walk out when a little guy dressed in jeans and a blue denim shirt strolled through the door.

I thought, *this guy's got to be the janitor.* So I asked him, "You going in that office?"

"Yes."

"Good, look I got to see some guy named Lumet and I've been here two fucking hours. I don't want to lose my job, so tell him Salerno has been waiting a long fucking time."

The little guy took one look at me then laughed and went into the office without saying another word. I was just getting ready to pack it in when Shirly Rich came into the room.

"Salerno, Mr. Lumet will see you now." News to my ears. I strolled into the next room—and sitting in the chair was the little guy in his blue denims.

"Who are you?" I blurted out.

"Who are you?" The little guy grinned. "I'm Sidney Lumet, the director. Where are you from?"

"Brooklyn."

"Have you ever acted before?"

"Yes, all my life."

Lumet smiled then handed me a script. "Here take this and go into the other room and study it." I waved him off. "Mr. Lumet, I got this. I've been looking at it for a couple of hours. Shirly gave it to me when I first got here."

Lumet looked at my resume. "How much time did you do?"

"Too much."

He smiled again. "Okay, let's do this."

"How do you want me to do this character?"

"Any way you want, Salerno. Just do it."

So I did, and when I was finished, Lumet just sat there studying me. Then after a while I said, "Look, I gotta get back to work." I got up to leave.

"Salerno, where are you going?"

"I told you, back to work."

"Don't you want to know what happened?"

I turned and looked at him. "What happened?"

"You got the part, that's what happened."

Hearing that, I was riveted to the floor. I didn't know what to say or what to do. Dumbfounded, scared, happy, you name it, all those good things.

I looked at Lumet not knowing what to say, I just blurted out. "Look Sidney, I'll need three hundred bucks. I gotta join S.A.G."

Lumet smiled again. "Roger, bring me in a check for three hundred. Salerno here needs to join S.A.G."

58

Lumet and Salerno

On my way out the door, Lumet stopped me. "Salerno, I need you for this part, so you have to be very careful."

"Sidney, I'm good. No more mob stuff, I'm done with that crap."

Lumet gave me that little-boy smile that I already loved. "I'm not talking street stuff, I mean the meat market. Very dangerous place to work."

"Sidney, no sweat."

"See you in a couple of weeks."

"Where do I go for work?"

"Roger will call you, but I know for sure the first scene will be shot right on the corner of 14 Street and Ninth Avenue."

I ran out of that building with the check in my hand, moving so fast that I never realized I left Solly's Cadillac parked on Madison Avenue. I just kept on running and running, back to the meat market. I finally arrived and ran in yelling the news to everybody I could see.

"I got the job! I got the job! I'm gonna be with Pacino in his new movie!" People were looking at me like I was a crazy man, especially running around the street in a bloody white coat and a greasy sailor hat.

This was before cell phones, and I didn't even have a coin to call my bride. My whole body was racked with anticipation. I ran to Junior's candy store and told him, "Junior, I just got a job in Pacino's new movie!"

He laughed and said, "Yeah, I got one too."

"Fuck you, Junior."

I ran out into the street and bumped into Charlie A, the bookie. "Charlie, I got a job in Pacino's new movie!"

Charlie laughed. "Good, maybe now you can pay me the money you owe me."

I waved him off, still running, then ran up the stairs into Bruno's trucking company. "Bruno, I scored a part in Pacino's new movie. I'm gonna be in it!" Bruno didn't have a lot to say.

I scooted into Frank's Restaurant. "Frankie, I got a job with Pacino in his new movie! Something called *Serpico*!"

"Good for you." Then he looked at me. "Wait. Pacino? Al Pacino? Are you okay?"

"I'm better than okay." I looked around the crowded restaurant. "What happened to your new waitress?"

"She took off with some actor she was shacking up with."

"Hm. Maybe I'll run into her in Hollywood."

For the rest of the day, I ran my heart out to spread the news, but mostly no one believed me. Me, in a major movie? It just sounded too weird. Exhausted, I ran into old man Knuckles. "Knuckles, I got a movie with Pacino. Al Pacino!"

"I know kid, I heard. It's all over the meat market. But you know what? Keep it to yourself. You will live longer."

"Knuckles, I can't. This is too amazing!"

By the time I reached Wexlor Meats, Solly was standing vigil in his usual spot. He held up his hand to stop me from shouting the news. "I heard. So why the long face?"

"Solly, I was so excited, I forgot your car."

"Where is it?"

"I left it in front of 600 Madison Avenue."

"Let's jump in a cab. Maybe it will still be there."

"Solly, don't you think that's a long-shot?"

"Yeah I do. Not only that, it would be two long-shots on the same day. Come on, move before I change my mind."

That brought a smile to my face and put a warm feeling in my heart. As we tumbled into the cab, me being a horse player, I thought *there is no fucking way Solly's Caddy will still be there. No way!*

But we scooted up Madison Avenue, where I watched a street cleaner go around a car and merge into the jammed street to reveal, lo and behold, Solly's Cadillac, sitting there like a beacon of light. Undisturbed. Not even a fucking ticket. That was the longshot of the day.

After work, I ran over to the acting studio to share my good fortune. The coach asked me if he had my consent to tell the class. I said okay.

"Salerno, the definition of consent is it must be freely-given, specific, informed, and unambiguous. It must be given by a clear affirmative act. It must be demonstrated that you mean what you say. But you must be able to withdraw it at any time."

What? Then I got it.

Flabbergasted, I realized this prick just auditioned for me right in front of all his wannabes. "Coach, thanks, that was cool. When I see Lumet, I'll ask him if he has a spot for you. Do I have your consent to do that?"

* * *

Up to this moment, I was so desperate for a new life that I had actually been planning to try selling pots door to door. My bride hung the pots I had already bought on the wall as a shrine for all to see what I "gave up" to become an actor. All was going well, even my cheap neighbor was civil when he heard what I was doing.

Getting back to the old routine was boring, now, because I had a constant fire going on in my belly. I knew the shoot was coming, but it couldn't come fast enough. At work, I cut into those hindquarters like there was no tomorrow.

Seeing me at work, Solly yelled, "Salerno, slow down! One slip and your career is over before you start."

Lumet's words resonated in my mind. "Salerno, be careful. Cutting meat is very dangerous."

Impatient as I was, I kept that advice in mind. Not all the meat men had all of their fingers, and I already knew acting work would be hard enough to find when you had all ten.

Later, I walked out of the cooler to catch a breath of fresh air, and while I stood there watching, Solly was talking to a black woman. I could see they were engrossed in a very deep conversation. She was talking and he was smiling. She was nodding and laughing. I thought *who the fuck is she?*

I didn't have to wait long. Solly spotted me and waved me over. "Salerno, say hello to Sammy, she is your costumer on the film." The costumer on the film. She was there to see me.

For the film.

Sammy then took me on the best shopping trip I ever had. First thing she had me outfitted in was a light beige suit, a pale sandy yellowish-brown color. This puppy made me look smooth. Sammy said the suit accentuated my natural color. I loved that. Then a chocolate high-quality shirt and a honey-brown tie of superior quality. It looked lovely topped off with a Panama hat. Very light-colored, lightweight, and breathable. It fit like a glove.

Meanwhile over at the shoe stand, Sammy picked out a simple oxford with closed lacing that had a line or two of stitching to accentuate the front of the shoe. Sammy said, "These shoes fit your character."

They were smooth and looked sleek. Sammy said, "Bottom line, these are the most simple, sleek, dress shoes money can buy."

The final touches were a six-hundred-dollar pair of sunglasses, a pinky ring, and to top it all off, a pack of Lucky Strike cigarettes. "Sammy, I like cigars. I want a big Havana like my old man smokes."

But Sammy walked away, saying, "Cigars make a man look like a pig." When I heard that, I actually had to agree. I couldn't wait to drop that line on my old man.

That day was one I will never forget. It wasn't about the clothing, the fancy glasses, or the free pack of cigarettes. It was the experience. When I got home, I told my bride, "Mrs. Salerno, you deserve the best."

And right then, I carried her up to bed.

59

P-Day

I got a call at work telling me to report to 14th Street and Ninth Avenue the next morning at 11:00 a.m. sharp. "Sidney wants to see you."

Sidney wants to see you. Sidney Lumet wanted to see me. How could any actor get a better phone call than that? My insides did a flip. I ran down the cooler shouting, "Solly, they're coming! They're coming! They're coming!"

"Who?"

"Lumet and Pacino! The whole fucking crew will be out there at eleven!"

Solly's six-foot-six frame came to attention. "Salerno, put the knife down and get off the cutting room floor. Now!"

That phone call was the beginning for me. I stepped out of my meat cutter's existence at that very moment. For the first time in my life, I enjoyed walking down the 14th Street Meat Market. The greasy sidewalk, the noise, the yelling, the butchers, the customers, the meat haulers, the hookers. It was all still there, but none of it was a threat to me anymore, because just two short blocks away were the movie trucks! I could see them already starting to invade 14th Street. In minutes, the trucks engulfed the intersection at 14th and 9th Avenue like an invading army. I heard police sirens in the distance. The closer I got to 9th Avenue, the louder the sirens became.

The Meat Market district was starting to really come alive. Participants of every persuasion started to emerge toward the sirens, an uncanny sound for that time of the day. Usually all you ever heard out there was the sound of ten-wheelers coming and going, engines struggling to pull heavy loads.

Meat cutters, meat handlers, and customers were all starting to take notice. They started gravitating toward the film set. Movie trucks clogged up the corner. Teamsters began to unload props and big film cameras.

Crowds gathered in clumps, gazing at all the activity. They shouted questions, wanting to know what was going on.

A teamster replied, "We're shooting a movie."

I heard a little girl ask, "Who's in it?"

"Al Pacino."

"Who's he?"

Maybe she didn't know, but plenty of other people did. Pacino's name started to spread like wildfire.

"Pacino is in this!"

"Pacino!"

"You see him?"

A lot of pushing and neck stretching started to ignite.

The Bruno brothers made their way into the crowd, and customers from Frank's Restaurant started to file out into the street.

Solly and all his workers strode in unison toward the corner, joined there by all the film workers. Junior and all his mobster buddies were out in force, carrying stools and chairs so they could sit around and observe.

Junior spotted me and yelled, "Come on guys, hurry the fuck up! Looks like Salerno wasn't bullshitting this time!"

Knuckles limped along, mumbling, "That Salerno, he pulled it off."

Charlie A yelped, "Maybe now I can get paid!"

Knuckles took offense at that. "Charlie, shut the fuck up, you got more money than God."

"Knuckles, you wanna pick up his tab?"

I moved myself into the crowd and away from those guys, but I didn't know where the fucking actors' trailers were. It was like the first day of school and not knowing where to go. I panicked! Looking around at all the chaos scared the shit outta me. I stretched my neck, searching for Sammy, then spotted her. She waved at me to follow her.

We finally wound up at the costume trailer to change. On that morning, in walked Richie Salerno, the meat cutter, and out walked "Rudy Corsaro, the mobster," straight into the lives of Al Pacino and Sydney Lumet.

Pacino was already in the trailer getting outfitted, talking with Lumet. When I walked in, he took one look at the newly-minted mobster, Rudy Corsaro, and said to Lumet, "Who the fuck is this guy?"

Lumet replied. "That's the new guy I was telling you about."

Pacino laughed. "He doesn't look like no new guy to me."

True to my old reputation as a big mouth, when Pacino started to put on his butcher clothes, I said, "Al, you look too clean. You need some bloody aprons. Mine are in Sammy's camper."

I made a quick call to Sammy, and in minutes she showed up with the bloody aprons. I watched Pacino putting one on. Then I smiled and told him, "Now you look the part."

All dressed and ready to go, we emerged from the trailer together. When we hit the street, there was a sea of white coats from the meat cutters standing around. Lumet shouted to me, "Who the hell are all these guys?"

Pacino just said, "Well, they aren't here for me."

"Al, these are my people. They came to see a punk turn into a prince."

"That so? Maybe you should take 'em everywhere you go."

I just smiled, but he was right. And in a way, I do.

AFTERWORD

When the film, *Serpico*, wrapped, I had no more doubts that if I did what's right in life, good things would happen. You just can't always see what direction they will come from.

I knew after my first year in prison—make that after my *first day* in prison—I was never going back to one of those hellholes. So the night when *Serpico* opened, and my mom and dad didn't show, I was hurt by it, but for the first time I was able to forgive them.

For me, this was a giant leap into understanding how to feel. Walking the path to forgiveness results in being able to love and let yourself be loved. I feel certain it was because of all those things that then and only then was I able to lay down a dark life and a darker mindset, go to Hollywood, and have a long and successful career. My many film acting credits can be found listed under the name **Richard Foronjy.**

- Richie Salerno
  New York City

For More News About Richie Salerno,
Signup For Our Newsletter:

http://wbp.bz/newsletter

Word-of-mouth is critical to an author's long-term success. If you appreciated this book please leave a review on the Amazon sales page:

http://wbp.bz/mobtomovies

**AVAILABLE FROM SALVATORE
LUCANIA AND WILDBLUE PRESS!**

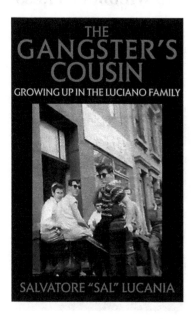

THE GANGSTER'S COUSIN by
SALVATORE LUCANIA

http://wbp.bz/tgca

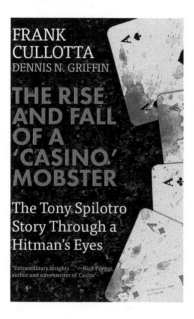

CPSIA information can be obtained
at www.ICGtesting.com
Printed in the USA
LVHW010501150920
666044LV00020B/2135